THEATER TIPS AND STRATEGIES
FOR JURY TRIALS

Second Edition

THEATER TIPS AND STRATEGIES FOR JURY TRIALS

Second Edition

David Ball, Ph.D.

Adjunct Professor of Law
Campbell University
Norman Adrian Wiggins
School of Law

Foreword by
Donald H. Beskind, Esq.

NATIONAL INSTITUTE FOR TRIAL ADVOCACY

Reproduction Permission
National Institute for Trial Advocacy
1602 North Ironwood
South Bend, Indiana 46635
(800) 225-6482
Fax (219) 282-1263
E-mail nita.1@nd.edu

Ball, David, *Theater Tips and Strategies for Jury Trials*, Second Edition (NITA, 1997).

ISBN 1-55681-531-X

THEATER TIPS AND STRATEGIES FOR JURY TRIALS

CONTENTS

FOREWORD

by Donald H. Beskind, Esq.

I am blessed by traveling in two worlds. Mostly I am a trial lawyer, but in my teaching at Duke and for NITA, my students and colleagues constantly expose me to ideas from the world outside of lawyers and lawsuits. David Ball is a friend from that world. He has filled all the chairs in professional theater—director, playwright, producer. He has taught theater at Carnegie-Mellon and chaired the theater department at Duke. And his book *Backwards and Forwards* is a standard text for theater students. David, fascinated with trials and seeing them as the ultimate theater, now fills a courtroom chair. As a professional trial consultant, he helps trial lawyers bring themselves and their cases to life. And in classrooms such as mine at Duke and in CLE programs across the country, he turns stage fright into stagecraft.

David's breadth of experience gives him a particularly broad view of what we do. Others help lawyers and law students with public speaking, communication, and movement. David does that, too, in his first chapters of this book. Trial lawyers with limited experience will find those chapters invaluable. Even those with considerable experience and success should skim those chapters. Some of this material will be familiar, but he includes new ideas worth a close look. An example is his suggestion about where to place the important phrase in direct and cross examination questions. David suggests putting the key phrase early in direct questions and late in those on cross because doing so leaves more time for your witness to think on direct and less time for their witness to think on cross.

Regardless of experience, every lawyer will find what David does in the rest of this book unique. He shows trial lawyers how to use concepts from theater to persuade and motivate. Visceral communication, story, point of view, forwards, backwards, and many others are concepts first used by successful writers, producers, and directors. For years experienced lawyers have employed some of these techniques such as looking at things as the jury sees them (point of view). Other techniques, such as backwards (which I leave to David to explain), are likely to seem strange at first, but eventually may become as common as the leading questions on cross. Whether known or novel, whether easily accepted or not, each idea in David's book will make you think about how you try your cases—from a new point of view.

Donald H. Beskind, Esq.
Durham, North Carolina

PREFACE

Jury trials and plays share one primary goal: audience persuasion. The techniques to achieve that goal were first created 2500 years ago by the ancient Greek juristors who invented trials and plays. Today on Broadway, people pay upwards of a hundred dollars per ticket to watch these techniques in action for just a few hours. But these techniques are most powerful when wielded in real courtrooms to convince real juries.

Every moment jurors are in the box they are being convinced, intentionally or not, consciously or not, your way or not. Even when you think no one is watching you, you and your case are *always* center stage. By using courtroom strategies based on scriptwriting, directing, and performance principles, you can influence and monitor how your jurors see and respond to everything on that stage.

Jurors are not lawyers and probably do not want to know any. Jurors usually come to court with no knowledge or concern about your case. They are *forced* to come; they have no personal reasons. And they are often suspicious of lawyers. They rarely arrive with any interest in you, your client, or your issues. Their default state is boredom. They just want to go home.

But we make them stay. So you need to know what makes them tick. Audiences and juries are 1) live, 2) in person, and 3) unable to answer back, make comments, or ask questions. They are not interactive. They:

    —can't go back and see or hear something again like a reader can;

    —are affected by communications well beyond the mere conveyance of words and information;

    —have attention and memory abilities that vary wildly;

    —*can be communicated to in ways that readers cannot*, because you are right there to do it.

Theater's techniques provide time-tested and reliable methods of live-audience persuasion. They can help you make jurors care, trust you, and want to help your client. They make jurors listen, contemplate, feel, and understand. They make jurors remember what you want them to remember and in the ways you want them to remember it. Most important, they help make jurors want what you want them to want, and motivate them to argue for your side effectively and tenaciously.

You don't have to be a born actor, director, or playwright to use these techniques. You just have to be a lawyer who wants to win cases.

ACKNOWLEDGMENTS FOR THE FIRST EDITION

Duke University and its School of Law provided me with the resources to write this book. I must particularly acknowledge the help of Duke's skilled law librarians, as well as the assistance of Debbie Selinsky at the University News Service, and the constant challenge of my students and colleagues at Duke in both theater and law. Dr. Leslie Banner, Special Assistant to Duke University's President during the writing of this text, was particularly invaluable, as was Duke Distinguished Professor Robert L. Hobbs, who has trained some of the best actors and lawyers in either business.

I am equally grateful for the input of my current students at Campbell University's Wiggins School of Law, and for the assistance of Campbell Law Professor Thomas P. Anderson. I also owe thanks to law students at the University of North Carolina at Chapel Hill.

Gary C. Johnson, whose counsel's table I have been privileged to share during some remarkable cases, has taught me much. In return I can offer only my admiration and respect.

I am indebted to the inspiration and teaching of Judge Charles L. Becton, and to the generous help and encouragement of attorney and professor Donald H. Beskind.

I owe thanks to attorneys Robert Brown, Jr., Alexander Charnes, Andrea A. Curcio, Anne Duvoison, William O. Faison, Robert B. Glenn, Jr., William S. Mills, Michael Nifong, Peter E. Tracy, Howard F. Twiggs, and the dozens of attorneys I have scrutinized in court without ever revealing who I was or what I was doing there, yet who were so generous afterwards with their time and attention when I started asking questions.

One of North Carolina's most skilled Attorneys General, Sherry L. Cornett, provided me with the highest level of expertise and guidance. The American Society of Trial Consultants provided research materials and considerable advice. My long-time friend Susan Macpherson of the National Jury Project offered suggestions important and wise enough to have changed the shape of this book. And Jury Clerk Sue Clayton at the Durham (North Carolina) County Courthouse provided more help than I can ever repay.

Susan Chapek, a theater professional of formidable talent, experience, and abilities, contributed to this project in crucial and continuing ways.

Jean Bryan at the North Carolina Academy of Trial Lawyers provided some excellent editorial assistance. NITA's copy editor Shelly Goethals showed me what needed improvement, and deftly got me to do it. And NITA's Jude Phillips is one of those rare graphic designers who knows how to make a book look like what it means.

Finally, but really foremost: every page has benefited from the expertise of Francis Marion University's extraordinary composition consultant, Professor Katharine M. Wilson. Better criticism than hers cannot be found, nor more motivating encouragement. With such counsel the best writers write brilliantly and the rest of us write our best.

ACKNOWLEDGMENTS FOR THE SECOND EDITION

Half of this edition's content is brand new, and most of the rest is considerably revised. This effort has been aided by the kindly offices of many.

I continue to be indebted to Duke University and its School of Law for support and assistance in the writing of the first edition, and now with this new edition as well.

NITA, the Association of Trial Lawyers of America, and the North Carolina Academy of Trial Lawyers continue to provide me with frequent opportunities to teach trial attorneys here in North Carolina and from coast to coast. I am grateful to the attorneys who have attended my workshops and seminars, and who have offered suggestions now incorporated into this edition.

Many jury, trial, and communication experts—notably Mary E. Ryan, V. Hale Starr, John A. Call, Robert Hirschhorn, Rodney Jew, Joshua Karton, John B. McConahay, and the astonishing folks from the National Jury Project (especially Beth Bonora, Elissa Krauss, Diane M. Wiley and my dear friend Susan Macpherson)—have been constant sources of ideas and inspiration. They have influenced my thinking so much that it is impossible for me to credit them for every one of their ideas I have drawn upon. The National Jury Project in particular is the inspiration for much of what is good in this book—as well as for what is good in general in my profession of jury and trial consulting.

Among those attorneys who have inspired and taught me, and with whom I have been privileged to teach, I am proud to number Gregory S. Cusimano, Donna R. Davis, Emmanuel Edem, James L. Gilbert, Howard L. Nations, Howard S. Richman, Lance Sears, Marcus Z. Shar, Thomas J. Vesper, and David A. Wenner. And those who know James J. Leonard, Jr., will understand why I single out this gentleman and genius for special thanks: he is an inspiration to everyone lucky enough to be taught by him.

To the group of attorneys I acknowledged in the first edition, I must add other extraordinary practitioners who have allowed me to observe them at work. For the privilege and for their input I am grateful to Douglas B. Abrams; Charles Bentley; Dan Blue; Joel H. Brewer; Guy R. Bucci; Irvin V. Cantor; William H. Elam; John M. Ervin, III; E.D. Gaskins, Jr.; Alexander M. Hall;

Samuel B. Ingram; John Alan Jones; Jimmie R. Keel; Carl S. Kravitz; A. LaFon LeGette, Jr.; Glenn B. Manning; Charles G. Monnett; Susan M. O'Malley; Martin A. Rosenberg; Annie L. Sullivan; Mary Ann Tally; Hoyt G. Tessener; Cressie H. Thigpen, Jr.; William L. Thorp; and Richard N. Watson.

Two virtuosi of jury voir dire—Joseph Blount Cheshire V and John R. Edwards—generously shared their knowledge with me as they have with many others. And if every attorney could have my experience of working with and learning from Wade E. Byrd, the quality of trial advocacy in America would improve ten times over.

I have also benefited from the input of the Honorable Anthony M. Brannon, the Honorable Thomas W. Ross, and the Honorable Gregory A. Weeks, judges who define the level of excellence of the North Carolina judiciary, and whose concern for skilled advocacy translates into superb advice.

I want to particularly acknowledge M. Gordon Widenhouse, Jr., for providing me with challenging opportunities and for being a powerful force for good in the legal community.

It is impossible to sufficiently thank Donald H. Beskind. I am far from alone in benefiting from his guidance; he is a constant source of support and instruction for many who seek his wisdom. His patience with beginners is matched only by his ability to help even the most experienced and sophisticated practitioners.

The folks at NITA deserve thanks on a daily basis. Publications Editor John M. Maciejczyk is the driving force behind a long shelf of new books that should be in every trial attorney's office; I'm proud to have *Theater Tips and Strategies for Jury Trials* in such splendid company. Mark Caldwell, along with Jean M. Molloy and Peg Hartman, provided me with an enviable string of teaching opportunities that substantially influenced this second edition.

Sherry L. Cornett, now (happily) Sherry L. Lindquist, has continued to be one of my most valued advisors.

For this second edition I again relied heavily on the best three guides any writer could hope for: Duke University's Dr. Leslie Banner, whose extraordinary rhetorical skills (and patience) provided the initial direction for this second edition; actress and director Susan Chapek, whose wisdom about writing and theater have bettered every page of this book and inspired some of my best work here and elsewhere; and Katharine M. Wilson, who, though her recent work has made her a rising star nationally in the professional writing community, has still found time to help transform my efforts.

For what is good in this second edition, the credit goes to those I have named. I would also be happy to lay at their feet the responsibility for whatever may be not so good—but honesty requires me to accept that blame myself.

PART ONE: METHODS

CHAPTER 1

The Leading Character: You

HOW YOU LOOK, HOW YOU TALK, WHAT YOU DO[1]

In the theater of the courtroom, you are one of the stars. How you look, how you talk, and what you do are largely in your control and determine how you will strike the jury.

The suggestions in this chapter should be practiced outside of court as well as in trial. Don't wait until you are in front of a jury to start trying, for example, to omit the "um's" that clutter your speech, or to start improving your posture. Whatever presentation skills or personal habits you want to develop or improve, practice them in everyday life. Merely understanding something is not enough. You have to practice. Good wine improves with age; good people improve with practice.

TALK—DON'T READ—DON'T SPEECHIFY

Talk to jurors and witnesses. Don't speechify. Talk to jurors the way you talk to friends in normal, personal conversations.

It is easy to learn the difference between talking and speechifying. First, make a speech to a friend. Then talk normally with your friend. You will feel the difference. Then monitor yourself in court. When you feel yourself speechifying, you will know to switch back to normal talking.

Practice: Take a friend to lunch and tell him about your case. Then in court, in opening statement, talk to the jury the same way you talked to your friend at lunch—the same words, the same tone, the same comfortable way. Don't read speeches. Don't recite from memory. Just talk. Glance at your notes when you must. The words will come.

You may write out your openings, closings, or questions as a means of preparation, but never read aloud what you have written. Reading anything aloud sounds false, stilted, and uninvolved. Instead, use what you have written

---

1. Many attorneys re-read or re-skim this chapter before every new trial. During pressure-filled court days, it is a reminder of what not to forget.

as the basis for creating skeletal—but no more than skeletal—notes. (See next section below, "Skeletal Notes.") Don't read speeches. Read jurors. Emulate this experienced trial attorney:

> As he spoke, the sweep of his gaze continued to survey the fourteen faces before him for signs. Unlike the multitudes of his colleagues at the trial bar who had condemned themselves to be less than great by bringing to the lectern reams of notes or prepared speeches to sum up a lawsuit, Shaw worked only with his memory and his wit, keeping his eyes ever on his audience. The slightest quizzical brow, a mere change of expression from a single juror, these would be a sign from which he could shift and bear down on a point, paraphrase it if he thought the first shot hadn't gotten through, or shift his topic if he caught attention starting to drift.[2]

When words are coming out of your mouth, your eyes should be on whomever you are talking to. In openings and closings you want to see the jurors you are talking to, because the visible—usually barely visible—reactions of jurors tell you what to say next, what to emphasize, what to say differently, and what to unsay. Reading to jurors instead of talking to them is like driving blindfolded. You may know the road, but you cannot know the traffic.

Working from Notes. If you need notes, maintain jury contact as follows: Before you glance down, stop talking. No one minds—or even notices—a brief pause. Look at your notes without speaking. Before you start talking again, look up.

When questioning witnesses, the best way to know your next question is to listen to the witness's last answer. But when you must look at your notes, first stop talking. Then glance at your notes. Don't talk again until you have looked up and re-established visual contact with the witness.

In other words, when talking to witnesses or anyone else, don't talk without looking at them. Here is the drill for questioning witnesses:

1) Establish eye contact with the witness.

2) Without looking away, ask a question.

3) Don't look at your notes. Watch the witness until the answer ends. (To write a note, wait until the answer ends.)

4) After the witness finishes answering, maintain eye contact for a very brief instant. This shows the witness that you are paying attention and makes the jury pay attention. If you seem too eager to get back into your notes, jurors conclude that you consider the witness's answer insignificant and they tend to pay less attention. (For the same reason, stand

---

2. F. Lee Bailey, *Secrets*, Stein and Day, 1978.

still during a witness's answer. Any movement on your part draws the jury's attention away from the witness.)[3]

On cross you can discomfit a witness by holding eye contact for an extra-long moment after each answer. This may cause the witness to either reveal something visually or fall into the common trap of saying something unintended just to fill the pause.

When you dive too quickly back into your notes for your next question, you miss the revealing things witnesses do between questions. You may miss seeing the witness become rattled or worried.

5) After the answer ends and you have maintained an extra instant of eye contact, try to determine your next question without resorting to your notes. Look down at your notes only if nothing comes to mind.

6) After you see the next question, look up at the witness before you speak.

7) After you re-establish witness eye contact, ask your next question.

Particularly on cross, some attorneys look at the jury as much as at the witness. This effective tactic can make jurors feel as if they are an active part of the process rather than just passive observers. It also allows you to monitor juror reactions to the testimony.

But be careful. During openings, closings, and testimony, looking at an individual juror for more than a few seconds at a time can make him uncomfortable. To prevent this, move your glance easily and comfortably from juror to juror, as if talking to friends at a gathering. You can practice group eye contact in any social situation: As you talk with the group, simply make visual contact with one person, then another, then the next. It will feel just as comfortable when you transfer that effort to jurors.

Because comfortable eye contact makes you feel (and look) like you are talking to real people, you will sound more natural. As a result, listeners will more easily trust you. Comfortable eye contact also helps you relax when you are nervous.

Skeletal notes. To prevent your notes from drawing too much of your attention, they should be single words or brief phrases, not full sentences. Don't write out, "And now, Mrs. Calumny, would you please tell us what you do for a living?" That long note takes too long to see. Worse, having it all written out keeps you from thinking on your feet. It lulls your mind, snags you into reading verbatim, and makes you sound fake. Over-reliance on notes also diminishes your rapport with the jury, undermines your credibility (because

---

3. Conversely, when you want to minimize the impact of an answer, ignore the witness and either scrutinize your notes or move as the witness speaks.

jurors think that the truth is easy to remember), makes it harder for jurors to listen, and makes it harder for you to monitor how the jury is reacting. A good note can be read instantly. Instead of writing out, "And now, Mrs. Calumny, would you please tell us what you do for a living?" just write:

"JOB?"

That's all you need. For each question or topic, a key word or phrase is always all you need. Anything more should be cast off like unnecessary crutches or you will look at your notes too often. Result: Jurors will wonder why you cannot go twenty words without looking at your notes.

The pile of paper from hell. When working from notes in opening or closing, *don't let jurors see your stack of papers*. Nothing disheartens a juror more after twenty minutes of a speech than seeing it is only half through.

It is particularly discouraging when you slide each discarded page to the bottom of the stack. The pile never gets smaller, so jurors think you are going to talk forever. When that is what they think, they don't listen carefully. They hope something will soar through the window and carry them (or you) away.

Solution: Place your papers on an angled stand so that jurors cannot see them. (But don't be a lectern prisoner. See p. 9, "Lecterns.")

Getting speaking experience. If speaking in public makes you nervous, the best—and perhaps only—solution is to speak in public a lot. Volunteer to speak at every community event that will have you, even if it is only talking to high school students interested in law careers. The more you speak publicly, the more comfortable you will become.

Bonus: When you speak at civic and other local group functions, your reputation will spread. People will even ask for your business card, so carry a supply.

POSTURE

Your mother was right: stand up straight. And sit up straight in your chair—not ramrod stiff, but comfortably up instead of saggingly over, down, or drooped. Jurors expect you to look like a lawyer, not like a teenager watching TV.

Jurors draw conclusions from how you carry yourself. You may be comfortable or think you look dashing when you slouch, but slouching makes you look tired, sloppy, un-alert, and uninvolved. Maybe arrogant or sneaky, too.

Be particularly careful as the trial day wears on and you tire. If you let yourself sag in your chair (even when just listening), you will look like you are sick of being in court.

If you have poor posture, get someone to help you improve it. If you droop when tired, have someone remind you, or leave yourself a reminder on your work pad.

Are you short? Never rest your arms on the arms of your chair. Your shoulders and clothes will hunch up around your neck, your head will jut forward as if it is about to drop off, the courtroom dog will growl at you, and your mother will not love you.

Are you tall? Learn decent chair posture or you will look like you have too many arms and legs. Sprawling or twisting around a chair does not make you look dramatic or casual. It makes you look silly.

WEIGHT SHIFTING, WALKING, FIDGETING

When you are on your feet, keep your weight evenly balanced on both legs. If you continually shift your weight from leg to leg, you will look nervous and insecure or as if you have to go to the bathroom. Maintain a solid stance with your weight evenly balanced side to side.

When you take a step, take it for a purpose and not just to relieve nervous tension. It is fine to take a few steps to get nearer to a particular section of the jury or to an exhibit, but if you are not actually going somewhere, stand still. Aimless wandering, even a step or two, makes you harder to listen to, distracts from whatever you are trying to do, and reduces your authority.

Stillness. Sitting at your table tapping a pencil, your fingers, or your foot makes you look bored or mentally absent. Don't wriggle. Don't take a step without a purpose. Don't wander. Don't fidget. Stillness conveys confidence and strength.

You rid yourself of wriggles, fidgets, and pointless wandering by monitoring yourself all the time, not just in court. Tell your friends to let you know when you are backsliding, and be nice to them when they do.

Caveat: "Stillness" does not mean stiffness. If you sit or stand stiffly you will alienate jurors. Simply maintain a relaxed, attentive stillness without nervous fidgeting.

HANDS

Performers as well as trial lawyers worry about what to do with their hands. But when you are fully engaged in asking (not reading) questions, or listening intently to answers (instead of checking notes for what to do next), or when you are *talking* to jurors about your case (instead of reading them a speech or reciting memorized lines), hands almost always take care of themselves. They move into action on their own to support your words with gestures that emphasize, clarify, and humanize.

If they don't, there is an easy solution: Simply let them hang at your sides, from where they will soon move naturally and spontaneously.

Mary Ryan, a leading jury and communications expert from Denver, suggests that you give your hands a job: "Their job is touching the sides of your pants or skirt." Send your hands down to do that job and you will feel like they are doing what they are supposed to do. You will automatically and almost instantly stop thinking about them. Soon, they will leave their "job" and start moving expressively as you talk.

There is nothing intrinsically wrong with the informal look of having your hands in your pockets, but pocketed hands tend to stay pocketed instead of moving into action. For the same reason, clasping your hands behind your back tends to inhibit them from helping you communicate.

Clasping your hands behind your back or in front of your crotch or breasts, or folding your arms across your chest, might make you feel comfortable but gives a distressingly different impression. When men clasp their hands in front of their crotches, they take on the most defensive male position known to humanity. It is a weak, insecure position that makes a man seem unsure of himself no matter how comfortable it may feel. The same thing happens when women "comfortably" fold their arms in front of their breasts. And if you are a man, folding your arms across your chest can strike observers as arrogant, hostile, or downright scared.

So do what Mary Ryan tells you: send your hands down to your sides and tell them to do their job of touching the sides of your pants or skirt.

When you are seated, put your hands on the table. Don't hide them in your lap. Don't fold them, and don't let them fiddle with table stuff. Rest one hand on each side of your note pad (give them the "job" of touching the edges of the pad), and as you get involved in your work they will soon be fine. Whenever you notice them fiddling with fingers or pens or anything else, or sneaking down toward your lap, send them back to their job of touching each side of your note pad.

What *not* to do with your hands:

> Don't cover your face. Don't even touch your face. You will look like you are trying to hide something other than your face—such as the truth.

> Don't rub your eyes. Don't fix or fiddle with your hair. Keep your fingers out of your ears. Don't pick your nose. You don't turn invisible when your opponent has the floor. Can you say with certainty that you have never picked at your cute little nose (or ears) in court? Someone does it in almost every trial.

Don't clean your fingernails. Don't pick (or suck) your teeth. Don't do *anything* in court that your mother would not want you to do in public.

Keep your hands in their own quadrants. Think of your body as being divided by a horizontal line at shoulder level and by a vertical line that bisects you in front from top to bottom. Don't let your right hand cross the vertical line to the left or your left hand cross to the right, or you will seem to be defensively closing yourself off. Don't let either hand rise above the horizontal line at your shoulders. If it does, it is going up there for no good purpose (catching a fly, or touching your face—or worse).

In other words, position your arms so that your body is open, not closed off.

SHIFTY EYES

This problem can be tricky to correct because it is often a lifelong habit. To change the direction in which you are looking, *don't move only your eyes. Turn your whole head.* This is especially hard to remember at the end of a long day when you are tired, but the jurors are tired too. The last thing they want to see is a shifty-eyed lawyer peering out of the corners of her eyes.

You can cure yourself of the shifty-eye habit only by paying attention to it all the time, not just in court.

HAIR

All of your face—ear to ear, hairline to throat—should be clearly visible, not only from the front but also from the sides, too, because jurors see you mainly from the sides. Cut, arrange, spray, pin, or nail your hair so it stays out of and away from your face. If your hair is long, pull it back so it cannot hide *any* of your face. Hair hanging below or forward of your ears blocks the view; so does hair jutting out over or hanging low on your forehead. It de-emphasizes and shadows your eyes—a sinister effect that your client does not want you to cultivate.

The more the jurors can see of your face, the more easily they will trust you—and even hear you.

Whatever you do to your hair, *do it so that it will stay done.* Don't push it out of your face in court. Don't adjust your hair in court at all or you will seem vain. Don't even touch your hair. Hair-play is interpreted as nervousness.

Beards and moustaches are okay if they communicate trustworthiness. But if they give you the slick look of a used car salesman, the scuzzy look of a hermit, or the crazed look of a mad scientist or a drama teacher, then shave! If you are not sure if your looks fit into one of those categories or something similarly inappropriate, send me a photo and I will tell you.

CLOTHING AND ACCESSORIES

Dress comfortably, unpretentiously, and—as your mother told you—to look nice. Look like a decent person any juror would want to have lunch with. Don't appear overly expensive but do look reasonably successful. For example, a nice wristwatch is fine but a gold Rolex is not. Don't wear $1,500 suits unless you have a reason to appear ostentatiously superior to your jurors.[4]

---

4.   Cars are not clothing, but they have the same effect if jurors see you arriving. Drive to court in something modest. A three-year-old Buick is more appropriate than a Rolls. On the other hand, don't drive a jalopy. If jurors think you have no money, they will think you are a bad lawyer.

Once in court, ignore your clothes. If, for example, you meticulously adjust your trouser legs each time you sit, or if you carefully smooth your skirt every five minutes, you will appear vain, which to some jurors means untrustworthy.

Select tasteful and unobtrusive accessories, including ties, jewelry, and rings. Avoid clunky bracelets and rings that clatter and bang. Don't fiddle with your jewelry. Be certain that your lapel pins cannot be misinterpreted as religious, political, or social movement symbols that might alienate some jurors. Not every juror wants to save whales; some might prefer to eat them.

Don't use an expensive-looking pen. Make sure no one at your table does. (Give your Mont Blanc to your opponent.) You needn't settle for a 49-cent Bic, but holding a 14-karat gold writing utensil is like waving a placard that says, "I'm overpaid and greedy, and I'm here for more money."

Some inexpensive pens look like they cost a lot. Don't use a pen that looks as if it cost more than lunch.[5] And don't chew on your pen. It's not your lunch. In fact, don't put your pen anywhere near your face. Pens leak, and neither your opponent nor the judge can be relied upon to tell you about the big blue splotch on your chin.

Clothing color can help emphasize your face. The more easily your face draws the juror's visual attention, the more closely the juror listens. If the courtroom walls are light, dark clothing helps frame your eyes and mouth. If you are light skinned, blond hair can be a problem because it draws focus away from your face. You can offset this by selecting jacket or shirt colors that emphasize your facial hues.

Perhaps in law school you failed your courses in clothing and color selection. If so, see a consultant for advice. In preparing a case, it is easy to ignore costumes, but remember that jurors have little to look at in court. What little they do see has enormous effect.

EYES AND EYEGLASSES

—Frames should emphasize your eyes, not hide them. Test: When you look in the mirror, your most obvious facial feature should be your eyes, not your glasses.

—Use anti-glare lenses so that reflections don't obscure the jury's view of your eyes. You don't want jurors to see reflected fluorescents where your eyeballs should be.[6]

—Use untinted lenses.

---

5.   And don't eat expensive lunches, but do eat where your jurors eat, and bring your client (unless he is being tried for a violent crime). It humanizes both of you to be seen eating. (Order a burger, not *lobster à la crème du pretentious gourmand*.)

6.   Caveat: Some anti-glare coatings have an ugly green hue. Find an optometrist who can provide the clear kind.

—Use high index (extra-thin) lenses.

—Don't wear half-frame reading glasses. The top of such frames crosses directly in front of your pupils. Worse, half-frame spectacles force you to peer over and down to see anything at a distance. That gives you an arch, snooty, or glaring look. (If you need glasses only for reading, use full-frame lenses graduated to a nonprescription upper half.)

EYE MAKEUP

Women may wish to use a little eye makeup to emphasize their eyes. The goal is to subtly draw the viewer's gaze toward the eyes.

LECTERNS

Lecterns are tools of the devil. They are not there to use; they are there to get you in trouble. Try to stay away from them.

Hiding behind a lectern is like covering your face with both hands and a stolen hat. In confines as small as a courtroom, only three kinds of people stand behind lecterns for more than a few minutes: those who are uncomfortable, those who have something to hide, and those who plan to talk too long. The only thing more harmful to effective communication than standing behind a lectern is standing behind a wall.

On the other hand, a lectern is a wonderful object for you to step out and around from, removing the barrier between you and the jury. Come around to the side shortly after you start your opening statement, for example. The move creates a trustful rapport.

Don't lean on the lectern. Don't wrap your arms around it; it is not your mother. You can touch it, but touching leads to leaning. If you are physically small, standing beside the lectern and lightly touching it creates a positive impression of taking up more space, thus making you seem more authoritative. But that impression evaporates if you end up leaning on the lectern, hugging it, or standing behind it.

If local custom requires you to stand behind a lectern, use every excuse to get away from it. Go to the easel to show something. Find a need to approach the witness. Get something from your table and later put it back on your table. Give a demonstration. Do all you can to get yourself out from behind the lectern. During a recess, hide the damnable thing!

REMOTE CONTROLS

Technology can hurt as well as help. Don't use remote controls for such display devices as VCRs, projection screens, and multimedia systems. There is no advantage to sitting in your chair rather than crossing the courtroom to show something to the jury.

Movement creates interest, authority, and emphasis. Even a mere walk over to snap off the overhead projector can provide effective punctuation to a visual display.

So before investing in high-tech display devices, be aware that you are paying for the privilege of being deprived of one of your most effective tactics: moving around the courtroom. This is especially true in jurisdictions where you cannot leave your table or lectern without reason to do so.

The moral: Be a couch potato at home, not a table potato in court.

YOUR JURY PERSONA

An imagined mental construct can improve the way you treat jurors. Choosing the right one depends on the kind of person you are.

For one possibility, think of the courtroom as your living room, and the jurors as guests you have invited into your home. As host, you want to make each guest feel welcome, special, and comfortable. You should be friendly, helpful, and caring. Show your guests they are important to you and your family. In your home you make sure that everyone is comfortable, feeling special, and well taken care of. If you make yourself feel that way in court about your jurors, you will automatically treat them well and constantly communicate warmth and trustworthiness.

The image of guests in your living room is not for everyone. If you hate having people coming to visit, think of some other easily imaginable, *familiar* situation with strong personal associations. Create in your mind's eye any situation that leads you to behave the way you want the jury to see you: courteous, considerate, welcoming, grateful, self-assured, nice, respectful, and so forth.

THE TEN COMMANDMENTS OF COURT CONDUCT

Thou shalt make the jury see and believe that:

I.   You are always comfortable and in control.
II. You are always prepared.
III. You are always aware of everything going on in court.
IV. You are never taken off guard.
V.   You are always a step ahead of everything, but you are never condescending.
VI. You are a professional officer of the court who takes the job seriously.
VII. You are trustworthy and care for the truth and justice above all things.
VIII. You consider the jury more important than yourself.

IX.   You consider your client more important than yourself.

X.   You consider your opponent your equal (neither superior nor inferior).

STAGE FRIGHT

Most stage fright is caused by the intense self-consciousness that can come from being concerned about how others will gauge your performance. This self-consciousness is involuntary, and it is physical as well as emotional. It is an inherent survival mechanism designed by nature to discourage the individual from acting alone when there are others present with whom to act in concert. Unfortunately, even though there are others present in a courtroom, conducting trial is not a group activity; you must do your part of it alone.

Stage fright is a *public* reaction. You have no stage fright when working alone at your desk. Stage fright rears its unnerving head only while you are being watched and evaluated by others.

Stage fright makes you uncomfortable and afraid. It interferes with concentration and leads to false mannerisms and errors in judgment. It can make you feel, look, and act like an amateur.

Actors and athletes (including the best and most experienced) frequently suffer from stage fright, often severe. Their methods of controlling it can help you in court.

1) Take a series of deep, slow breaths. You can subtly do this at counsel's table. Inhale and exhale slowly. Deep, slow breathing comforts you. By altering your body chemistry enough to reduce your visceral urge to hide or flee, deep breathing diminishes stage fright.

Deep breathing means drawing air all the way down into your diaphragm as if you are trying to fill your stomach instead of your chest. If your chest moves as you breathe, aim lower, down below your diaphragm. Your navel, not your chest, will move. (Practice this. You already do it perfectly in your sleep.)

2) Don't let yourself be rushed by the people or situation around you. Try not to be bullied by the press of time and expectation. Realize that time and events are dependent on you; you are not dependent on them. If you feel that the judge wants you to hurry along, let it be her problem, not yours—at least until your stage fright goes away. When you think, work, and speak at your own pace, and make the pace of time and events dependent on you, you gain a feeling of control that reduces stage fright.

3) Pretend that the people watching you are other people, unintimidating to you in any circumstance (your kid brother's little friends or the people who finished at the bottom of your law class).

4) Think of yourself as a member of a trial team rather than as one person whose work is on the line.

5) Concentrate on the details of the task at hand. For example, in jury voir dire, concentrate 110 percent on the process of getting that prospective juror to talk to you. Scrutinize the prospective. Try to project yourself right inside that prospective. Focus all your attention on your specific goal.

The self-consciousness that causes stage fright occurs when your attention is concentrated onto yourself, like the sun through a magnifying glass. The most effective remedy is to direct your attention onto something else. This requires something strong enough to distract your attention from yourself, such as the importance and intricacy of the task at hand. If you direct your full concentration onto the task at hand, you will have little attention left to focus upon yourself. This will dilute your self-consciousness.

Here is the stage-fright drill:

—breathe slowly and deeply,

—don't let yourself feel hurried,

—pretend that the people observing you are folks who cannot intimidate you,

—think of yourself as a member of a team, and

—forcefully concentrate your attention onto the task at hand.

Result: The energy that your stage fright was flinging off in all directions will begin to refocus onto the work you are supposed to be doing.

TABLE

Does your counsel table make the impression you want it to, or is it a mess? Does it give off an air of professionalism and organization, or does it look like a teenager's closet? Utter neatness might be unnerving because some clutter is to be expected in the midst of trial. All your memo pads need not be lined up and squared off, but utter messiness can make you seem scatterbrained, undisciplined, uncaring, frenetic, disorganized, and even untrustworthy.

Can you use something on your table as a tantalizer,[7] such as a corner of an interesting photo you have not yet introduced? A demonstrative model obviously covered has the effect of a package that says, "Hey, kid! Don't open me till Christmas."

It is okay to have a cup of water on your table even though jurors don't (and think they cannot) ask for any,[8] but not coffee! Jurors longing for a coffee

---

7. See Chapter 7, "Forwards Creating Tension," page 127.
8. In voir dire or opening, you might tell jurors they can get water by asking the bailiff.

break who smell your coffee and see you glugging away will be thinking about something other than the case.

GENDER

If you are male and work with a female co-counsel or paralegal, treat her as your equal or you will alienate some jurors. Even if you have no negative feelings about women, monitor your behavior and have others observe you to be sure you are not inadvertently doing something that could send a negative message. This is a particular danger if you are the senior colleague, because attitudes and behaviors of "seniority" easily and clearly manifest themselves. Some jurors will ascribe such attitudes and behaviors to your feelings about women rather than about younger colleagues.

For example, consider the physical gestures you use to get a colleague's attention or to indicate that you want her to come closer so you can talk. Would you make that gesture to your boss or to the judge? Such a gesture may be acceptable in your office, if your relationship is such that your colleague would tell you if it bothered her. But jurors know nothing about your office relationship. They just see you crooking your finger to beckon your colleague over to you. Such in-court behavior sends indelible messages that may not reflect your actual feelings. Be careful.

On the other hand, if you do have problems considering women equal, it is better not to work with women colleagues at all because over the course of trial it will be impossible to conceal that bias. Many jurors who have had bad experiences with such attitudes are keenly sensitive to them and spot them no matter how well concealed you think they are.

Of course, advising you not to work with women if you consider them your inferiors is unfair to women because it reduces the number of opportunities for them. But it is even more unfair to create a situation in which jurors lean against your client because of your apparent sexist behavior.

Oddly enough, women can be just as guilty of sexist behavior toward other women. Not so oddly, this can alienate jurors even more than a man's sexist behavior.

YOU ARE WHAT YOU SAY (How you talk)

Jurors gauge character largely by sound. The word "personality" means "by the sound." Next time you talk to a stranger on the phone, notice how much you quickly conclude about him just by how he sounds.

Give substantial consideration not only to the words you choose, but to how you sound when you say them.

Avoid legalese. If the entire Western world can get along without saying "pursuant," so can you. One of America's best jury consultants describes her job as "teaching lawyers English as a second language." This is because speaking legalese is a habit not easily broken, despite the urging of every jury consultant, trial skills teacher, and advocacy textbook.

It is bad enough to use technical terms such as "voir dire." It is even worse to use terms to mean something other than their commonly understood meanings, such as "interest." Consider the harm you do when you tell the jury, "Our medical expert has no interest in this case."

Talk like a normal person, not like a lawyer. "Did you have occasion pursuant to the foregoing to . . ." does not have the effect you intend. Jurors don't know "compensatory" from "punitive." Many don't know what "plaintiff" means, or what you're talking about when you call some witnesses "your witnesses" and others "your opponent's witnesses." Then you make matters worse at the end of your direct examination when you say "your witness" to your opponent when you are referring to *your* witness. That just confused you, so how do you think jurors feel?

Many jurors are unsure whether "subsequent" means before or after. Some attorneys use "pursuant" and "subsequent" interchangeably. The only thing worse than using legalese is using it incorrectly.

Remember when you first encountered the definition of hearsay? Did you understand it without rereading it several times? Of course not. Yet lawyers and judges expect jurors to understand such obscurity delivered orally and without the advantage of reading it even once, much less hearing it again or rereading it.

You use legalese so often that it is easy for you to think it is English. So while Shakespeare's Hamlet says:

To be or not to be, that is the question.

Counsel's Hamlet might say:

Have I occasion, if anything, to be? Alternatively, subsequently, and secondarily, might there come a point in time when I have not occasion to be? At the instant point in time, the aforementioned is the probative issue. Whether pursuantly . . . .

When jurors don't *easily* understand you, they stop listening. Worse, they trust you less, because honesty means clear talk, and legalese is not clear.

Legalese is like medicalese. Would you understand if your doctor said you were suffering from, say, *pimelosis extremis, pes planovalgus,* or *sebaceoustica custicus?* You cure the first (fat) by exercise and dieting, the second (flat feet) by a shoe insert, and the third (pimples) by surviving adolescence—so are they worth the obfuscation?

Like other bad habits, you can break your legalese habit only by eliminating it in every situation, not just in court. Don't talk to judges or other lawyers in legalese, don't use legalese in your office, and don't think to yourself in legalese. Never again in your life should you say anything like "pursuant" or "perpetrator"[9] or "at that point in time" or "*in mens rea*" or "vehicle" or "proponent" or "damages" to mean money. Talking that way in front of a jury is self-sabotage.

When you must use legal language, tell your jurors what it means every time you use it. Just because you explain in opening what "punitive" or "liability" means does not mean they will remember during testimony.[10]

Send fifty dollars to my publisher (NITA) every time you let yourself say trash like "pursuant" or "herein" or "testatrix." Especially don't say "testatrix." As with all legalese, jurors will get the wrong idea.

Sentences: shape, length, impact point.

SHAPE: To be clear and effective, speak in plain sentences. Plain means linear. Linear means in a straight line. When you speak a sentence that does not progress in a straight line, you confuse people.[11]

Think to yourself, not out loud. Don't make half starts, then stop, go back, turn around, repeat, recycle, take a snooze, correct yourself, weave, refer to side issues and qualifications, or retract.

Develop the habit of saying one thing at a time or you will end up with swamp mud. For example:

> Is it true, sir—and it was raining that day, you said yesterday, or this morning, and that night, too—that going so fast, driving, because you were late, in the car with rain, it was hard driving, given that the rain had started to freeze and that the road was slick and you had driven your whole life, all of it, in the South where there was never much of snow before when the defendant got into the car that was yours to start with at the light, isn't that right?

I heard a lawyer ask this question in court. Verbatim. The witness answered, "Yes." Who knows at what? Jurors snickered. Afterward, counsel told me, "Oh, they knew what I meant." Not likely, but I knew what the snicker meant.

---

9. Some prosecutors think that saying "perpetrator" gives them an authoritative air. Maybe. But it's not as authoritative as saying "killer" or "thief" or "rapist."

10. Be careful with all specialized language, not just legalese. For example, a medical test that reveals bad news is called "positive," and one that reveals good news is called "negative." But it is just the opposite for pregnancy tests—if you want to be pregnant. If you don't, then it is the opposite of the opposite. See how confusing it gets? So don't use such language. When you have to use it, define it: "When the doctor said that your biopsy was negative, *that you did not have cancer*, what did you do?"

11. Compare: Sentences confuse people that don't progress in a straight line when you speak them.

You cannot fix an early flaw in a sentence by revising it later in the same sentence. Stop, figure out what you want to say, start again, and say it linearly—one thing at a time.[12]

LENGTH: Your sentences—particularly questions to witnesses—should be like contest entries: twenty-five words or less (fifteen or less on cross). Limit yourself to one thought per sentence and one sentence per question.

Sentence fragments? Good things. Especially for emphasis. But sparingly.

IMPACT POINT AND EMPHASIS: The impact point is the word or phrase that conveys your sentence's main concern. For clarity and emphasis, place your impact point near the end of the sentence. When you ask, "Did John park the car under the tree at noon?" your main concern—the impact point—is the time ("at noon"). If "under the tree" is the main concern, then ask, "Did John park the car at noon under the tree?" The impact point belongs as close to the end as possible without twisting syntax, because once you state your main concern, jurors tend to stop listening.

In one sense, the purpose of a sentence is to get to your impact point. Once you have gotten to it, end the sentence. New trial lawyers get understandably nervous and sometimes ramble beyond their impact points. Older trial lawyers do, too.

On cross, placing your impact point at the end of the question leaves the witness no time to think. "When you entered the office, it was the only time you *saw the corpse*, right?" Zap! She's got to answer with no time to think. If she considers before answering, her hesitation creates suspicion. (Conversely, if you say, "The only time you saw the corpse was when you entered the vice president's outer office just after the plant opened on May 17, 1987, right?" the witness has five seconds to think.)

On direct, especially with a nervous witness, reverse the principle: Place your impact point early in the question so that your own witness has time to formulate an answer while you are finishing the question. Say, "What did you see when you entered the vice president's outer office just after the plant opened on the morning of May 17, 1987?" That word order gives your witness five seconds to think.

You can put greater significance on an impact point or anything else by emphasizing it *vocally* (as I just did by italicizing "vocally"). Vocal emphasis tells the listener what is important. It can be accomplished by increasing volume on a specific word or phrase. "Where were you *Saturday night?*"

For even greater emphasis on an impact point or anything else, pause slightly just before you say it. "Where were you . . . *Saturday night?*

---

12. If your courtroom uses a real court reporter, don't say "Strike that" when you stop. Instead, say "*Please* strike that." Jurors don't like attorneys who are rude to the support staff.

Change of pace also provides emphasis. For example, zip quickly through "Where-were-you" and then slowly speak one word at a time: ". . . Saturday . . . night?"

Use these emphasis techniques often but with a delicate touch. They work best and can be used over and over when subtly employed. Think of these emphasis techniques as *oral italics*.

With or without emphasis, remember the principle of the impact point: Once jurors have heard the main concern of a sentence, they listen less carefully until the next sentence starts.

Never say isn't, didn't, shouldn't, wouldn't, couldn't. When speaking aloud, use -n't contractions only when the contraction's vowel sound is different from the vowel sound in the word's uncontracted form. "Don't" is okay because "do" has a different vowel sound than "don't." But "didn't" and "did" have the same vowel sound. A cough in the courtroom or a turn of your head can obscure the -n't, causing "didn't" to be heard as "did."

You will never know that the jurors misheard you. They may never know you said the opposite of what they heard.

Unintended insults. Phrasing can contain embedded insults you don't intend. For example, don't say to jurors in voir dire, "If you don't understand I'll explain it to you again." They *will* understand that you think they are stupid. Say instead, "If I don't say it clearly the first time, let me know and I'll try it again." Put the blame for failure on yourself.

Don't call women "girls" and don't call young African American men "boys." Whether or not you mean offense, many jurors will take offense.

Further, beware of negative descriptions that might inadvertently apply to jurors. Don't say, "He doddered around like an old man" if you have elderly jurors. Don't say, "Fat guy" if you have an obese juror. Don't say, "He was not smart enough to finish high school" unless you are certain all your jurors (and their parents and children) graduated.

Proper names. The name you call your client, opponent party, or a witness can be persuasive. So can the tone in which you speak it.

Don't say, "my client." "Client" implies a business transaction. Use a proper name, first or last as appropriate. And know your client's name! Saying, "Mr., uh . . . Jones" implies that this case is unimportant to you.

Refer to your opposing party as "Mr. _____" (or Mrs., Miss, or Ms.) or, better yet, "the intruder," "the corporation," "the speeder," "the stalker," "that man," "the defendant," or "my opponent's client."

Tone of voice carries persuasive weight. Keep this in mind every time you speak your client's name. Don't exaggerate your tone, but make it clear that you trust, like, or sympathize with your client. This is important because jurors believe you know the "real truth" of the case. So if they hear you address your client with trust, respect, and affection, they will assume you have good reason for doing so. Use the opposite principle against your opponent party.

If you have children, think about how they sound when calling you "daddy" or "mommy." The tone contains a world of meaning and feeling. Think how you would say, "Your Honor" to a respected Justice of the U.S. Supreme Court. The tone carries as much weight as the name or title itself.

Word choice. To the plaintiff, there is no such thing as an "accident"; there are wrecks, catastrophes, and disasters. To the defendant there are no wrecks, catastrophes, or disasters. There are only accidents, incidents, and mishaps.

—Opposing counsel is not a "good lawyer," but "highly skilled." "Highly skilled" implies that something besides truth and facts is being used against your client.

—Your client's business organization is a "company" or a "store." The opposition's is a "corporation."

Your choice of word or phrase controls how jurors understand and remember. This is not a lightweight consideration. Was Vietnam a "peacekeeping mission" or a "war"? Are Moonies a "religion" or a "cult"? Is abortion a "right" or a "murder"? Language is not empty words.

Jurors don't read, they listen. They have no chance to meditate on your choice of words. Thus, the effect of your word choice infiltrates jurors' minds almost without their knowing. The result can be a cumulative effect of great impact —either for or against you.

Empty words (uh . . . and . . . and so . . . um . . . yes, and . . . okay). Avoid empty connector words:

COUNSEL   Would you tell the court your name, please?

WITNESS   Ella Angelina Franklin.

COUNSEL   *Okay . . . and . . .* where do you live?

WITNESS   24 Hennepin Street in St. Paul.

COUNSEL   *Okay . . . and . . .* what is your occupation?

WITNESS   I'm retired.

COUNSEL   *Yes, retired, okay . . . and* what did you do before you retired?

WITNESS   I was a private investigator. I had my own business.

COUNSEL   *Okay, yes, okay . . .* and did you . . . ?

Every "okay" (or other empty word) makes jurors think you are having to organize your thoughts on the run, and they wonder what kind of dunce needs to organize thoughts about such simple information. Moreover, the monotonous rhythm of your empty repetitions distracts from the sense and impact of what you are saying.

COUNSEL   *Okay* . . . and did you see anything when you opened the door?
WITNESS   Blood, just blood at first.
COUNSEL   *Okay* . . . then what?
WITNESS   And then Mr. Coffin lying sort of against the wall.
COUNSEL   *Okay* . . . lying against the wall. *Okay.* Did you see anything else?
WITNESS   There was broken glass all over the place.
COUNSEL   *Okay* . . . .

It is nice to know that counsel thinks it is *okay* that Mr. Coffin was lying against the wall, that it is *okay* the witness's name is Ella Franklin, and that everything else is *okay* too.

There is nothing wrong with thinking between questions. It shows the jury that you are really listening to the witness. But don't display your need to think about organizing yourself. Keep quiet while you are thinking. Nothing is wrong with a little pause.

"Uh" and "um" do the same thing as "okay." So does "I see" over and over.

Unplanned repetition of a witness's answer is as pointless as using empty words such as "uh" and "I see." Repeat the words of an answer solely to emphasize them. Such strategic repetition is called "looping" or "reflection" or "pickups." It is an effective emphasizer. For example,

Q   How many glasses of wine did you drink?

A   Three.

Q   And after *you drank those three glasses of wine*, what did you do?

A   I ordered a beer.

Q   And what did you do *with the beer you ordered*?

Such looping emphasizes the three glasses of wine and the beer, but not if you have been looping at random when you are not trying to emphasize anything. Be highly selective when choosing which words of an answer, if any, to repeat in the next question.

Vocal quality. If you have a relatively high-pitched voice (most women and some men), make a conscious effort to lower, not raise, your pitch when you strive for emphasis. Only operatic sopranos can convey strength of purpose by using high-pitched sounds. Further, too much talking at the higher end of your range strains your voice, resulting in hoarse or harsh tones (like Bill Clinton toward the end of his 1992 presidential campaign).

Higher voices are more directional than low (they aim rather than disperse), so if you have a high voice, turn your head directly toward whomever you want to hear you best. And talk slightly louder when you turn away.

Regardless of the pitch of your voice, take the same precautions if the room acoustics are hollow: Direct your voice toward whomever you want to hear it best. That almost always means the jury.

If you have a small voice, consider vocal training for volume and projection. Most older courtrooms' acoustics, and even some new courtrooms', are unkind to small voices. Different kinds of wall surfaces reflect and absorb unequal amounts of various pitches and resonances, so deeper and stronger voices are affected differently than higher and smaller voices. Until recently, public chambers were designed only with deeper and stronger voices in mind. (Sound amplification does not always help; some sound systems merely amplify the problem.)

In courtrooms with microphones, avoid turning away from the jury to speak into the microphone. Situate your microphone between the jury and yourself so that you need not turn away from the jury to talk. This also gives you reason to look at the jury more often. (Adjust your witness's microphone in the same way, and give your witness advance practice using it. See Chapter 2, p. 27.)

Women (and others) are usually interrupted. Studies show that many people, especially women, are interrupted so regularly that speaking without interruption feels unnatural to them.[13] This is a disadvantage when it comes to delivering openings and closings. Get as much practice as you can speaking uninterruptedly in real life. It may drive your friends mad, but that is what friends are for.

Breathing. You can improve vocal power, resonance, and emotional weight (and calm your nerves) by taking larger-than-usual breaths before talking. Breathe down into your diaphragm as if you're trying to fill your stomach, not your chest, with air. Do this all the time, not just when you are in court, to make it habit.

Mispronunciation. Mispronunciation is like bad breath: Even your best friends won't tell you. Bribe them to tell you every time.

For example, in most areas of the country it is substandard usage to omit the 'g' in *recognize*. If you live in such an area and don't say that 'g' ("reco'nize"), you want your friends, colleagues, or assistants to tell you.

Some mistakes are not limited by geographical region, such as the common error regarding the word "the." It should be pronounced "thee" before words that start with a vowel sound: th_ee_ engine, not th_uh_ engine. Th_ee_ ice cream. Th_ee_ attorney. Before words that start with consonants, it is pronounced th_uh_: th_uh_ lawyer, th_uh_ puddle, th_uh_ motor.

---

13. *You Just Don't Understand*, Deborah Tannen, Ballantine Books, 1991. Chapter 7, pages 188-215.

You needn't speak standard, generic, or even unflawed English. But in some regions certain errors communicate ignorance or pretentiousness. Identify the usages in your area that give impressions you don't wish to convey, and avoid those usages.

Etcetera is not *eKcetera*. Etc.

Distinct vocal quality. In high school plays and other amateur theater, almost all the actors talk the same way—the same volume, the same speed, the same pitch, the same inflections. People automatically pick up each other's speech patterns. That is why people from Brooklyn sound like other people from Brooklyn.

In court, pay attention to how your opponent talks so that you can avoid sounding the same. If you want jurors to be alert to what you say, don't sound like others around you—particularly not like your opponent.

Strengthen and warm up your voice. Vocal sound is created largely by vocal muscles—muscles that can be strengthened. Here's an easy but effective strengthening exercise that can also serve as a warm-up: read out loud for ten minutes a day, every day. Read loudly enough for court. Read material you have not read before so that you get simultaneous practice at presenting new material from text. Read at varying pitch levels—high sounds, bass sounds, medium-range sounds—to strengthen your voice beyond its current narrow range. This will give you greater vocal variety in court, making you more expressive and attention-holding.

In this reading exercise, articulate extra carefully. Pronounce every consonant and don't slur vowels. You may feel as if you are over-articulating, but you are merely offsetting your natural tendency to under-articulate—so that in court you will become more audible and authoritative.

Your daily ten minutes of reading aloud will quickly improve your vocal strength, expressiveness, endurance, and richness of tone. Don't stop after just a few weeks or months. The benefits of this exercise continue and increase for as long as you continue doing it, even years into the future.

There are dozens of other exercises, but most should be expertly chosen for your own particular voice. The vocal coach from a local college drama department can help. For serious speaking problems (such as a lisp), see a speech pathologist. For severe voice problems (such as frequent hoarseness or strain), see a physician who specializes in voice.

WARM-UPS: Because your vocal and speaking apparatuses are muscular, a good warm-up helps you prepare each day for court. A warm-up also prepares you mentally and emotionally to get up and "perform."

Some actors use Lewis Carroll's poem *Jabberwocky* to ready their voices. It is best done within an hour of the time you get to court. Speak the poem as directed below at the start of each stanza. Use a full voice and over-articulate.

Exaggerate the consonants and voice the vowels clearly and richly. The goal
is to warm up your voice at high, medium, and low pitches and to limber up
your lips and tongue, which is essential for clear articulation. *Caveat:* Do not
strain by going too high, too low, or too loud. Stay within a note or two of your
comfortable range. If you feel strain in your throat, ease up.

And don't worry that *Jabberwocky* doesn't make immediate sense. It is not
necessarily supposed to.

Jabberwocky
by Lewis Carroll
(The Warm-up Poem)

SLOW SPEED, LOW PITCH:
> *'Twas brillig, and the slithy toves*
> *Did gyre and gimble in the wabe;*
> *All mimsy were the borogoves,*
> *And the mome raths outgrabe.*

SLOW SPEED, HIGH PITCH:
> *Beware the Jabberwock, my son!*
> *The jaws that bite, the claws that catch!*
> *Beware the Jubjub bird, and shun*
> *The frumious Bandersnatch!*

FAST SPEED, HIGH PITCH:
> *He took his vorpal sword in hand;*
> *Long time the manxome foe he sought*
> *So rested he by the Tumtum tree,*
> *And stood awhile in thought.*

NORMAL SPEED, START PITCH HIGH, THEN DROP TO LOW:
> *And, as in uffish thought he stood,*
> *The Jabberwock, with eyes of flame,*
> *Came whiffling through the tulgey wood,*
> *And burbled as it came!*

SUPER-FAST SPEED, ANY PITCH (emphasize consonants):
> *One, two! One, two! And through and through*
> *The vorpal blade went snicker-snack!*
> *He left it dead, and with its head*
> *He went galumphing back.*

SLOW SPEED, HIGH PITCH (drag out and exaggerate vowels):
And hast thou slain the Jabberwock?
Come to my arms, my beamish boy!
O frabjous day! Callooh! Callay!
He chortled in his joy.

NORMAL SPEED, NORMAL PITCH, FULL AND RICH VOICE:
'Twas brillig, and the slithy toves
Did gyre and gimble in the wabe;
All mimsy were the borogoves,
And the mome raths outgrabe.

Don't do this in front of your client.

Images.   A trial attorney without images is like an art book without pictures.

An image is a word picture that uses something we know, or can easily imagine, or that can easily be explained, to *describe, make coherent,* or *organize* something we don't know or that cannot easily be explained. For example, WE KNOW that deer run fast but we DON'T KNOW how Joe Smith runs. "Joe Smith runs like a deer" uses what we know (how deer run) to explain what we don't know (how Joe runs).

An image communicates more than raw information. It also elicits the listener's own personal associations. "She came into the room like a cool summer breeze after a hot day's work" conveys the same raw information to everyone but evokes different associations from each listener. The way one person thinks of a cool summer breeze is different from the way another does. "A hot day's work" means one thing to an Alabama farmer, another to a Manhattan cop, and something else to a worker in a steel mill. Everyone receives the same raw information and spontaneously individualizes it.

Because images evoke each juror's own thoughts, feelings, and associations, they allow you to have a private little chat with each juror.

Images are free. They take no time. In fact, by communicating concisely they save time. And images are interesting. They help keep jurors alert.

Jurors remember images and repeat them in deliberations. When one of your images pops up in deliberations, it is the next best thing to your being there yourself to carry on your case.

In cases dealing with complicated matters, images help you communicate with jurors who lack the background, intelligence, or training to easily learn a complex concept. For example, "The unanticipated outward vector of combined stresses on the fission chamber's brittle ceramic containment partition acted like *a rock smashing through your living-room window.*" It's hard to match the clarity and effectiveness of that image (the rock smashing through the window) with any other kind of explanation.

PASSION

Movies, TV, radio talk shows, and real life all teach jurors that people are passionate when arguing for what they believe. Jurors should see that your work is driven by your feelings as well as your professional obligations. Conduct your case as if your client were your best friend or a loved one up against outrageous opposition. Make yourself feel that the stakes are your own. Because jurors assume that you know "the real truth," they are influenced by the level of your emotional commitment. If you are dispassionate and uncaring, they will conclude that you know or suspect something negative about your case or your client that you are not revealing.

Do not let the routine of your job or the formality of the courtroom mask your commitment. It may be your thousandth case, but it is the jury's first.

On defense, don't calmly accept the fact that the state or the plaintiff has brought this outrageous case against your client. On offense, don't be dispassionate about the defendant's devastating misdeeds. If you display no passion, jurors will assume that you have no belief in your client.

Information, logic, and law are not enough. Show jurors that you deeply care about this case and your client. The courtroom is no place to hide your feelings.

Caveat: "Passion" does not mean ranting and raving, nor necessarily even raising your voice. It means a deep emotional commitment that drives what you say and do. It is an emotional energy fueled by the righteousness of your cause and by your commitment to your client. You can display passion in ways that suit your personal style and that you are comfortable with, the same ways you exhibit passion in real life. That can be anything from Dustin-Hoffman-quiet-and-intense to Sylvester-Stallone-enormous to Holly-Hunter-exuberant to Meryl-Streep-thoughtful, as long as it is really you.

To help you generate passion, decide how the case relates to you personally. Ask yourself how the opposition's contentions offend your personal sense of right and wrong, assault your values and beliefs, or threaten you *personally*. Wage battle not just for your client but for yourself. Your real and personal commitment to the issues (not to your fee) must be continual, potent, and visible.

TEN MORE COMMANDMENTS

    I.   Thou shalt keep your head up.

    II.   Thou shalt get your hands away from your face.

   III. Thou shalt not talk to the floor.

IV. Thou shalt *keep* your hands away from your face.

V. Thou shalt not talk to your notes.

VI. Thou shalt darn well get thine hands from thine face!

VI. Thou shalt not stare at your tabletop.

VII. Thou shalt not speak to your feet or anyone else's.

VIII. Thou shalt keep your head up so that jurors can always see your eyes.

IX. and X. Thou shalt banish thine hands from thine face all the days of thine career.

BE YOURSELF

It is hard to be yourself when trying to do everything this book is telling you to do. But you must! Don't be different in trial from the way you are in real life. As you hear about new trial skills, use them in ways that help you to be yourself. Only when you are yourself are you credible and persuasive. Theater and movie audiences don't believe obvious acting. Neither do juries.

Pretend that your two closest friends are on the jury. Make sure you do nothing that would surprise them. Stay in character—and the character to stay in is *you.*

✠ CHAPTER 2 ✠

YOUR CAST REHEARSALS:
THE TEN COMMANDMENTS OF WITNESS PREPARATION

Most people are terrified of having to speak in public—especially in the unfamiliar, imposing, and stressful setting of a deposition or a courtroom. The prospect of direct examination can be nerve-wracking, and the prospect of cross-examination can be terrifying. Result: unclear and ineffective testimony. Remedy: gentle guidance and extensive practice. Discussion is never sufficient preparation for testifying or any other difficult activity. Actors don't just memorize lines; they rehearse. Athletes don't merely study play charts; they run plays. Being a witness is just as hard. Guided practice is essential.

Not only does practice help a witness, but it also alerts you to problems you may not be able to solve, so you know ahead of time what you will have to contend with in court.

Some attorneys do not prepare witnesses, fearing damage if the witness is cross-examined about it. But badly presented, inadvertently ambiguous, or unclear testimony is far more damaging. There are effective ways to handle your opponent's attempt to use preparation for impeachment (see page 31 below, "Prepare for Cross"). But there are no effective ways to handle testimony that goes badly because the witness was unprepared.

The only danger of practice is that witnesses might memorize answers. Caution them not to, and don't let them write down any answers. Stay alert for any tendency to memorize.

When acting coaches work with new actors, the results are often rapid and marked. Some of their approaches will help you with your witnesses. These approaches are the foundation of the Ten Commandments of Witness Preparation:

I. THOU SHALT PRACTICE IN PROPER CONDITIONS

The room. Practicing under courtroom conditions helps the witness relax enough to be clear and thorough on the stand. Practice sessions in an office do not replicate courtroom conditions. If you cannot get access to a courtroom, use some other large room and approximate the furniture, especially the relative locations of counsels, the witness, the judge, and the jury.

Microphones. If the courtroom has a witness microphone, use one for practice. Have the witness practice the process of taking the stand and adjusting the microphone so that it is between herself and the jury (see page 20), and close enough to her that she need not lean forward to speak into it.

Clothing. Witnesses should practice in the same clothes they plan to wear for court. This allows you to make changes, if necessary, and it helps witnesses get used to doing it the "real" way. Practice testimony in jeans and a sweatshirt is misleadingly relaxed.

In court—and thus in rehearsal—witnesses should dress appropriately but comfortably in clothing they have worn before, so that they will feel natural and at ease. Court is an awkward place for many people, and unfamiliar clothing compounds the discomfort.

Tell your witnesses not to dress too warmly. Jurors will not notice if a witness is a little chilly, but witnesses who dress too warmly will sweat. Jurors sometimes think that sweating reveals dishonesty.

Have your witnesses dress appropriately with respect both to court and to who they are. Don't let a car mechanic dress like a bank president. Don't let parents dress up a child like Little Lord Fauntleroy. Aside from making a false impression, inappropriate clothing makes the witness self-conscious—which, in turn, makes it harder for him to be clear.

To avoid unpleasant surprises on court day, some lawyers keep a suitcase of plain shirts, blouses, skirts, etc., of various sizes, in case a witness shows up dressed like a rock star or fugitive.

Rehearsal jury. For a final practice session, provide the witness with a jury by assembling a small group to watch and listen. Even three or four people can be enough to give your witness an idea of what it is like to talk to jurors. These practice jurors can also tell you how your witness comes across.

Seriousness of practice. The tone at practice should reflect courtroom formality. No casualness. Don't allow anyone to think, "Well, it's just a dry run so it doesn't count." The point of practice is to re-create the physical, emotional, and mental conditions of the real thing. No jokes, no jeans, no doughnuts.

II. THOU SHALT BEGIN CAUTIOUSLY

Begin without giving advice. Start by asking some of the questions you will ask in court. Don't give any advice or suggestions. Just let the witness start answering questions. Ask a variety of question types—questions that require short answers, questions that elicit longer answers, routine questions such as name and occupation, substantive questions, etc. Observe what the witness does. Then—still with no advance advice—have someone else cross-examine in the way you anticipate your opponent will.[1] If you don't know how your opponent cross-examines, find out.

This uninfluenced, uncoached first view reveals a witness's natural weaknesses, and—more importantly—natural strengths. If you give advice before you see what a witness does naturally, you can mask useful qualities. A witness struggling to follow your instructions cannot do what comes naturally, so you never see what "natural" might have been. You could be throwing away something good.

Begin positively. Make your first critique almost entirely positive. Don't try to fix everything all at once. Give one or two *easy* suggestions for improvement, such as "talk louder" or "look at the jury when you answer." When the witness follows those suggestions and improves, he will gain confidence in himself, in the coaching process, and in you as a coach. That sets the stage for attacking harder problems.

Tell them early: Hands away from face. This is a good suggestion to offer early. Once is never enough. Say it over and over. Explain that when he covers his face with his hand, he seems sneaky. Make a point of this even if it is not a problem in practice. Some people do it only when nervous—such as in court.

III. THOU SHALT MAKE SUGGESTIONS WITH CARE

Know when to shut up. When giving advice, stop the instant the witness indicates understanding. Even though you will want to complete or fine-tune your suggestion, don't. When you get that nod or grunt of understanding, STOP! Even if you are in mid-phrase, and even if you think the witness has misunderstood, shut up, get out of the way, and let the witness try it. If the witness understood wrongly or incompletely, it will be obvious when he tries it, and you can explain again.

There are several reasons to stop talking as soon as the witness indicates understanding:

> —It helps keep the focus of the practice session on the witness instead of on you. This is of paramount importance when coaching.

> —It keeps your talking to a minimum and the witness's practice to a maximum.

---

1. Don't practice cross-examining the witness yourself. No matter how clearly you explain that it is just practice, no one likes to be cross-examined. When you cross your witness, you risk alienating her. You demonstrate that you can easily transform into her enemy, and that makes you hard to trust.

—Often a witness who misunderstands your advice will say or do something in a better way than you had in mind.

—Once a witness has the idea, continued explanation is more likely to confuse than clarify.

Give suggestions in private. When observers are present, take your witness into another room or speak quietly so that no one else hears. That way, on the next attempt the witness will not feel the pressure of everyone in the room evaluating the result.

Mention good with bad. With every negative criticism, mention something good. People who think they are doing well are more likely to improve. You can always find something good to say. For example, "Good jury contact that time," or, "Good, you stayed calm on that one." Then you can say, "But you're still going too fast."

Avoid false praise. A witness who has a good voice, or an impressive appearance, or is especially articulate and convincing and responds well to questions, should be told you think so. It creates confidence, and confidence bolsters the witness's ability to think and speak clearly.

But avoid false praise. You have to live later with what you say now. False praise can reinforce a weakness that might later appear full-blown in court.

In general, give praise as deserved, but never lie. Good coaching requires trust.

Keep it simple. Give no more than two corrective suggestions at a time. Don't barrage the witness by piling on advice to talk louder, answer succinctly, sit up straight, make eye contact, tell the truth, relax, breathe, don't fidget, remember Grandma's testimony, don't wear a sweatshirt, think before answering, talk into the microphone, and keep hands away from face. That is too much to think about; it calls for a juggling act, not testimony. No one can assimilate all that at once.

Give two suggestions at most. Let the witness try them and get comfortable with them. Then give the next two.

Think of yourself as a coach whose player is on the bench for a short rest. Don't itemize all her failings. Focus solely on the worst problem or two that she can fix, tell her how, and send her back into the game.

Compliment looks. Many people worry about their looks. Even people who look fine worry that they are fat, skinny, stupid-looking, gawky, or whatever. Don't fib to relieve those worries, but do find positive things to say about appearance. For example, "You have a good authoritative look on the stand," or, "Don't be afraid to stop and think about your answer. You look fine just thinking. Very credible." When you make witnesses feel confident about how they look, they do their task more effectively.

IV. THOU SHALT DEVELOP YOUR COACHING SKILLS

Know your witness. The effective coach maximizes each witness's own characteristics. Don't try to make your witness into someone different. If you do, the witness will not be natural and genuine.

Avoid delusions of superiority. Unfortunately, when many perfectly nice people start teaching or coaching, they suddenly become dogmatic, know-it-all, and arrogant. This can happen to you without your even realizing it. Be careful not to intimidate or embarrass. Don't show off your knowledge and skills. A coaching session is about the witness, not the coach.

Listen to your witness. Coaching is a two-way street. Ask the witness how she thinks she's doing. Ask what she's finding useful about what you have to say and what is not helping as much. If you make your witness comfortable telling you what she thinks, she will provide information that shows you how to proceed.

Be patient. When you find yourself losing hope or patience, remind yourself how you felt when you first had to talk in a formal, public situation with a lot at stake. What may now seem easy to you was hard at first, and it can be nightmarishly difficult for your beginner.

Use an alternate coach. Not every coach is best for everyone. When you are making insufficient progress with a particular witness, someone else might be a more effective coach.

Acting teacher disease: Acting teachers often assume that when a student makes no headway, it must be the student's fault. "After all," reasons the teacher, "I have trained hundreds of students successfully. If this one doesn't improve, it must be his own fault, not mine." But coaching is such an individual process that some personalities will not mesh with yours. That renders you an ineffective coach for that witness. Don't blame the witness; just try a different coach.

Watch like a director. When practicing, try to see your witness as the jury will. Forget what you know about the case, about the law, about the witness, and about trials. Focus solely on how this witness will strike lay jurors. This will suggest adjustments you can help the witness make.

Don't mistake improvement for excellence. When practicing, generously praise improvement but don't mistake improvement for excellence—an easy error to make. Just because a witness gets better does not mean she's good enough. Know in advance how far you hope to get, and don't be satisfied until you get there.

Don't be intimidated by impressive personages. Some witnesses may be powerful, impressive, wise, or successful people who impress or intimidate you or for whom you have great respect. You might feel impolite or presumptuous telling such people that they need preparation. But when you think so well of a witness, it is easy to forget that a courtroom might unnerve her, no matter how confident she may seem everywhere else. Without coaching, your favorite NFL quarterback, the dean of your law school, or the most imposing judge you know could turn out to be nervous or inept on the witness stand.

Allow them their feelings. Because you are the lawyer and witnesses are mere humans, they might conceal their negative reactions or hurt feelings when you critique them. Explain to them that it is normal and okay to be annoyed at being told, say, to use clearer language, which way to look when talking, or to speak up. Explain that your intention is not to make them feel badly but to prepare them for a new situation.

Explain context. With an intelligent witness, it is often wise to explain how her particular testimony fits your overall case. This minimizes voluntary, time-consuming digressions on the stand and helps the witness focus her testimony. (Caveat: what you tell a witness is not privileged if she is not your client.)

With a witness you trust less, it might be better to explain nothing about the case. Instead, keep her focused on the sliver of knowledge her testimony is intended to bring out.

Prepare for cross. Prepare the witness to stay calm even when opposing counsel tries to shake him. Ask a colleague[2] to give the witness a cross more blistering than you expect. Help the witness see where and how to stay calm, slow, polite (as appropriate), and confident. Teach him a statement he can repeat to calm himself when he gets rattled (such as, "It's that attorney's job to rattle all witnesses. It's got nothing to do with me personally; ignore it.")

In practice, ask every question your opponent might possibly come up with. Discuss the answers. Remind the witness:

—To tell the truth.

—To answer only what was asked.

—That you will come back on redirect and fix any damage.

—That the worst thing the witness can do is to twist the truth.

On cross, your opponent may ask if you prepared the witness. Tell your witness to answer truthfully, "Yes, to help me be clear." She can also say that you went through her testimony with her so she would be less nervous speaking in public. With many witnesses, there will be other good reasons for preparation. For example, "It's hard for me to talk about these things, so I wanted to do it in private before having to do it in public."

---

2. See footnote 1, p. 28.

Prepare for non-leading questions on direct. Give the witness plenty of practice responding to your non-leading questions so that in court you need not lead. When you lead your own witness (especially an expert), you de-emphasize his testimony and make jurors think that you don't trust him to speak for himself.

For the same reason, think twice about objecting when your opponent leads her own witnesses. If she wants to undermine juror confidence in her own witness and de-emphasize his testimony, let her. If you object, she will simply ask the same question in a non-leading way and the answer will emerge anyway. It will be more credible because it comes from the witness, and it will be emphasized and more damaging because your objection makes jurors think you fear the answer. Your objection can make jurors think that even a completely harmless answer somehow damages your case.[3]

Criticize in practice, praise in performance. During practice, offer praise and any necessary negative criticism. In court, provide only praise. You can say, "Good." You can say, "Thank you for being so clear and informative." You can nod and smile. You can look satisfied.

V. THOU SHALT HELP YOUR WITNESS TO LOOK GOOD

Making eye contact. Teach your witness not to talk into space, to the floor or ceiling, at listeners' shirt fronts, or off into a distant corner—or he will be harder for jurors to listen to, and may even seem dishonest. You want your witness's gaze *up* and *forward*, directed at counsel or jurors.

Talking to floors, corners, and walls is usually a result of nervousness. Since most witnesses are not as nervous in practice as in court, you may not spot the problem until too late. So provide guidance in this area even if it is not a problem in practice.

Tell your witness that when you say, "Please tell us," it is a reminder to look at the jury. Also explain that to reinforce the reminder, you may accompany those words with a gesture directing the witness's attention toward the jury.

Whenever speaking, the witness should be looking at someone—at jurors if you think it appropriate, or at counsel.[4] Caution the witness not to stare at one or just a few jurors, but to look comfortably from juror to juror, then at

---

3. See Chapter 9, p. 150, "Objections."
4. In some regions of the country, such as the rural South, talking to the floor or off to the side of the person being addressed is a deeply ingrained social behavior that manifests itself when the speaker perceives himself to be in a lower social class than the listener. Under such conditions, it will be difficult for you to get the witness to talk directly to counsel or to the jury. Sometimes it is effective to explain that talking face-to-face in these circumstances is proper and expected.

counsel, then at the jurors again. Individual jurors become uncomfortable if they are looked at too long.

Waving at Mom. Kids in school plays who wave at Mom in the audience lose credibility, but it is cute. Witnesses who look at you while your opponent has them on cross lose credibility—and it is not cute.

Your witness may look at you when he is insecure about the damage an upcoming answer might do. Juries spot this and your opponent may point it out. Tell your witnesses in advance that they need not worry; you will come back on redirect to fix any damage. Give your witnesses sufficient confidence that they don't feel the need to dart panicky looks at you while they are on cross.

In court, if your witness looks at you on cross, smile and look confident. Let the witness and the jury see that you think he is doing fine.

Sitting like a human. Teach—and show—your witnesses that when they slouch, they look like bad guys. And casually crossed legs are okay, but not that double pretzel twist some people do when tense.

Give the kid a cigar. Theater directors know that the best way to keep young actors from looking and feeling nervous on stage is to put usable props in their hands. The pathetic little kid who just wants to pee his pants and go hide often becomes an entertaining performer the instant he gets a cigar, cane, monocle, stuffed dog, or bloody knife. Props give young actors something to focus on besides themselves. That outer-directed focus reduces nervousness.

Starting in practice, give your witness something to show or demonstrate, especially early in her testimony. As long as it does not involve a complex demonstration that can be botched, the result will be a more assured witness.

VI. THOU SHALT HELP YOUR WITNESS TO SOUND GOOD

Breathing. Explain that full, relaxed breathing gives good vocal support and helps relaxation and concentration. Encourage your witness to regularly practice deep breathing up until testimony day.

Volume. Remind witnesses as often as necessary—even in trial—to keep their volume up. The court reporter will complain when a witness gets too quiet, but court reporters sit close and usually have good hearing. Jurors are farther away and some may be hearing impaired. You need more volume from witnesses than the reporter settles for.

Low volume hurts not just because some jurors will not hear, but also because some will interpret low volume as a sign of uncertainty or even dishonesty. They think forthrightness has a loud voice.

Articulation. Lack of volume is not the only cause of inaudibility. Slurred consonants have the same effect as ear plugs, especially within the hollow acoustics of many courtrooms. Practice with your witnesses to speak distinctly—not over-enunciating, but speaking more clearly than they think necessary. If a witness backslides in court and starts slurring again, simply say, "Please slow down and speak more distinctly so we can hear."

Because you already know what your witness is going to say, you may think he is understandable when, in fact, he is not. Slurred sounds—even though you understand them—should signal you that the jury might not understand them.

Sentence fade. When speaking in public, some people tend to drop their volume and intensity at the ends of sentences. "Yes, John came home at about five o'clock" sounds like "Yes, John came home 'bout ffffv . . . ." Even when the final words remain audible, their diminishing volume decreases emphasis. Moreover, this speaking pattern sets up a monotonously predictable sound rhythm that makes the jury tune out.

You can fix this problem by pointing it out in practice. If it crops up again in court, which is likely, simply say, "Please speak up at the ends of your sentences."

Water and bathroom. Tell your witnesses that a small sip of water every few minutes is helpful when speaking in public. (Keep this in mind for yourself as you progress through the court day.) This is particularly helpful for nervous or tense speakers because their throats tend to go dry.

Caveat: Frequent, hasty sips can make a witness seem nervous. Water should be taken slowly, almost thoughtfully.

Second caveat: Don't make a nervous witness pour her own water. Do it for her.

Tell your witness in advance it is okay to ask for a bathroom break, though some jurors may interpret it as a sign that the witness needs time to think.

If your witness does ask for a bathroom break, *make sure that neither you nor anyone on your trial team accompanies her.* This arouses juror suspicions: Will you discuss the testimony? If the witness needs assistance, ask the bailiff or a court clerk. If all else fails, send your paralegal, but don't go yourself.

VII. THOU SHALT SHOW EXAMPLES

Imagine how hard it would be for an actor to perform if he had never seen a play or movie. It is just as hard for a witness to testify if he has never seen a trial except on *Perry Mason* or *L.A. Law.*

Videotapes of actual in-court testimony are readily available. Court TV's video library (800 888-4580) is an inexpensive, convenient source. And there are always current trials on Court TV or at the local courthouse. Have your witnesses watch so they will know what to expect.

VIII. THOU SHALT GET MORE FROM EXPERTS

Ask your expert witness:

—What areas of her field relevant to this case does she usually have the most trouble making clear to laypersons? Then help her find ways to explain those areas clearly. Analogies and visual displays are particularly helpful.

—What areas of her field relevant to this case does she usually find to be the least interesting to laypersons? If these are areas that you want the jury to focus on and remember, then help her find engaging, effective ways of talking about them. Again, analogies and visual displays are helpful.

—What areas of her field does she usually find to be the most interesting to laypersons? Even if such areas are not directly relevant to your case, you might briefly involve them to draw the jury in to listening to the rest of her testimony.

IX. THOU SHALT USE VIDEOTAPE[5]

A three-step videotaping session can help your witness with clarity and presentation on the stand as well as in deposition.

Tape one: Before saying a word to the witness about how to be a witness, videotape twenty minutes of his practice testimony. Then, with the camera off and before viewing the tape, discuss with the witness how he would like to be seen by the jury. Identify two or three desirable qualities such as authoritativeness, credibility, sympathy, efficiency, decency, humaneness, or whatever else might be effective. Then identify two or three qualities you both agree should be avoided, such as arrogance, evasiveness, wordiness, uncertainty, moroseness, overt defensiveness, etc.

During these discussions, and while working on the witness's manner of presentation, don't discuss testimony *content*. Handle that separately. Witnesses can have difficulty gaining lasting improvement if you burden them with both content and manner during the same working sessions. If you treat content and manner separately, most witnesses can improve at both.

While identifying positive and negative qualities, be certain you are engaging in a two-way discussion rather than giving one-way instruction. You want the witness to be an active part of the process, not just passively accepting of what you say. By enlisting the witness as a collaborator rather than an underling, you give him confidence and better prepare him for the solo voyage of testifying in court.

---

5. Absent clear law in your jurisdiction as to whether witness preparation videotapes are discoverable, it is prudent to assume that they are.

If the witness has trouble identifying particular qualities that you want him to have or to avoid, *ask him how he feels about those particular qualities in other people*: "Does arrogance make you angry?" "What is it about arrogance in others that bothers you?" "Does it seem rude when people are arrogant?" "Do you like to do business with arrogant people? Why not?" "Who do you know who is arrogant?" "What conclusions do you draw about people when they act arrogantly?" This usually gets your witness to tell you what is wrong with arrogance.

If he says, "No, arrogance doesn't bother me," ask, "Why do you suppose it bothers so many other people?"

Your goal is to work with the witness to develop a list of the two or three positive qualities you most want to encourage and the two or three negative qualities you most want to avoid. Don't try to work with or even mention more.

Note that you have yet to tell the witness how to do anything or not to do anything (you have not said, "Be more forthcoming," or "Don't be arrogant"). For now, avoid the temptation to do so.

Once you have lists of mutually agreed-upon positive and negative qualities, view the first videotape. Stop at appropriate moments to point out the presence or absence of the qualities on the lists. Discuss what he is doing right, and point out specific behaviors that might seem to jurors to match any of the negative qualities on your list.

That is all you should do during this viewing, except for providing some mild praise for encouragement. It is still too early to tell the witness what to do.

Be especially careful to resist the temptation to mention qualities or problems that are not on your lists. Take notes and deal with them in a later session.

Tape two: After viewing the first tape and pointing out the presence or absence of the qualities on your lists, again tape the witness in testimony. Most witnesses start to self-correct at this point. Their problems diminish and their strengths begin to appear.

Play the second tape back right away, and now—*for the first time*—offer suggestions on how to make even greater improvements than the witness did on his own.

Tape three: Let him try it yet again. Tape, view, and discuss how well he followed your suggestions. There will almost always be some improvement, and you will also be able to spot what needs to be addressed next, preferably a few days later.

Opposition rebukes: Prepare your witness for the possibility of your opponent attacking him in court for having worked with a video camera. Possible responses: "Seeing myself on video made me less nervous about taking the stand," or "I could see for myself that I'd be okay on the stand." If you ask your witness what he got out of the videotape preparation, his answers—such as "I'm less nervous now"—will often be the basis for useful responses to your opponent's attacks.

X. THOU SHALT EVALUATE THINE COACHING

To be a better coach next time, ask all your witnesses after trial which parts of your coaching they found helpful and why. Find out what was not helpful. Ask what else they wish you had done to help prepare them.

⚶ CHAPTER 3 ⚶

YOUR AUDIENCE: JURY VOIR DIRE

Brief History of Jury Selection. You will conduct better voir dires if you understand the historical forces that made voir dire necessary for obtaining a balanced cross-section of jurors. When the ancient Greeks invented juries 2,500 years ago, cross-sectional balance was assured by size—500 jurors per case. Statistics minimized the influence of jurors who could not be fair because of particular biases. With so many jurors, biases on either side of any issue were outweighed by the enormous number of unbiased jurors in the middle, and jury size assured that biases would be present on *both* sides of any issue and thus cancel each other out.

For example, in a self-defense case, 50 arms-control activists who disapproved of keeping spears in the home might have been prejudicially hostile to the spear-owning homeowner who had skewed an intruder. But their bias was outweighed by the 400 other jurors who were neutral on that issue.

Moreover, if a large jury contained strong proponents of spear control, they were almost certainly balanced by members of the NSA (National Spear Association) who strongly favored the right to bear spears. Extremes were offset and consequently neutralized by their corresponding opposite extremes.

Over the centuries as juries grew smaller and majority rule gave way to unanimous or near-unanimous requirements, the statistical dynamics changed. With fewer jurors, the chances decreased that any extreme would be balanced by its opposite counterpart on the jury. And whereas 50 jurors could barely influence a majority-seeking jury of 500, two or three jurors can hang or sway a unanimity-seeking jury of twelve or six. Even a single juror can do so.

Since we no longer seat hundreds of jurors on a single case, we use adversarial peremptory and cause challenges instead of relying on statistics to create a balanced jury. Each side removes those jurors who are potentially most hostile to its cause. Political pressures to decrease the number of peremptory challenges ignore the statistical fact that, without adversarial peremptories, the uncontrollable tyranny of random chance makes it nearly impossible to obtain a balanced jury. Thus, attorneys on both sides, judges concerned with fairness instead of saving time, and citizens who understand the value of balanced juries must fight efforts to reduce the number of peremptory strikes. Any argument against adequate peremptory challenges must rest on some agenda other than fairness.

Difficulty of Jury Selection. When counsel is provided with an adequate number of peremptory challenges, squandering them is among the most common causes of losing cases. Jury de-selection must be done skillfully and with an understanding of jury psychology and group decision-making dynamics.

The difficulty of skillfully conducting voir dire lies not in how hard it is, but in how different it is from everything else you do. Voir dire requires skills, preparation, mindset, and processes that you use at no other time in a case. But if you are intelligent enough to have mastered enough law and procedure to engage in anything as monstrously complex as a trial, you can master the methods of voir dire.

ATTITUDES

A juror coming into court brings attitudes that do not change during trial. Some of these attitudes will affect how the juror perceives and eventually decides the case.

A juror's particular attitudes are the result of a combination of life experiences (they do not change during trial) and inherent personality traits (they never change). You cannot always discover inherent personality traits during voir dire, but you can easily find out about a juror's life experiences. Just ask.

Because life experiences shape attitudes that govern juror responses, you can examine life experiences to determine what attitudes they might have created. For example, if you ask, "Have you ever been blamed for something you did not do?" and learn that Mrs. Jones was fired from a job after being wrongfully accused, you can infer that she is probably suspicious of accusations and thus will probably demand a higher burden of proof than other jurors. Her *life experience* (being fired) gave rise to an *attitude* (suspicion of accusations) that controls how she responds to something in the case (the burden of proof). Because nothing during trial is going to alter her life experience of having been fired, her attitude about accusations and the burden of proof will not be changed by anything she hears in court.

Some judges may not allow you to ask how a juror feels about burden of proof, but few judges bar questions concerning jurors' case-relevant life experiences (though you may have to show the judge the relevance). So you can find out that Mrs. Jones was fired without proof of wrongdoing. Even if you cannot ask her how she feels about what happened, you can safely assume that it left scars.

If you had started by asking her directly about the burden of proof, her answer would have been less informative and less reliable than what you could infer from the fact that she was unjustly fired. ("Mrs. Jones, tell me what you think about the burden of proof," or worse yet, "Mrs. Jones, will you be able to obey the judge when she instructs you about the burden of proof?")

Nothing in trial can outweigh this juror's life experience. Its scars will continue to control her attitudes about accusations and burdens of proof long after the trial ends—and probably for the rest of her life.[1] This does not mean you can be certain how any juror will vote in deliberations, but you can predict which way a juror will *probably lean* when it comes to case issues related to her particular attitudes.

Voir dire's most important goal is to gather information about life experiences because life experiences provide clues to the attitudes that can affect jurors' responses.

SOFTER BIASES

There are softer biases which, unlike attitudes, can change—some more easily than others. Soft biases present themselves in such forms as opinions, proclivities, or even temporary moods. Because they vary in strength, the possibility and difficulty of changing soft biases vary correspondingly.

You can discover soft biases by using the same techniques you use to discover immutable attitudes. For example, demographics (see next section) can provide clues for follow-up questioning. And because life experiences create soft biases and attitudes, identifying life experiences can reveal both.

Because a soft bias can be changed during trial, whereas an attitude will remain constant, you must differentiate between them. For example, if a juror seems uncomfortable discussing his perceptions of the crime rate among black males, you must determine whether he is a racist (which is an attitude) or simply nervous about recent local unrest in his neighborhood (which is a soft bias). Mistaking one for the other can result in a wasted peremptory or in a juror you cannot afford to have.[2]

Evaluating soft bias. Once you identify a harmful soft bias, determine whether your case contains the kinds of facts and arguments that can change it. If not, you must treat the soft bias as an immutable attitude. For example, you may discover that a juror has the soft bias of believing that policemen always tell the truth. You can change that bias if you have, say, a convincing

---

1. To deal with immutable attitudes that are bad for your case, see Chapter 4, p. 69, "Bad Attitudes."
2. Like so much else in voir dire, the distinction between attitude and soft bias is best pursued via open-ended questioning as described below, p. 47, and self-confession, pp. 49-50.

way to impeach the police witness in question. If not, then for all practical purposes that soft bias is an attitude.

Step one: Ferret out the soft biases and differentiate them from attitudes. *Step two*: Determine whether you have the ammunition to change the soft biases.

Caveat: It is risky to try to change soft biases during voir dire. You don't yet have the standing to disagree with jurors, and doing so can harden soft biases into a real problem for you later. Some jurors will resent you for trying to impose your point of view, and you may alienate yourself even from jurors who don't share that soft bias but are listening to the interchange.

The purpose of discovering soft biases in voir dire is not to argue against them right then but to decide whether you have the ammunition to change them later, once you have sufficient standing with the jurors to attempt to do so.

DEMOGRAPHICS AND PHYSICAL CHARACTERISTICS

Because demographic groupings (such as "middle-aged white mothers") and physical characteristics (such as "expensive-looking haircuts") are easier to spot than attitudes or even life experiences, it is tempting to rely on them (as in, "strike anyone with an expensive-looking haircut"). But demographic groupings and physical characteristics can rarely do more than alert you to possibilities. They show you where to probe for particular life experiences that can reveal relevant attitudes. This makes it worthwhile to examine each juror's demographic and physical characteristics, but only for clues to *possible* attitudes.[3]

For example, a plaintiff's personal injury attorney should avoid jurors who believe that bad things happen solely because God wills them. Such a belief is an attitude that will not likely change during trial. The demographics-driven solution is to strike every born-again Christian. But some born-again Christians also believe that when a person does something wrong, it is up to *other people* to right the wrong, even though God willed the wrong in the first place. Such folks can be excellent plaintiff's jurors. The moral: Demographics provide inadequate information to intelligently strike, but they can usefully guide your voir dire questioning.[4]

Here are some common demographic assumptions:

---

3. Relying too much on demographic groupings can also entangle you in Batson and its progeny—the U.S. Supreme Court and other decisions that forbid the use of peremptory challenges based on race or other cognizable groups.
4. Exceptions are obvious: Med mal plaintiffs don't want *any* doctor—no matter her expressed attitudes—on the jury, and criminal defendants should almost always avoid having policemen on the jury. Just be careful to maintain a high threshold for "obvious."

—Blacks are soft on criminals.

—Orientals value education.

—Bankers and businessmen banish emotion from their decision-making.

—Artists are emotional and liberal.

—Social workers care about people.

Here are some common assumptions based on physical characteristics:

—People in ties are bad plaintiff jurors.

—Obese folks are people-friendly.

—Jurors who lean forward and smile when you question them must like you.

—People who lean back while you question them and fold their arms over their chests don't like you.

All such assumptions can lead you astray, so if you have a black prospective juror, question her about her attitudes toward crime. Maybe she believes that most victims of crime are black, and thus she is harder on black criminals than a white juror might be. If you have Oriental jurors, ask about their educational achievements and their family's. Question thoroughly enough to determine whether the businessman incorporates emotion into his decision-making process and whether the artist fits the stereotype (emotional and liberal) or stands outside it.[5] Find out if the social worker still respects and likes the people she was trained to help. The man may be wearing a tie because he is going to his office later if he does not get stuck on a jury. The woman leaning forward and smiling while you question her may hate you so much that she feels obliged to cover her hostility.

Often, your demographics-based or visual-based expectations will be borne out, but not always. Moral: Demographics and physical characteristics can guide follow-up questioning, but they are a dangerous shortcut.

As a guide, *occupation* is among the most revealing of demographic groupings because it so heavily determines life experiences, including day-to-day lifestyles. But even with so revealing a demographic as occupation, don't jump to conclusions. For example, it is tempting to make the demographics-based assumption that teachers value education. But some don't. A weary, embittered veteran of the classroom who no longer values education can carry enormous weight on that topic during deliberations. She can thus profoundly influence other jurors' reactions to, say, an injured plaintiff's proposal for

---

5. Question *every* juror on such demographics-based topics. If you question, say, only the black juror about her attitudes on crime, you will seem to be offensively operating out of a stereotypical framework.

special education or to a defendant's mitigation argument (lack of education) in a capital case.

IMPROVING VOIR DIRE CONDITIONS

Before looking at how to shape questions to uncover attitudes and ways of seeing, first consider the limitations under which you conduct voir dire. Problem areas may include the allowable topics and form of questions, the time allotted to voir dire, who asks the questions, and the order of strikes. These and several auxiliary matters vary from jurisdiction to jurisdiction. Improvement is often possible.

Many judges are surprisingly open to intelligently supported motions for better conditions. For example, if your jurisdiction does not usually allow attorney questioning, or requires you to exercise peremptories before having questioned the whole panel (a system that belongs in a casino, not court), or severely limits the form or topics of questions, it is worth moving for improvements.

If your judge customarily introduces voir dire by announcing, "This is a search for fair jurors," you can probably get her also (or instead) to encourage jurors to be forthcoming and tell the truth.[6]

If some of your questions might be uncomfortable for jurors to answer in open-court voir dire, you may be allowed sequestered questioning of individual jurors, or supplementary pre-voir dire written questionnaires.[7] Judges are more likely to grant either if you:

—Show case-specific need for the information and explain how a questionnaire or sequestered voir dire questioning is necessary to reveal that information.

—Specify the precise questions to be asked.

—Indicate other courts in which it has been done.

—Show how it will save time.

Some jurisdictions do not routinely provide a venire list in advance, even when there is no issue of juror security. However, many judges, if asked, would be willing to override such an inane withholding of information, as long as you can show that there is no real or perceived potential threat to juror safety.

Improvements are often granted even in highly limiting jurisdictions. For example, many judges who typically do all voir dire questioning themselves don't really care who does it. They have merely been following custom, not statute or even local rules. They may even prefer that you do the questioning.

---

6. To understand the harm done when the judge says she is seeking fair jurors, see pp. 46-47 below, "Fairness questions."
7. See below, p. 52, "Use a pre-voir dire questionnaire."

But you have to make the request. The worst a judge can say is no, and there is every chance she will say yes.

Judges are more likely to grant improvements when counsel argues in terms of the court's own concerns and priorities:

—Saving time.

—Helping both sides intelligently exercise peremptories.

—Understanding your proposal in relationship to existing law, rules, and custom.

—Being fairer to both sides.

—Removing the least fair jurors.

—Producing a fairer jury.

—Easy logistics (for example, propose a simple system for question-naires to be xeroxed and distributed to all parties and the court).

—Indication of other courts that have used your proposed improve-ments.

Few judges will resent intelligently supported requests for voir dire im-provements. Even if your requests are all turned down, sane judges will not get angry or vengefully rule against you later on other matters. In fact, the passive listening that makes up most of a judge's day can be so boring that you help it go faster by giving the judge something challenging to think about. So don't hesitate to make motions for improvements. The judge knows that you know your case better than she does, so she relies on you to make the motions you need and to support them well enough for her to gauge their necessity and rationale.

When to ask: Don't wait until the day of trial. Begin the process during pretrial conferences. You are asking the judge to alter customary procedure. While many judges will seriously consider an intelligent request to do so, it is difficult for them to grant a last-minute request. In limine is too late.

Written briefs bolster your request by providing something palpable to help the judge consider your request. In these matters, an oral motion is not worth the paper on which it is written.

For further guidance: For detailed guidance in identifying voir dire improve-ments and petitioning for them, several readily available books are helpful. The clearest and most useful is Chapter 2 of the National Jury Project's *Jurywork* (published by Clark Boardman Callaghan). Also see Chapters 3 and 5 of Starr & McCormick's *Jury Selection* (Little, Brown), and Chapter 7 of Bennett & Hirschhorn's *Bennett's Guide to Jury Selection and Trial Dynamics* (West Publishing). These books also provide comprehensive guidance for planning, wording, presenting, and evaluating the responses to the kind of voir dire questioning suggested in this chapter.

Statutes and Case Law. Have all statutes and case law applicable to voir dire outlined and at your fingertips. This will make it more possible to ask the questions you want, and to prevail in your objections to your opponent's questions. Judges have broad discretion in voir dire and are more likely to respond your way when you can quickly cite supporting statutes or precedents.

DE-SELECTION (How to tell who to get rid of)[8]

You do not select jurors. You only de-select the worst and try to avoid revealing the best.

In some jurisdictions, you are in the preposterous position of having to strike before you know anything about the replacements.[9] And in every jurisdiction, you must rely mainly on what prospective jurors *choose* to tell you. Even under the best conditions, the uncertainties of voir dire are a messy business. Messy jobs are best accomplished with methodical tools. You can't stir goulash with a sponge rubber spoon.

Preparatory lists. Five methodical preparation steps will get you started.

(1) List the *key evidence and pivotal issues* of your case. (For example: a theory of negligence that centers on the installation of a shoddy front door lock.)

(2) List *attitudes and ways of seeing* that might affect how jurors respond to your key evidence and pivotal issues. (Continuing the example: jurors' attitudes about personal safety may affect how they respond to the issue of a shoddy lock.)

(3) List *life experiences* that can give rise to and help you spot the attitudes listed in 2. (A victim of violence, such as someone who was mugged, probably has strong attitudes about personal safety.)

(4) List *demographic and other factors* that can help you spot jurors who might have had the kinds of life experiences in 3 or who might have the attitudes in 2. (*Elderly people living alone* are likely to worry about issues of personal safety.)[10]

(5) List *questions* that will uncover the attitudes listed in 2. "How many of you wear seat belts all the time?" immediately followed by, "Mr. Jones,

---

8. Suggestions in this and following sections assume a voir dire system in which the attorneys do the questioning. For judge-conducted voir dire, many of the same principles can be adapted.
9. See previous section on improving voir dire conditions.
10. Other examples: Parents of school-age children are more likely than others to expect schools to provide absolutely safe facilities. Relatives of physicians are more likely than others to believe there is a litigation crisis.

why do—or why don't—you?" can reveal attitudes regarding personal safety.[11]

These five lists will help you ask the right questions of the right people and effectively evaluate the responses. You will be able to distinguish between jurors who are likely to take seriously the installation of a shoddy lock and those who will probably think it is not so serious. The lists will keep you from frittering away time and juror patience with useless questions such as, "Is there anyone here who cannot be fair?" Such a question cannot come from your lists.

Fairness questions. Generalized "fairness" questions are pointless and often harmful.

Q   Can you be fair even though my client is African American?

A   Yes.

All you have learned is that the respondent is more comfortable answering "yes" than "no." The answer does not help you tell a Martin Luther King from a Mark Furman.[12] The only possible answers are "yes," "maybe," or "no." You almost always get "yes" followed by silence, and learn nothing. Juror after juror answers "yes!" An eavesdropping Martian would conclude that racism has vanished from America.

Fairness questions yield unreliable answers because people rarely confess to their bigotry or anything else that might be socially frowned upon in that particular situation, especially in the intimidating environs of the courtroom. Moreover, people are often blind to their own biases.[13]

When you tell prospective jurors that you are seeking *fair* jurors, it is easy for them to think you are lying. Although you are indeed seeking fair jurors, it might appear otherwise when jurors who don't yet understand the case see whom you select and whom you drop.

Moreover, when you (or the judge) say that the goal is to find fair jurors, some jurors will shade their answers to meet with approval. Other jurors will shade their answers to avoid having to serve.

---

11. Another example: If list 2 includes attitudes toward authority, you might ask, "Mr. Smith, when do you think it's okay to disobey your boss?"

12. Furman was the racist cop in the O.J. Simpson criminal case.

13. A further problem with fairness questions: When counsel or the court accepts a juror's implausible answer, every juror immediately learns that honesty is neither expected nor valued here—because jurors are knowingly allowed to give whatever impressions they wish to give, rather than the truth. Judges particularly should be aware of this because it undermines the entire process of voir dire and does not help much with the rest of trial either. It even erodes public confidence in the justice system.

    When you accept obviously false answers to fairness questions, jurors can conclude that you are gullible, and, therefore, untrustworthy. "After all," they reason, "if you accept deceptive answers from prospective jurors, who knows what deception you might have accepted from your client or witnesses?"

Instead of saying "fair," some attorneys explain that they are seeking jurors who can best judge the case strictly according to the evidence and the law. Others prefer the option of simply not explaining what they are seeking. Whichever your choice, don't say you are looking for fair jurors if your selections are liable to make jurors think that you did not mean what you said.

Exception: The National Jury Project's Susan Macpherson wisely points out one use for saying that you need fair jurors. Sometimes a juror's bias is so strong and you so short of peremptory challenges that all you can do is ask him to be aware of his bias and to try to keep it out of his decision-making. This might motivate the juror to at least try to be fair. For example, "Mr. White, though you feel like young black males are committing all the crimes these days, can I count on you not to convict Joe Defendant for what others have done, but instead to do your best to be fair to Joe by considering only the evidence in this case?" If you have developed some rapport with that juror during voir dire and place that question squarely in his lap, he may feel a responsibility to not only answer honestly but (if he answers "yes") to later try to abide by his answer. Of course, if he answers "no," challenge him for cause.

You can go further and ask jurors if they are willing to monitor each other in deliberations so that a particular bias or topic (such as worry over the litigation crisis or sympathy for the victim) does not get factored into the decision-making process. For example, "Mrs. White, during deliberations, if you hear others talking about how much crime is committed these days by young black men, will you be willing to remind everyone that that opinion has no fair place in your decision-making? Will you be able do that?" (But be cautious when eliciting promises from jurors during voir dire. See p. 64 below, "Getting Assurances from Jurors.")

Indirect questions. Because direct fairness questions do not work, you must instead ask questions that address the issue indirectly. To uncover potential racist attitudes, ask, for example, about the juror's children. What grade are they in? Public or private school? What do you like about the school? Any problems in that school? Any recent changes? Have you ever considered changing schools? What would you look for in a new school?

Or ask about the juror's neighborhood. Strengths? Problems? Changes over recent years?

The goal of such questioning is to gain sufficient information so that it is you and not the juror who decides whether the juror can be fair to your client.

Open-ended vs. close-ended questions. The above questions are not only indirect but most are open-ended. Questions are open-ended when they suggest no particular answer and cannot be answered in only a word or phrase. Because "What's your job?" is close-ended, it shuts people up after a word or two. "Tell us about your workday" is open-ended and gets people talking.

Close-ended questions have some limited use in voir dire: They can nail down a challenge for cause, launch a new topic, or introduce the weaknesses of your case.

To prepare the way for a challenge for cause: "*So it's hard for you to trust doctors?*" "Yes." "*You've mistrusted them since your operation?*" "Yes." "*Eleven years?*" "Yes." "*Do you think you'll start trusting them again in the next few days?*" "Not likely." Etc.

To launch a new topic: "*Do you believe policemen always tell the truth?*" "Sure." "*Do you think there are ever pressures on policemen to shade the truth one way or the other?*" "I guess." Now start open-ended questioning: "*What do you think some of those pressures might be?*" This sets the stage for this juror and others to give opinions.

To use close-ended questions for introducing case weaknesses in voir dire, see page 62 below, "Introducing Weaknesses During Voir Dire."

For most other purposes, a close-ended question such as "Has the publicity about this case caused you to form an opinion?" is inferior to an open-ended question like, "What opinions have you formed about this case?" "Do you believe a person is innocent until proven guilty?" is inferior to "When someone is accused of a crime, why is it so easy to believe the person is guilty?"

Even when looking for biographical information, use open-ended questions to get jurors talking. No matter what jurors say, the more they talk, the more you learn.

Q   What kind of work do you do?

A   Dogcatcher.

Not much there. Ask it a different way:

Q   Tell us what your work day's like.

A   I'm a dogcatcher.

Q   I've never known a dogcatcher. What's involved?

A   Well, you know, I drive a truck around the city all day and pick up people's stray or dangerous dogs.

That can lead to:

Q   I'll bet you run into lots of problems with a job like that.

A   Yeah, sometimes.

Q   Like what, for example?

A   Well, I get bit all the time, one time a lady even bit me because I got her poodle.

If you get twenty seconds of conversation going, you will learn something, even if no relevant attitudes or characteristics are mentioned. How people sound is revealing no matter what they are saying.

Avoid questions that start with the following:
—"Do you agree that . . . ?"
—"Does anyone here . . . ?"
—"Do you . . . ?"
—"Is . . . ?"

Never say, "I take it by your silence that [for example] none of you has ever been in a dangerous situation." Instead, when faced with that awful silence after you ask a group question, ask, "Mr. Jones, what about you, what experiences have you had that put you in dangerous situations?"

Ask questions that start with:
—"What . . . ?"
—"Why . . . ?"
—"How . . . ?"
—"Tell us about . . ."
—"Please explain . . ."

If you have trouble asking open-ended questions, practice by sitting down with a friend and trying to ask a dozen open-ended questions in a row. Practice twice a week until you can do it easily and automatically every time.

The most useless voir dires are those in which counsel asks close-ended questions to which everyone knows the answers before any of the jurors open their mouths. "Is there anyone here who does not agree that Sally Smith deserves a fair trial? . . . I take it by your silence that you all agree." All you can ever take by a jury's silence is that they don't want to talk to you.

The best voir dires are those in which you use open-ended questions to such an extent that you do only ten percent of the talking. The jurors do the rest.[14]

OTHER VOIR DIRE STRATEGIES. In addition to well planned open-ended questioning, consider the following strategies when appropriate:

Getting jurors to talk: counsel's confession. The attitudes and softer biases you need to discover are often the very ones jurors are most reluctant to reveal. As Raleigh attorney Joseph Blount Chesire V points out, one way to overcome that reluctance is to confess to having some of the same kind of bias yourself.

For example, you might say, "Mrs. Smith, sometimes I find myself thinking that when someone gets hurt these days, maybe they complain too much, and maybe they just ought to learn to play the hand they've been dealt instead of trying to find someone to blame it on. Do you ever feel that way? Tell me about it." If she answers "yes" to such a question, ask open-ended follow-ups such as,

---

14. See Application F, p. 205, "Conducting Voir Dire."

"Why?" If she answers "no," ask her if she knows people who think that way, and why.[15]

Or, "We all like to think we judge everybody the same, but I remember when I first went to a doctor who had a foreign accent. It crossed my mind to wonder if she was any good. Mr. Johnson, did that ever happen to you? That you maybe realized you had some feelings like that about foreigners or some other group of people?"

This kind of questioning allows jurors to reveal their biases because you have just done so yourself. In other words, you are asking how a juror might be like you, not different from you. This is a powerful information-gathering tool that opens the way for more information in voir dire, enhances your credibility, and lays the groundwork for better rapport.

Caveat: Be sure that your self-confession cannot anger anyone on the venire panel. For example, some jurors will understandably take offense if you say, "Going to a black doctor makes me nervous," or "I admit I've made some assumptions about Jews and money." To avoid this, ask yourself how a member of the group might feel hearing you confess to such feelings. If you don't like the answer, try it another way.

Voir dire deliberations. Raleigh attorney John R. Edwards describes a superb voir dire technique that gets jurors to deliberate with each other in voir dire. This is the most productive information-gathering method you can employ. To use it, wait for a juror's statement that seems open to debate, such as, "People who keep guns in the home are asking for trouble and deserve whatever they get." Then simply ask another juror, "Mr. Jones, what's your opinion about that?" And keep asking until you find a juror who disagrees with Mr. Jones.

This method has many benefits. First, disagreement among jurors reveals a range of juror attitudes. Second, you will see how strongly the jurors hold their particular views, as well as their general malleability and willingness to compromise. Third, as these jurors interact with each other you will see how they will probably interact with each other in deliberations. (Be on the lookout for jurors who are likely to despise each other. If they are both on the jury, they decrease the chance of a unanimous verdict.) Fourth, you will see who the leaders are (see p. 55 below, "Identifying leaders").

---

15. If the judge does not want you to ask about the opinions of people the juror knows, argue that such opinions can unfairly influence how she might want the case to come out. When she deliberates, she may fear that her friends will be angry at her for having been on a jury that decided in a way they disapprove of.

For example, a juror may have no bias of her own concerning lawsuits against physicians, but she might worry that her physician acquaintances and maybe even her own doctor will harbor ill feelings toward her if she has helped decide a multi-million-dollar medical-negligence verdict. That juror knows she will have to associate with her physician acquaintances long after this trial ends.

To get jurors to debate with each other, use open-ended follow-up questions. When a juror expresses an opinion (such as, "I don't like using money to compensate for pain and suffering"), don't merely ask another juror, "Do you agree?" Ask her what she thinks. Don't accept, "I think the same thing." Follow that up with, "Could you tell me exactly what you agreed with?" or, "I'd like to hear your opinion in your own words, if that's okay with you."

When a juror disagrees with another juror, leapfrog your follow-up questions to involve even more jurors. For example, "Mrs. Johnson, do you agree with Mr. Jones and Mr. Green, or do you agree with Mrs. Brown and Mr. Black?" followed by "Why is that?" You should be doing almost none of the talking. And by no means should you get pulled into the debate.

Because the jurors do all the talking, this is the easiest kind of voir dire to conduct. And because they talk and even argue with each other, it is also the most useful.

Once you get jurors debating in voir dire, ask how their life experiences relate to the subject of the debate. For example, "Mr. Jones, you seem sure that people should not keep guns in the home. Have you been in homes where there were guns?" and "Who do you know who was hurt by a hand gun?" Eliciting the jurors' own life experiences helps you gauge how strongly each juror believes what he is saying. (See p. 39, "Attitudes.")

Co-counsel should participate in voir dire so that you both build rapport with jurors. Moreover, sharing voir dire makes jurors see you as equals—and, thus, later they will pay as much attention to the evidence co-counsel presents as to the evidence you present.

To share voir dire with co-counsel, you may need to request permission. Offer case-specific reasons why sharing will result in a more efficient voir dire, more complete information from jurors, and a saving of court time. For example, point out that co-counsel has focused heavily on a particular aspect of the case, so that she can question the jurors more efficiently in that regard and thus more quickly frame follow-up questions that cannot be planned in advance.[16]

Among the many fine suggestions made by Robert B. Hirschhorn (president of one of the nation's premier trial consulting firms, Cathy E. Bennett & Associates, Inc., in Galveston), one of the most intriguing is to *consider having your client ask one or two questions in jury voir dire.* A brief interchange between your client and each prospective juror helps reveal which jurors are uncomfortable with your client and where there is rapport. In fact, the interchange can build rapport.

---

16. See also Application A, p. 187, "Working with Co-Counsel."

Not every client can be put in such a position, and no client should be put in this position without careful preparation. The pressure of participating in voir dire is more than some clients can handle. Not everyone has the necessary communication abilities and personality traits. The enormous nervous tension of participating in voir dire can make your client seem like anything but a person who is in the right.

For clients with the appropriate personality and skills to come across reasonably well in the unnerving process of participating in voir dire, provide ample role-playing sessions with strangers acting as jurors. This will give you an indication of how your client will do in a real voir dire, and the advance practice will produce better results in court.

Look at your prospective jurors—and don't wait until they are in the courtroom. Send assistants out to watch jurors arriving at the courthouse (to see what kinds of cars they drive), coming up the elevator, and going into the waiting room. Note clothing, jewelry, shoes, reading materials, demeanor, etc. How do the jurors socialize with each other? Who are the talkers and leaders? (See below, p. 55, "Identifying leaders.") What are the jurors' apparent feelings about having to be here?

This advance look provides information to help you decide what questions to ask and which jurors will be more influential than others. If local rules force you to exercise strikes before questioning the entire panel (see p. 43 above, "Improving Voir Dire Conditions"), this advance look helps you gauge your chances for improvement when considering who to eliminate.

Collect jury clerk information. The clerk's venire list sometimes includes such useful information as address, race, occupation, marital status, age, education level, etc. Such things provide attitude clues that help you decide which questions to ask of which jurors. Jury lists also give you an advance overview of the jury panel, which can somewhat mitigate the gamble when you are forced to exercise strikes before having questioned everyone.

Other government information. Once you have the jury clerk's list, you can seek further information from tax records (such as real estate valuation), election records (such as party affiliation and in which elections each juror voted), and civil actions (to learn which jurors have been involved in lawsuits). Prosecutors can obtain criminal histories, and defense should seek to see those materials.

Use a pre-voir dire supplemental questionnaire. The court often allows questionnaires because they save courtroom time and can spare jurors the discomfort of answering sensitive questions (such as medical history inquiries or questions about alcohol use) in open court. Questionnaires also provide demographic and other data on which to base oral voir dire questions. Even a one-page questionnaire can cover extensive personal and occupational information, names of witnesses and parties jurors might know, and juror experiences that might relate to the case ("Have you ever been a patient at the Central Union Hospital?").

Jury studies. Anything that helps you understand juries is helpful, both for voir dire and for the remainder of trial. There are published jury studies about language perception and usage, community values and attitudes, juror psychology, how jurors listen and make decisions, and so forth.

But beware! Juries operate in secret, so most studies are based either upon what jurors choose to say afterward or upon the results of surrogate juries. The former is unreliable because there are many reasons jurors may not be accurate or forthcoming. And though surrogate juries can provide a wealth of useful information, in inept hands the results can be misleading.

For example, one study was based on surrogate juries composed of faculty and students at one of America's most expensive, prestigious, upscale, racially unmixed universities. The only time you could rely on the results of such a study would be if you had an all-white jury of highly educated, upper-middle-class jurors watching a case they believe is pretend, who don't have to put up with the inconvenience of time or circumstance that a real trial entails, who have none of the sense of moral or civic duty that a real trial arouses, and who are all either twenty years old or the professors of those twenty-year-olds. Because the study's "juries" so little resembled real juries, the results must not be taken seriously.

Before accepting the conclusions of any jury study, examine its methods. The internal mysteries of the jury are not easily revealed.

Be especially careful to question secondhand reports. When someone tells you what a study says, look for yourself. It may not say what you were told it says. For example, you have probably been told about a study which showed that 80 percent of jurors make up their minds by the end of opening. The study referred to is *The American Jury* (Harry Kalven, Jr., and Hans Zeisel). But that study says no such thing. It does not even discuss the topic. Dr. Zeisel himself vigorously repudiated the grapevine misreporting of his work ("A Jury Hoax: The Superpower of the Opening Statement," *Litigation*, Summer, 1988). But customarily reliable and well-meaning teachers and lawyers continue to misreport it even though no research indicates that jurors decide by the end of opening, and even though the Kalven/Zeisel study does not say they do.

Gender and Race. Whichever your sex, try to use an assistant or colleague in voir dire (and if possible throughout trial) who is the opposite sex. Men and women judge people differently. In voir dire, you want every perspective you can get.

It is equally important to apply the same considerations to race when the venire includes different races.

Fighting for rapport. If you have trouble establishing rapport in voir dire with a particular juror, don't stop questioning that juror. Keep trying to break the ice. If you cannot get through, you want to know it now, not halfway through testimony or after the verdict. Bad rapport during voir dire's two-way interchange rarely improves during the one-way communication of the rest of the trial.

In voir dire, compare your rapport with each juror to your opponent's rapport with the same jurors.[17] A prospective juror who is closed off to you and open to your opponent may stay that way throughout trial. A strike may be appropriate.

On the other hand, if a particular juror is obviously good for your side, your opponent will probably get rid of her. Before that happens, you can still use her to educate other jurors and help glean information about them. Once you know you are going to lose her, elicit her points of view, such as "Big industries don't care about public safety." While she is answering, you or a colleague should watch other prospective jurors for clues as to who agrees and who disagrees. Then ask those jurors how they feel about what she said. (See p. 50, "Voir dire deliberations.")

Influence of leaders. In deliberations, a single leader can carry the decision-making weight of several—sometimes of many—followers. Leaders often control the verdict. They are hard to persuade (either by you in trial or by other jurors in deliberations), but they are adept at persuading others. They have more power in deliberations than you ever have in trial, because, unlike you, they are present in deliberations, perceived by other jurors as having no stake in the outcome, able to participate in individual dialogue with every juror, and can enlist other jurors to help persuade those who disagree.

Even when most of the jurors start deliberations on your side, they often defer to leaders' opinions. You can start nine to three in your favor and lose; it happens more often than you think. Here is one way that it happens: The leader lets everyone have their say and then adds her authoritative weight until one or two of your jurors switch sides. A third, seeing others changing, is likely to follow. Now it is a balanced fight in terms of numbers, but because the leader is against you, it is not balanced in terms of weight. One by one, the followers slide over to the leader and her accumulated supporters. Each shift increases the pressure on the remaining holdouts. What should have been an easy decision turns into a tight race which you may well lose.

That is why keeping a harmful leader on the jury is lethal.

One common but harmful voir dire strategy is to strike jurors who have terrible qualities but are weak in terms of group impact—and to simultaneously

---

17. If you are forced to decide on jurors before your opponent questions them, petition for both sides to question before either side strikes. See p. 43, "Improving Voir Dire Conditions."

keep a leader who has only moderately bad qualities, in hopes that your "better" jurors will adequately contend with those moderately bad qualities. But leaders are not easily overridden. So don't waste precious peremptories on bad jurors who will have minimal group impact, unless their negative qualities fall into the "absolute" category (as a plaintiff must consider a doctor's son in a med mal case). The evaluation of every juror requires a balanced consideration of leadership strength and good-or-bad qualities. You must weigh each within the context of the other.

Another common error is to retain a harmful leader in the hope that your favorable leader will balance her. But leaders do not cancel each other out. At best, a battle of leaders is utterly unpredictable. Moreover, even if you don't lose your leader to an opposition strike, you may lose him to illness during trial. That leaves you with a leader against you and none for you. You will lose.

When it comes to hostile leaders, take no chances. Seating an opposition leader on the jury is not as bad as seating your opponent's mother. But it is close.

Identifying leaders. There are many ways to identify leaders. One of the easiest is by occupation. A leader in the workplace is often a leader on the jury. Managers, teachers, supervisors, administrators, bosses, and organizers are among those likely to be jury leaders. As you learn each juror's occupation, consider what human relationships are involved. Is leadership part of the job? How many people are under him? How often is he in decision-making situations? What is his level of responsibility and decision making? How much coordinating does he do? How much is he involved in leading groups that are charged with making decisions? How much do other people listen to him?

Even if leadership is not part of the job, familiarity with a work-connected activity can unexpectedly make a juror a "single-topic leader," if that work-connected activity is related to the case. For example, a taxi driver could be regarded as a reliable authority on matters such as dangerous nighttime neighborhoods or hospital emergency rooms. An office clerk might be regarded as authoritative when it comes to business machines. Such authority elevates an otherwise non-leader to a person with a leader's weight and status on that particular topic. (Particular life experiences can also make a juror a single-topic leader; see below.)

Articulate people, especially those who talk easily and a lot, are usually leaders because deliberations are mainly a speaking event. To identify articulate and expressive people, ask open-ended voir dire questions. Leaders are those who answer most fully and confidently.

People with charisma are often jury leaders because other jurors voluntarily gravitate to their way of thinking.

People who are popular are often jury leaders even when they do not try to be. They are popular because they are well liked, so other jurors try to please them.

Celebrities, including local celebrities, tend to be leaders.

People who easily offer opinions tend to be jury leaders, *if they listen as readily as they speak.* Jurors allow themselves to be led by democratic coordinators who are good listeners. Jurors want to follow a respectful person who has the self-confidence not to bully and who will prevent others from bullying. Such a democratic leader holds great power in deliberations because other jurors allow themselves to be coordinated by her, and many will eventually gravitate toward her opinions.

Problem solvers become jury leaders, as do take-charge people, as long as they seem to be able to do so without stifling open discussion. Organizers are leaders but not necessarily opinion leaders. Because they are interested primarily in leading the progress of a group's activity (such as making a difficult decision), they are likely to be consensus makers and as such are often responsible for compromise verdicts.

If you need unanimity, be wary of jurors who take stands in voir dire that seem intentionally different from those expressed by other jurors. This can indicate a common personality type that seeks stature by trying to lead people away from a popular side to his or her own side.

As with occupation, life experiences can create single-topic leaders. With or without other leadership qualities, some jurors are disproportionately influential on topics relating to their own life experiences. This is true even if they do not seek to influence others; it is a matter of how other jurors regard them. A juror who has had extensive or recent surgery can become influential on the medical issues in your case. A juror who cares for an invalid at home will be considered an authority on home care. Even a juror who was bonked in the head by a baseball 30 years ago might be regarded as an "expert" on post-concussion behavior (*"I got slammed and walked away just fine"*).

It is important to ask jurors about their spare-time activities because volunteers and people with special training can also be single-topic leaders. For example, a library volunteer knows not only about books but about working with the public. In case-related matters concerning working with the public, jurors may defer to that library volunteer's opinions. Even someone who has merely taken a Red Cross CPR course can be a strong influence on the jury's choice of which expert cardiologist to believe.

A juror with prior jury experience often carries more weight than first-timers. She is also likely choice for foreperson. While the position of foreperson is not always influential, a foreperson with prior jury service usually is.

Ask them. Come right out and ask prospective jurors to tell you the situations in which they are regarded as leaders, and which as followers. Their responses are not completely reliable, but will provide clues to be followed up.

Some leadership signs are subtle. When jurors are returning to the box after a recess, followers tend to sit down and look straight ahead. Leaders may check around to see if everyone is back in their seats. During voir dire recesses, observe how jurors behave with each other. Those who talk most are potential leaders. Also be on the lookout for people who take the initiative in such simple matters as seating arrangements, holding doors, and even pushing the elevator button. Have an associate hang around the hallway to observe who seems to be leading such decision-making processes as where to go for lunch. (Of course, make sure your associate does not interact with any prospective jurors.)

Caveat: Do not eliminate someone as a potential leader simply because she does not seem likely to lead a person like you. A juror who is deferential to you might exert considerable control over other sorts of people. Leadership is a comparative quality. In a room of lieutenants, the general is boss—but a roomful of sergeants heeds the lieutenant.

For the same reason, consider the makeup of the jury as a whole before concluding whether or not someone is a leader. Also consider gender and race. For example, can the woman who is a potential leader on your behalf hold sway over the particular men who are also going to be on the jury?

Even after voir dire, observe which jurors emerge as leaders over the course of trial. It is usually those you expected, but not always. Whoever they turn out to be, monitor them during trial to be sure they are paying attention during your important points. Without ignoring other jurors, focus the delivery of your important points on the leaders. Develop and maintain good rapport with the leaders. In opening and closing, talk to them. When prudent and appropriate, coach your key witnesses to make contact with them during key points in testimony. And make sure your visual exhibits are aimed at them.

Jury consultants. Jury and trial consultants are a readily available voir dire resource.[18] Your case needn't be big for a consultant to be affordable. In a few hours, a consultant can help you identify what to look for in voir dire, provide questions to help you find it, and make suggestions for getting prospective jurors to talk.

---

18. The American Society of Trial Consultants provides an annotated directory of members, their locations, and the services they provide. Call (410) 830-2448.

Depending on your needs and resources, consultants can also provide pretrial jury research that includes focus groups and surrogate juries, community analyses and surveys, and other voir dire and trial services.[19]

Jury and trial consultants also help identify and test pivotal issues of a case, guide case presentation, prepare witnesses, create and test visuals, and provide a wide range of other services. If you have never worked with a trial consultant, a good way to begin is to enlist their services for voir dire.

GET TO KNOW YOUR AUDIENCE

Information learned about jurors in voir dire tells you more than whom to eliminate. What you learn in voir dire also helps you tailor your case presentation to the jurors who are seated.

Playwrights and screenwriters write best when they know who they are writing for. Shakespeare, Moliere, Sophocles, and most other major dramatists tailored their plays to audiences they knew well. Few great plays have been written for anonymous, generic crowds.

Because audiences vary, the ways to affect them vary. Material that brings down the house in one place can empty the house in another. The world has different colors of paint because there is no generic favorite color.

In real life, you choose your tactics, tone, arguments, and evidence according to whom you are addressing: your law partner, your spouse, your teenager, your auto mechanic, your great-grandma, your dad, or your dog. You deal differently with each because people (and dogs) vary. Jurors vary, too. Find out in voir dire what they are like and then tailor your case to them.

Suppose, for example, that your client is an attorney suing for defamation. Among the seated jurors are several skilled manual laborers. Instead of saying in opening statement, "An attorney without a good name is like a doctor without medicine," change your comparison to, "Ruining an attorney's name is like chopping off a steelworker's arms. No one will employ him again." Every juror will understand your image, but it will have personal and, therefore, extra impact on your manual laborers because they understand the comparison

---

19. Not every pretrial jury research tool is equally useful. Surveys are expensive and often yield little useful information; they are best used for such purposes as deciding whether to seek change-of-venue and supporting the motion to do so. They consume resources that can almost always be put to better use—such as focus groups. "Drive-bys" are popular but overrated. They are popular because they are easy, but they are neither cost-efficient nor time-efficient. They entail a visual look at the homes of prospective jurors. Inferences are based on neighborhood, vehicles, condition of yard and house, and whatever other clues can be gathered by driving by and looking. Much of what can be predicted about juror behavior on the basis of what a home looks like can be better predicted by pretrial questionnaires and good voir dire observation and questioning. By far, the best research tool is the focus group or mock trial. (See Application D, p. 196, "Focus Groups, Mock Trials.")

personally. It also shows them—perhaps unexpectedly—that they have something in common with your client.

Warning: Don't pretend to *be* like your jurors. Mimicry is insulting. Simply choose terms they have reason to respond to.

Tailoring is not merely a matter of how you talk. What you learn in voir dire can help you modify and shape your themes and arguments, decide which evidence to emphasize, and choose which witnesses to call.

The particular kind of tailoring explained below in Chapter 4 (dealing with harmful juror attitudes) is a case-pivotal use of this technique and requires special emphasis on finding out all you can in voir dire. But every bit of tailoring you do, case-pivotal or not, will help your case presentation fit your jury.

During voir dire, have an assistant take thorough notes. Don't throw away the notes when voir dire ends. Use them to guide your thinking for the rest of the trial. (Also see Chapter 4, p. 74, "Tape Recording Voir Dire.")

Remember: there is no one-size-fits-all audience. Voir dire is where to get the precise measure of each particular juror.

EDUCATING JURORS: TWO TEACHING TOOLS

It is ethical to educate jurors in voir dire only if the "education" is an unavoidable by-product of a legitimate bias-seeking question. Based on this, you can employ two objection-resistant teaching tools.

The first teaching tool is low impact. It can be used to introduce information and themes but not to persuade. The second tool is high impact and can persuade.

The low-impact teaching tool consists of *voir dire questions that seek bias and simultaneously—as an unavoidable consequence of seeking bias—communicate*. For example, you might ask:

Q   Mrs. Jones, have you ever been accused of anything you did not do?

This question seeks bias, but at the same time (and unavoidably) it announces your major theme. The bias is one that you need to know about because people who have never been unjustly accused of anything tend to demand a lower burden of proof than others.

Note that this first method merely announces information and themes. It is informative but does not by itself persuade. It informs jurors of your theme (unjust accusations) but does little to persuade jurors of its validity.

Whereas the first method embeds *within the question* the matter you want the jury to hear, the high-impact teaching tool—the persuasive one—relies on matter embedded within the jurors' responses. Therefore, this method is called "response teaching." It uses questions that, as an unavoidable consequence of seeking bias, elicit responses you want the jury to hear—responses that get jurors thinking the way you want them to think.

> Q Mr. Smith, why were you so quick to believe your son had stolen your wallet?

Your question genuinely seeks bias: does Mr. Smith jump to conclusions based on insufficient evidence? But his answer will do more than reveal the presence or absence of that bias. It will also initiate juror discussion of how easily and why people jump to conclusions about guilt. By means of that discussion, the jurors will educate each other.

You can encourage such a discussion by appropriate follow-up questions such as, "Mrs. Jones, what kinds of conclusions have you ever jumped to?" or "Mr. Green, what kinds of unfair conclusions have others jumped to about you?" Ask about such possibilities in both their personal and work lives. Because such questioning elicits discussion of life experiences, the jurors relate themselves to the consequences of jumping to conclusions. This is both revealing and persuasive.

It is persuasive because *everything that is said comes from jurors, not from you.* You have a stake in the case, but jurors do not. Therefore, what they say to each other is more credible than what you say.

Another benefit is that jurors will provide their own vocabulary and terms, which you can pick up and use throughout trial. Jurors' language often communicates to jurors better than yours does.

Another example of response teaching: "Mr. Black, do you encourage your little girl to squeal on her friends when they do something wrong?" followed by "Why?" or "Why not?" You can use Mr. Black's (or some other juror's) answer to lead jurors into a discussion and possibly debate about why children hate squealers. You can easily shift from children to adults, and then (either directly or by implication) to the unwillingness of physicians to testify against colleagues in the same locale. You never need to make an affirmative statement; just ask questions: "Mrs. Green, we've been hearing why children don't like to squeal. Do you think any of those reasons explain why adults don't like to either? Which ones? Why?"

Origin. This kind of response teaching is a group application of the Socratic method of individual questioning. Socrates invented his method at the same time that his countrymen were inventing jury trials and theater in ancient Greece. The Socratic method is so powerful a persuader that throughout history it has been regarded as dangerous. Socrates himself was put to death, not merely for what he thought, but because his method of response teaching was so convincingly and memorably persuasive.

Good-faith bias seeking. Note that both kinds of teaching tools—questions that educate and Socratic group-response questions eliciting answers that educate—must be good-faith attempts on your part to uncover bias. This is an ethical imperative. It is also a jury matter. If you sneak information in via questions that are merely transparent pretenses at seeking bias, the judge will have reason to stop you and jurors will conclude that you are a sneak. Worse, they will assume that a sneak in voir dire will be a sneak throughout trial. So to protect your credibility (not to mention your ethical standing), ask questions that are genuinely bias-seeking. Along the way, you can educate.

To educate or not to educate? Experts disagree over the advisability of educating jurors during voir dire. Some argue that voir dire should be used solely for gathering information on which to base de-selection. Others say that key points should be established as early as possible, which means during voir dire.

It is undeniable that you need to gain as much information as possible for strike decisions. It is also undeniable that educating jurors can hinder the information-gathering process. But Socratic response questioning eliminates the need to choose between the two because it allows juror education to enhance information gathering, and vice versa.

Undesirable educating. There are some topics you may not want jurors to hear each other discuss. If you are a prosecutor, you may not want a juror discussing the reasons he distrusts the local cops. He might enlighten and persuade other jurors. The solution: a pre-voir dire supplemental written questionnaire. (See p. 52.)

Caveat: For reasons covered in the next section, unless you use the second teaching tool (Socratic response), *voir dire is a low-impact time to convey information.* Anything you say in voir dire that you want to stand out in jurors' minds later on must be emphatically reinforced during opening and testimony. This is because information conveyed in voir dire by any means other than Socratic response questions is muted. Such information can form an effective backdrop for certain issues[20] or serve as a low-key introduction to negative information that you must bring out but wish to downplay (such as your case's liabilities). Unless you use Socratic questioning, nothing you bring out in voir dire will have as strong an impact as initially presenting it later in trial.

On the other hand, Socratic response questions elicit answers that educate and persuade, and thereby provide high impact—so high that in some circumstances what the jurors talk about may not need to be mentioned again. For example, if you ask questions that get jurors to talk about why they think it is hard for children and adults to be squealers or whistle-blowers, it may suffice later merely to ask a hostile expert, "Doctor, you don't like to squeal on other

---

20. Creating backdrop (or context) helps jurors notice and remember information coming up later, but the backdrop itself has no impact and is not memorable. It merely provides a framework (context) for upcoming material.

doctors, do you?" The jurors will make the conclusion you want because in voir dire you had them (not you) talking about why folks are reluctant to tattle on acquaintances or co-workers.

INTRODUCING WEAKNESSES DURING VOIR DIRE

Breaking the "law of primacy." The "law of primacy" is a highly touted communications principle, and, as such, is frequently taught to trial attorneys. But it is often taught incorrectly, and the result is hogwash. Those who incorrectly teach primacy claim that placing an assertion first creates impact and memorableness. In fact, the opposite is often true.

Accurately expressed, the law of primacy holds that whatever listeners first *believe* is what they tend to continue believing. But primacy does not make them believe it. In actuality, placing an assertion first—before facts—radically diminishes and can altogether destroy the assertion's credibility.

The misconception that primacy creates emphasis, memorability, or credibility is based on a profound misunderstanding of audience perception. Without powerful methods for creating impact and memorableness, primacy—especially during voir dire—has the opposite effect from what many teachers claim. It subordinates material. As a result, primacy is a good way to introduce and subordinate your case weaknesses.

To prove to yourself that primacy is ineffective, think back to your last few CLE courses. Is your strongest memory the material that was presented first? Do you even remember the material that was presented first?

When experienced playwrights or screenwriters want to subordinate instead of emphasize something, they place it in the script's first ten or fifteen minutes. They know better than to put anything crucial at or near the beginning unless it is intrinsically spectacular or made memorable by the use of other attention-grabbing techniques. During the early moments of a play or movie, audience members are concerned with themselves and their own lives. They are not yet fully involved with what is on stage or screen.

Prospective jurors are the same. During voir dire, they are concerned with themselves and not yet involved with the case. They don't yet have any emotional investment in the case. This is why you can subordinate your case liabilities by introducing them in voir dire. To do so, use the first teaching tool (never the second) described in the preceding section: bias-seeking Socratic questions with your message embedded in the question, *not in the answer.*

To introduce but downplay your case weaknesses in voir dire, NEVER use Socratic response questions. If your client has used illegal drugs, you don't want jurors educating each other about the harmful effects of such drugs, or you highlight rather than downplay that case weakness.

Downplay further by using close-ended bias-seeking questions. Open-ended questions get jurors talking, which is exactly what you don't want them to do with respect to the liabilities of your case. Ask a close-ended question such as, "Mr. Jones, if you knew that Mr. Client once used illegal drugs, would that make it hard for you to be a juror in this case?" Such a question is a terrible information-gathering device, but it efficiently conveys your case weakness. In fact, in group voir dire you need ask it of only one juror (as long as all the other jurors—including those waiting in the gallery to be called into the box—have heard it).

There are many reasons to reveal your case's liabilities in voir dire:

—You can choose a low-impact manner of presentation. If you leave your opponent the opportunity to introduce your weaknesses, she will do it in the most harmful way possible, such as by hurling it in your client's face on cross. That is a powerful tactic only if the weakness is news to the jury. If it is old news (because you introduced it in voir dire), the tactic is limp.

—You gain juror trust because jurors see that you are hiding nothing, not even information that hurts your case. When you leave negative information for your opponent to bring up, jurors can conclude that you were either unaware of it or trying to hide it. Either conclusion undermines your credibility.

—In voir dire, prospective jurors have no context for harmful information, so it carries less significance than it would if it were to come up for the first time later. (See Chapter 7, p. 115, "Context.")

Prospective jurors have no involvement yet with the case. They don't even know if they will be a part of it. Thus, nothing they hear now will have as much impact as if they first hear about it later.

Mentioning your weaknesses as far ahead as possible from jury deliberations relegates your liabilities to the long-distant past. As "given circumstances" from the start, they tend to fade into the background.

By introducing the weaknesses yourself, you establish the language that will be used during trial to describe them. If you say "driving under the influence," your opponent may seem to be exaggerating when she later calls it "drunk driving." But if she mentions drunk driving first, then "driving under the influence" may seem artificial.

In summary, early mention dilutes harmful information into the stew of everything else jurors have on their minds during voir dire. They are inundated and intimidated by a barrage of questions and unfamiliar expectations. They are worried about how long they will be stuck here, whether they are being well regarded by others in the courtroom, and whether they will be accepted. They are hoping they don't have to sit next to the weird-looking person. They are thinking about how to coordinate their outside lives with court. During this period of preoccupation, jurors pay the least attention to new information.

Thus, weaknesses revealed in voir dire (unless via Socratic questioning) have little impact and will be old news by the time jurors are ready to focus on them later.

GETTING ASSURANCES FROM JURORS

Conventional wisdom would have you obtain assurances from jurors in voir dire. But except in particular circumstances (see p. 46 above, "Fairness questions"), it can be a dangerous practice. Jurors resent being asked to guarantee what they will do later or how they will think in deliberations. This is because in voir dire they don't yet know much about the case, and they know you are aware of that.

It is even more dangerous to call in promises in closing, because jurors leaning against you will feel that you tricked them. Those are the very jurors you can least afford to alienate.

Some attorneys report success in asking jurors for assurances in voir dire, but it requires skill and well-established rapport. Otherwise, this sophisticated strategy can blow up in your face. For example, you might ask, "Mr. Jones, if I show you that Doctor Smith was at fault, can you assure me that you will have no trouble finding against him?" Mr. Jones looks you in the eye and swears, "Yes." That seems like an innocent enough exchange. But if Mr. Jones either happens to have a bias in favor of doctors or starts to lean in favor of Doctor Smith as the case goes on, then your question propels him into taking pains to view every piece of evidence in the best possible light for the doctor. Having aggressively viewed all the accumulated evidence in that light, it is likely that by the end of the case, Mr. Jones will never agree that you showed the doctor to be at fault.

If you had not asked Mr. Jones for that assurance, he would have had less motive to view the evidence in a light favorable to the doctor.

HOW TO CONDUCT YOURSELF DURING VOIR DIRE

Make yourself the host-in-chief of the courtroom. Welcome prospective jurors by making them feel that you—you *personally* and not the system in general—consider them the most important part of the process. Show real and individual respect, not just rote politeness.

As host, take upon yourself the duty of introducing to the jurors everyone who has not yet been introduced: you, your client, your opponents, the court reporter, the bailiff, the clerks, the eagle glaring down from the flagpole, and even the judge.[21] This makes the jurors feel that you are cordially in charge and at their service.

---

21. You can introduce everyone via legitimate voir dire questions to check for conflicts of interest resulting from a juror's knowing someone. "This is Ms. Felicity Wright, the court reporter. Do any of you know her?"

During voir dire, prospective jurors are intimidated. Treating them warmly and well relaxes them, thus creating appreciation for and rapport with you and making it easier for them to talk freely.

Starting in voir dire and continuing until the last syllable of your closing, let jurors see that you acknowledge and appreciate that they are the whole point of the process. You have to treat the judge deferentially, but she is less important to the outcome of your case than are the jurors. From a jury perspective, the reason to treat the judge well is that jurors gauge you partly on your behavior toward the judge.

Think of prospective jurors as no less than your equals. With some jurors that can be difficult, but if you let yourself believe that you are superior, some jurors will spot and resent it.

It is particularly easy for you to feel (and thus inadvertently display) superiority. Court is your home ground whereas jurors are neophytes—court freshmen. But if you want to win jurors to your side, give them real respect, not freshman beanies. If you cannot get over feeling that most of your prospective jurors are inferior, single out one or two you *can* respect and generalize that feeling to the others.

Encourage answers. When questioning prospective jurors, don't act as if you expect (or want) a particular kind of answer. If you get an answer you don't like, *encourage the juror to say more.* Answers you don't like are exactly what you need to hear. As the juror speaks, nod slowly to get more (a quick nod will cut her off). Without being dishonest, exhibit approval of whatever you can about the answer: its frankness, for example, or its articulateness. Behave as if the answer is reasonable and important, and you want to hear more.

Don't argue. Don't disagree with anything a juror says in voir dire. It is an argument you cannot win. You will lose even more seriously if you seem to win, because the juror will want to see you proven wrong during trial. You don't have to falsely agree with anything, but never get drawn into disagreeing. You can rarely change a juror's mind in voir dire.

Exception: When pursuing challenge for cause, it may be necessary to confront a juror who is denying evidence of bias. For example, you are arguing when you point out a contradiction in his statements: "Mr. Johnson, you say you're able to follow the law, but you also say that money compensation for pain and suffering is wrong. So if the law says you're supposed to consider money for pain and suffering, you cannot follow that law, can you?"

Under such limited circumstances, you may have to argue with jurors. But most often, arguing with jurors is a futile and potentially damaging pursuit.

Talk loud. If there are prospective jurors behind you in the gallery while you are questioning the current group in the jury box, talk loudly and clearly enough to be heard by those behind you. Turn around from time to time to include them. Jury voir dire is the first step of your persuasive process, so take care that no prospective juror misses any of it. They will appreciate the attention. Bonus: in a strike-before-everyone-is-questioned system, talking to the remaining prospectives lets you turn and see them, thus giving you some idea of your chances of improving the jury if you strike.

Dangerous questions. Watch out for inadvertently impertinent or prying questions. This is often a matter of wording. For example, if someone has adolescent or adult children, don't ask, "What do they do?" If they are in jail, you have caused embarrassment. Word the question in a way that allows the juror to dodge: "Are your sons employed?" The juror will answer, "No, they are all in jail except for little Billy who's on the lam" only if he wants to. He can also just say, "No." In that case, don't reflexively ask, "Well then, what do they do?"

Prying. Attorneys often start voir dire by saying, "I'm not trying to pry," and then they go right ahead and pry. Don't deny in advance what you know you're going to do.

Be careful when excusing jurors. The remaining jurors are watching and this is their first impression of you in a difficult situation. Handle it well. Be truly considerate about the feelings of those you challenge peremptorily or for cause. Even if the excused juror does not want to be on the jury, being rejected is insulting. Don't use a boilerplate apology, and don't speak as if it is routine. Look at those you excuse. Make honest eye contact. Thank them face-to-face for their time and trouble and for their frankness in answering your questions. The remaining jurors will like you better for it. But they will lose trust in you if they see you trying to slink out of an awkward moment by avoiding eye contact with your victim and taking refuge in legalese formality.

Keep 'em on their toes. Most of voir dire is boring for jurors because they have no reason to listen. Their minds wander, making it less likely that they will have visible reactions and harder for you to get them talking when you finally get around to them.

To keep jurors alert, question them in random order instead of predictably across the back row and then the front. Jump around. Don't ask every juror the same question; use different wording to get at the same information. And don't sequence your questions in the same order to every juror.

By randomly sequencing what you ask and whom you question, and by varying the wording of your questions, you keep jurors alert and provide them less chance to formulate answers in advance. Their answers will be more spontaneous and therefore more revealing.

Caveat: Keep track of jurors when questioning in random order. Jurors are insulted when you miss them. Be especially careful to keep track of what you have covered with each juror and what you have yet to cover. Otherwise, you will have to base your peremptory challenges on guesswork instead of analysis.

Group questions. For purposes of gathering information, most group questions are useless. In fact they are harmful because they efficiently mask the very information you seek. Yet judges prefer group questions because they save time. In fact, it takes longer to ask group questions to get everything you need than it does to ask individual questions of each juror.

Many judges do not realize how much their insistence on group questions damages the information-gathering process and, consequently, counsel's ability to exercise intelligent challenges. Try to explain to your judge that jurors are neither frank nor forthcoming in response to group questions. Thus, group questions yield less information. And because you have to ask so many of them, they can take more time than individual questioning, not less.

Watch jurors carefully so that you miss no responses to your group queries. For example, "We're calling an expert witness named Dr. Jekyll. How many of you know him?" Two or three hands may shoot up, distracting you from shy Juror Stevenson back in the corner who raises his hand just a little. Mr. Stevenson raises his hand just a little because he is uncomfortable saying he knows Dr. Jekyll, who botched a diagnosis on his daughter last year. But you don't see shy Mr. Stevenson's hand, so you ask him no follow-up questions and he ends up on your jury—the last person in town to trust your Dr. Jekyll on the stand or anyplace else.

Not only can missing a juror response deprive you of learning something you need to know, but it can make a juror think you find him insignificant.

There is another reason to monitor the whole jury. When questioning one juror, others sometimes visually reveal reactions to the question or its answer. If possible, have an associate watch jurors so that both questioning and scanning get full attention. When a juror reacts to something another juror says, use the reaction to launch questions such as, "Mrs. Shelley, you look like you agreed with Mr. Stevenson. What did he say that you agreed with most?"

Don't stop reacting. Be careful how you visibly react while your opponent is questioning jurors. You lose credibility when you display, for example, sympathy when a juror mentions her accident injury if minutes later, when your opponent is questioning her, you have no reaction to her revelation that her mother just died.

Your visible responses are obvious and important all through the trial, not just during an answer to one of your own questions. You don't disappear from sight just by sitting down and not talking.

The ultimate question: Do you like each other? When you don't like a juror, or when you think a juror does not like you, heed your instincts. If you would not want to spend time together, then why would you want to have a trial together? Carefully consider the wisdom of keeping a juror when one of you seems to dislike the other.

And beware jurors who make a great show of liking you. People who try hard to show that they like you sometimes have hidden reasons for doing so. Carefully question such jurors. Observe them at every opportunity to see if their demeanor is equally exaggerated with everyone. If you are the only target, be suspicious.

✠ CHAPTER 4 ✠

YOUR AUDIENCE: JURORS DURING TRIAL

BAD ATTITUDES

A trial is a permanent marriage (and vice versa). The jurors are yours for the duration—for better or for worse. There is no use cursing the bad ones. They are not going to pack up and move out.

Throughout trial, you must deal skillfully and attentively with those jurors you did not strike or successfully challenge for cause, yet whose attitudes can hurt your case. Fortunately, your opponent has the same problem. So if you take steps to deal with jurors' bad attitudes and your opponent does not, your advantage will grow as trial progresses.

Dealing with jurors who have harmful attitudes is a two-step process. *Step one*: Identify in voir dire and make a catalog (a "Bad List," explained below) of every pre-existing harmful attitude that jurors reveal or that you even suspect might be there. *Step two*: In trial, show the jury how those particular bad attitudes either are irrelevant to the case or actually support your side of the case. This two-step process works so often that it is always worth doing.

When you ignore a bad attitude, it does greater and greater damage as the trial progresses. This is because a bad-attitude juror sees each new argument and piece of evidence in the light of her attitude, thus continually reinforcing her initial feelings and making her think that the case is about her attitude. Result: She turns more and more against you.

The jurors' process of making up their minds is well underway before the end of voir dire and continues throughout trial. When pre-existing bad attitudes are governing that process, you must interfere. But to interfere effectively, you must first understand why pre-existing bad attitudes ruin cases. It is not because counsel fails to change harmful juror attitudes, but because attitudes—harmful or otherwise—do not change. Hoping they will change or trying to change them never works. Few attitudes *ever* change. Those that do change do so only once or twice in a person's lifetime.

Etymologically, "attitude" originally meant an unchanging, internal orientation that directs external activity or position. A gyroscope's internal "attitude" prevents its external position from changing. As we use the word today, "attitude" is a fixed state of mind that shapes opinions and behavior. Jurors' attitudes derive from their life experiences and inherent personality traits. And nothing during trial changes a juror's life experiences or inherent personality traits.

Even after sitting on a case for months, jurors emerge from deliberations with the same attitudes they brought to voir dire. So if Juror #4 is a Scrooge who believes money should not be given unless it is tangibly justified to the half penny, he will not turn bountiful in deliberations when deciding on compensation for intangibles like pain and suffering.

Speaking of Scrooge: In *A Christmas Carol*, Scrooge's attitudes do change—after a dark night of lonely terror, a chained visitor from hell, three ghosts dragging him through the sky, traumatic reconfrontation with his entire life, and the graveyard vision of his own solitary death. That is what it takes to change attitudes, so if that is your case content you have nothing to worry about. Otherwise, you have to deal with harmful attitudes, not try to change them. Here is how:

BAD LIST. *Step one:* During voir dire, list every pre-existing bad attitude you discover or suspect. After voir dire, cross out the attitudes that disappeared via challenges. Result: a master *Bad List* of the pre-existing harmful attitudes that will sit on this case.

Step two: Use the Bad List as a constant reminder of those harmful attitudes. Throughout trial, deal with each bad attitude whenever something comes up that might elicit a juror response that could involve that bad attitude.

Your Bad List allows you to use the two methods described below to reduce the harmful effects of many bad attitudes and sometimes overcome them entirely. Both methods rely upon the fact that the behavior that results from any attitude is dependent on context. Vary context and the behavior alters. Thus, when a juror accepts a new way of seeing the relationship between her attitude and the circumstances at hand, her resulting decision-making behavior can be meliorated or even turned in your favor.

Method 1: Separate the attitude. This first method consists of showing that the attitude is not relevant. Though you have little chance of changing a juror's attitude, you might be able to persuade her that her attitude does not actually apply to this case. Jurors rarely see this non-connection on their own, because the very attitude in question does not let them. It is your burden to show them.

For example, you are defending an alleged rapist. Juror #7 was the best of a bad batch so you kept her despite her firm belief (i.e., attitude) that men are prone to violence against women. Her firm belief gives her a tendency to see everything in a light favorable to the prosecution.

As she sees each piece of evidence in its best prosecution light, her attitude will intensify her feelings against your client. Every time she looks at him, she will see the embodiment of the villain of her attitude. He will look worse and worse to her as trial goes on. She may go so far as to carry his image home at night in her mind and grow eager to inflict punishment. Long before deliberations, Juror #7 will know what her job is.

You must interrupt that process. You cannot wait until closing because by then her attitude and your client have inextricably merged in her mind.

Contradicting her attitude will only harden it and validate her assumption that this trial is about that attitude. Otherwise, she will reason, why would you be contradicting it? Instead of contradicting her attitude, your task is gentler, and it is crucial that you do it gently: you must disentangle the issues of guilt or innocence from the issues of violence against women. *Without putting her on the defensive about her attitude*, gently rescue the issues of your case from her attitude's clutches.

For example: "This case is not about what was done. It is about *whether John Smith did it*. The State claims he did. We say no. There was a rape—but who was the rapist?"

It sounds obvious, but it works. It cannot be left to the juror's own thought process and it cannot be a minor part of your presentation. It must be a repeating theme. Even if it fails to persuade Juror #7 that her attitude has nothing to do with the case, it will affect other jurors. They will less likely be swayed by her. They will better resist her stance and be better armed to argue her out of her stance. And she will be more open to their persuasive efforts than to yours.

None of this is hard as long as you remember Juror #7 and other jurors with harmful attitudes. Remind yourself by frequently revisiting your Bad List, which among other things indicates that "*Juror #7 believes men are prone to violence against women*." With every possible argument and witness, highlight the distinction between the bad attitude and the real issue: "So, officer, you looked at everything at the crime scene, but nothing you saw shed light on who did it?"

Treat that distinction as a theme. It became a theme when Juror #7 was seated, and will stay a theme for the duration of the case because that is how long her attitude will be on the jury. As a theme, it should be referred to throughout trial, whenever the evidence or an argument makes it relevant.

Method 1 works with civil cases, too. Consider a med mal case juror who adamantly believes in protecting the medical profession. Such a juror may well lean toward the defense even if the plaintiff convinces him that the defendant did something wrong. But the juror can become a decent plaintiff's juror—or at least neutral—if plaintiff's counsel dissociates the defendant from the group that the juror wants to protect.

For example, if the plaintiff is contending that the defendant doctor prescribed medication without considering its commonly dangerous side effects, plaintiff's counsel can probably get both sides' experts to say that responsible doctors (including themselves) *always* consider the dangerous side effects. This lets counsel show that no one—not even doctors—considers anyone who has done what the defendant allegedly did to be part of the group (responsible doctors) that deserves protection. Thus, if counsel ultimately shows that the defendant did it, the juror will feel no need to protect him.

Counsel makes no attempt to alter the juror's attitude, but instead renders it irrelevant in this case by excluding the defendant from the attitude's concern. And regardless of how far this approach helps counsel get, it gives other jurors a way to deal with the juror in question.

Method 2: Use the attitude. Whereas the first method *disconnects* a bad attitude, this second method consists of showing that a bad attitude is *directly connected* to the issues, and that it supports your side, not your opponent's.

Continuing the rape-case example: You cannot change Juror #7's attitude, but you can use it to draw her closer to a neutral stance. You might suggest a scenario that her attitude will abhor: *If your client is wrongfully convicted, the real rapist will be out walking the streets grateful for what Juror #7 did.*

This proposed scenario redirects the motivating effects of her attitude squarely onto scrutinizing the evidence to determine whether your client is the rapist. That levels the playing field. The horror of rape and men's violence now attach to the consequences of making the wrong decision. Result: Her mental energies focus on the question of who committed the crime, rather than just punishing someone.

Even if this method does not turn Juror #7 neutral, it arms the other jurors to contend with her.

The principle: Turn the cutting edge of a harmful pre-existing attitude away from your client and slice it through a pivotal spot in your opponent's case. In the example, turn the cutting edge of Juror #7's attitude away from wanting to punish your client and aim it at whether the evidence proves it *was* your client.[1]

---

1. Method 2 works with civil as well as criminal cases. Continuing the example of plaintiff dealing with a pro-medical-profession juror: Emphasize that the defendant's negligence undermines the medical profession, because the profession itself created—in part for its own protection—the standards of care that the defendant violated. To do their jobs well, physicians rely heavily on every doctor applying these standards and on redressing any violations. This argument provides a way for the juror's pro-physician attitude to support the plaintiff's case. The argument also shows that siding with the defendant would be a slap in the medical profession's face because the profession's own standards were violated.

Sometimes this technique entails suggesting a scenario that the juror's attitude will abhor (such as the real rapist going free). It might also entail emphasizing something about the case to refocus its relationship to a juror's attitude. For example, if you fear that a juror's law-and-order attitude predisposes him to believe police testimony, emphasize that the police have laws and rules to obey, but the investigator did not obey them.

These tactics do not in themselves convert a juror to your side. But they open the door. Juror #7 will not stand up and demand the immediate release of your client, but she may start viewing the evidence more fairly rather than automatically interpreting all of it in a light favorable to the state. This gives you a chance with her, and ultimately, if the state's evidence fails the burden, she may be your strongest ally.

It works because you showed her the greatest possible affront to her attitude: the consequences of a mistaken conviction. The real rapist would go free to rape again.

(Warning: While trying to disarm one attitude, take care not to raise the hackles of other attitudes. In the rape example, when showing how bad it would be to convict the wrong person, don't make the fatal error of playing down the seriousness of the rape itself. Instead, use the rape's seriousness to emphasize the horror of allowing the real rapist to go free.)

In such cases, this method of disarming harmful attitudes can help accomplish four things:

1. It raises the burden of proof (Juror #7 may not convict so easily).

2. It enlists the bad attitude to help create a level playing field on which real issues of the case can battle.

3. It gives other jurors a motive and a way to deal with the juror who has the bad attitude.

4. It repositions the case so that whenever your opponent emphasizes the horror of the deed, he further shifts the effects of the juror's bad attitude away from blind punishment and onto whether your client committed the rape.

While not all these benefits are possible in every kind of case, other benefits arise in their place.

Both methods (separating the bad attitude from the case and enlisting the bad attitude to support your side) require careful preparation and continuous execution. You have to decide how to use each witness, argument, and piece of evidence to deal with every attitude on your Bad List. Much of this preparation cannot be done until after voir dire. But the effort is often worthwhile.

TAPE RECORDING VOIR DIRE. Particularly in a long trial, it is useful to make an audio recording of voir dire (if permitted). It is during voir dire that you hear about harmful attitudes. After voir dire, edit out the jurors who were not seated. While voir dire is still fresh in your mind, dub onto the tape the names of the seated jurors so that you know who is talking. Frequent use of jurors' names during voir dire makes this easier.

Over the days of trial, play the tape for yourself, en route to court in the morning, for example. This keeps you focused on the jurors you have—their helpful attitudes and harmful ones, as well as their other characteristics that should remain in your mind throughout trial. Playing some of the tape every morning reminds you that the jurors are the primary force in the room, and that you must pay special attention to those jurors with bad attitudes.

BAD ATTITUDES AND VOIR DIRE DECISIONS. Not every bad attitude can be neutralized. When deciding whom to strike, consider whether or not your case contains the necessary material to neutralize a juror's bad attitude. Because you cannot get rid of every juror with a bad attitude, you should conserve your strikes for jurors with attitudes you know you cannot neutralize. The effect of racial bias, for example, is as rarely neutralized in court as it is in real life.

GOOD LIST. In addition to your Bad List, make a Good List. A Good List includes juror attitudes revealed in voir dire that are good for you and bad for your opponent.

Use your Good List the same way you use your Bad List: to create themes to deal with each entry and to remind you throughout trial to present those themes. With every appropriate witness, argument, and piece of evidence, emphasize how each "good" attitude directly relates to your case and show how it applies.

For example, in defending the rape case you may have a juror who is strongly opposed to drinking. If so, the fact that the only eyewitness had been drinking becomes more important than you might have initially gauged it to be. (But be careful. If the eyewitness is the victim, don't shift blame for the rape onto her, such as by suggesting that her drinking somehow contributed to the rape. That can conflict with strong attitudes that other jurors hold.)

Using both a Bad List and a Good List keeps your jurors foremost in your mind throughout trial. Because jurors are the whole reason you are in court instead of in a star chamber, the more they are at the forefront of your attention, the better.

GIVING JURORS YOUR TOOLS

Your ultimate goal is to prepare the jurors who are leaning your way to argue on your behalf during deliberations. You are the coach and your jurors are your team. Throughout trial, you have to provide arguments, evidence, catch phrases, verbal images, small stories, and main points worded so that jurors can readily use them. You should also provide visuals that jurors can easily use to argue for you in deliberations.

Without effective tools, jurors on your side can be easily intimidated—first into silence and then into changing their minds. If you give them usable tools, they are more likely to speak up in deliberations. Once they have stated their support, it is harder for other jurors to dissuade them. So provide tools to make it easy for your jurors to speak up. They can win your case for you. (See Chapter 10, p. 157, "Favorable Jurors.")

SHOWOFFS AND HAMS

If you take visible delight in winning technical spats with your opponent, jurors will conclude (correctly?) that you are more interested in the adventure of the game than in what happens to your client. That makes jurors suspicious of your motives and, consequently, of you. Concentrate on substance, not squabble.

Any kind of showing off—arrogance, visible delight in winning technical spats, imperiousness with witnesses, even the wrong choice of clothing—antagonizes jurors. Audiences and jurors are repelled by egotistical posturing.

An actor who shows off is a ham. A ham is the back end of a pig. No one likes listening to a ham whether it is on a pig, on a stage, or on a case. When actors or lawyers are hams, no one likes them and no one believes them.

PEEKING

Jurors see everything. They see what you do, what you don't do, and what you don't intend for them to see. At any given moment, at least one or two jurors are watching you. You don't turn invisible just because you are not talking.

Theater audiences display a deeply entrenched human propensity: peeking. Audiences peek at whatever they are not supposed to focus on or even see. If a backstage curtain is open a mere crack, patrons ignore Hamlet on stage and instead watch the stagehand scratching and chewing.

During trial, jurors have an abundance of mental free time. They are always looking for something, anything, to fill it. Often, they interpret what they see as clues. Whatever one juror notices, she shares with the others, so that every little thing you do is sooner or later known by the whole jury. Both in and out of the courtroom, assume that jurors are peeking. Make sure they see what you want them to see.

BONUS JURY POINTS

Be on the lookout for unexpected scoring opportunities. For example, "Your Honor, I have more questions for this witness but I'm at the end of a section now. Even though it's a few minutes early, this might be a good time for morning recess so the jury can get to the coffee bar before it closes at eleven." Even if the judge says no, your efforts will be appreciated.

SARDINING JURORS

Weigh the cost of being responsible for cramming the jurors into their little room while you argue out of their presence. Don't underestimate how slowly time goes for a TV-era jury dismissed to that little room. (Legend has it that one jurisdiction dealt with this problem by putting video games in the jury room, but then had trouble getting the jurors back into the courtroom.)

How would guests in your home feel if you suddenly shoved them into a closet with nothing to do for forty-five minutes, without explanation, and over and over? Your kids would love to see you do that to Aunt Nelly and her poodles, but think twice before doing it continually to a jury.

Even when they are not forced to leave the courtroom, jurors become annoyed and suspicious when your objections constantly result in bench conferences. Consider the cost of appearing to be the one who is always interrupting the jurors' hearing of the case. Jurors start wondering what you are trying to hide. Even if the real cause is your opponent's improper questions, jurors do not usually make that connection. They simply see a direct cause and effect: You object and everything grinds to another halt.

IGNORING JURORS

Jurors are the sole reason you are in court. Remember them as you question a witness, listen to testimony, wait through an opponent's speeches and questions, or argue at the bench.

When you do not look at jurors frequently, you violate a cardinal rule of persuasion: You cannot persuade people you don't look at. When you don't look at jurors, you appear to be shutting them out of your circle of communication. So draw them into your circle of communication at every opportunity. Share an open glance with them after a significant piece of testimony. Between questions, look at the jurors as if you are trying to determine what they would ask if they were allowed to.

Constantly ask yourself, "What is the jury doing, thinking, and seeing right now?"

Constantly remind yourself of the jury. Before you open your mouth to speak, consider the effect your words will have on the jury.

Observe and evaluate everything about you and your case as seen through the jurors' eyes. There is no other measure.

HIDE NOTHING

Do all you can to show jurors that you will hide nothing, good or bad. This means, for example, that you should avoid objecting in the presence of the jury unless absolutely essential, because every objection makes jurors think that you have something to hide. (See Chapter 9, p. 150, "Objections.")

You should also avoid cutting off your opponent's witnesses when they are trying to answer a question on cross.

ASSUME A WORST-CASE JUROR

Imagine that an extraordinarily articulate and persuasive juror is giving your opponent the fullest benefit of the doubt at every turn. Pretend that this frightening juror will find something to disagree with or disbelieve about everything you bring to court, and that in deliberations she will forcefully point out all your weaknesses.

Shape and execute your case with that juror in mind. This will keep you from being easily satisfied with yourself. You will take the extra trouble to make an effective chart instead of relying on an easier-to-prepare verbal explanation. You will cover each issue from multiple angles. And you will more realistically gauge how your opponent's case is going.

It is an old theater trick: Please the grouch in the audience and everyone else is a piece of cake.

DON'T BE FOOLED BY APPARENT SUPPORT

You never know who your worst-case juror might be. No matter how carefully even the most perceptive observer watches jurors, there is no way to know for sure when a juror is disagreeing with you. Some jurors who give the impression of agreeing with you may, in fact, merely like you or enjoy listening to you, even though they are far from convinced that your side is in the right. That can lull you into assuming that you needn't work very hard to get them to agree with you.

Other jurors who seem to be agreeing with you may just be polite. They smile and nod, but inside they disagree with every syllable you say. This is more common in some parts of the country (the South, for example) than in others. In some contexts, it is a charming, civilized remnant of old-fashioned manners. In court, it is a lethal obstacle to assessing juries. Don't be fooled by it. Assume that no matter how the jurors appear, more than half disagree with you. This will keep you on your toes.

THE EFFECT OF TELEVISION TIME ON JURORS

You are used to lengthy law school and CLE lectures, but jurors watch TV, which has altered everyone's attention span. Even people who don't watch television are conditioned by the culture it has created. The six-minute segment, the thirty-second commercial, and the seven-second news bite have accustomed us to briefer chunks of input than a generation ago. Even church sermons are short these days (unless they are highly theatrical or full of jokes).

Ministers know that no souls are saved—*and no minds are changed*—after twenty minutes.

Yet attorneys still go on forever—for an hour or even three or four! Unaccustomed to long listening, jurors may look attentive but their minds are out to lunch.

Persuasion requires focus. Nothing that takes several hours to say is focused. Today's jurors cannot stay tuned.

Some gifted speakers can hold a TV-era audience for hours. Don't talk more than thirty or forty minutes unless you are one of those gifted speakers. If not, here are some ways to save time:

—Never talk about any issue that will not help determine the outcome of the case.

—Never use ten words when three will do.

—Monitor the jurors to know when they are bored. When they are bored, it means they are ahead of you or they don't care about what you are doing. They have stopped listening, so you have nothing to lose by moving on quickly.

—Be well organized. Don't make jurors wait while you bumble around searching for a page, a document, a piece of evidence, or your next question.

—After you decide how long your opening or closing needs to be, trim it to half that length. It will be twice as good.

Tennessee attorney Donna Davis, who is also a leading trial skills teacher, suggests that you segment everything you present into six-minute (or shorter) chunks—a typical TV unit of time. Create the segmentation by such means as inserting a visual at appropriate intervals, or changing topics, or altering the means of your presentation (for example, after six minutes of long, narrative answers, switch to short-answer questions). Structuring your case into six-minute chunks eases the listening task of most of today's TV-conditioned jurors. (Perhaps the next step will be commercials between witnesses.)

LITTLE LIES

Don't promise to be brief if you are going to question or talk for a long time. It is either a lie or a mistake, and you don't want the jury to catch you at either. Because jurors assume that you know the real and full truth of the case, you need them to trust you. They will not trust you about anything if they see you twist (or mistake) reality over minor matters such as how long you are going to talk.

INNOCENT UNTIL PROVEN GUILTY (The forgotten burden)

This topic is for criminal defense, so prosecutors should eavesdrop.

Innocence is boring, but guilt is a visceral.[2] People happily decide "guilty!" based on six-word headlines ("Rock star accused of molesting child").

Most jurors believe that innocence does not come to court. The impulse to presume guilt is so strong that you cannot overcome it merely by asking, "You understand my client is innocent until proven guilty?" Throughout trial, you must educate and persuade jurors about the presumption of innocence and reasonable doubt. Prisons are full of clients whose lawyers failed to do that and thereby eased the state's burden.

The presumption of innocence is an alien notion, partly because of inherent human attitudes and partly because television and movie dramas as well as most crime fiction emphasize pursuit and prosecution of the guilty, not protection of the accused. Even when someone is wrongly accused, the "happy ending" is that the true perpetrator is found out. A not-guilty ending is unsatisfying dramatically unless someone else is accused and convicted. This has deeply conditioned jurors. Show business has no stake in protecting the innocent.

The investigation of *possible* guilt is the main focus of the first half of *Hamlet*. But the audience, already having reached its own conclusion, is yelling for revenge before they even know whether there has been a crime. Even professional directors and literature professors ignore any question of the King's guilt. They "know" that if he was accused, he must have done it. Don't expect better from jurors.

"*What if* the defendant did not do it?" should keep your jurors awake at night. But because jurors worry more about becoming a victim of a crime than being unjustly accused of one, they are more concerned with punishing the guilty than protecting the innocent. Instructions from the judge are never enough. You have to make it your primary concern at every moment of trial.

The best way to do this varies from jurisdiction to jurisdiction because what you can say about it varies. Use an explanation that incorporates some of the language of your jurisdiction's statute, such as:

> If there are *competing reasonable theories*, reasonable doubt requires choosing the theory favorable to the defendant.

This (or whatever is appropriate to your jurisdiction's statutes) should be an omnipresent theme. Implant it in voir dire, if possible, by open-ended questioning (using the statute's language) as to what each juror thinks are the reasons for the doctrine of reasonable doubt, or via questions concerning their own experiences of being falsely accused. Then point out that in each juror's experience of being falsely accused there were "competing theories" of what actually happened—the juror's and the person's who accused him. Then

---

2. See Chapter 6.

emphasize your competing theory in opening. During testimony, gather evidence that supports your competing theory and use the language of the statute in your questions (for example, "So, Officer, would it be as *reasonable* to assume that the shot was fired at three o'clock as to assume it was fired at four o'clock?"). Then structure your closing around the concept of competing theories as they emerged in this case.[3]

During a criminal trial, jurors think that the main issue is "Did he do it?" Change that to "Are we certain beyond a reasonable doubt?" It is useless to bring up reasonable doubt for the first time in closing. YOU WANT JURORS SPOTTING REASONABLE DOUBTS AS EARLY AS POSSIBLE.

DON'T LET THE SHERIFF YELL BAD GUY

When your witness or your client is a prisoner, be sure the handcuffs are removed *outside* the courtroom. And don't allow the sheriff to leave the cuffs in the jury's sight (such as by twirling them from his wrist, leaving them tucked into his belt, or holding them in his teeth—a practice I have seen) while bringing in the prisoner. The point of removing the handcuffs in advance is so they will not prejudice the jury. But the sheriff is usually on the state's side and *wants* to prejudice the jury. Don't let him.

If he does it with your client or a pivotal witness, move for a mistrial. Handcuffs are an impossible bell to unring. They make a visual, visceral, and real statement, backed with all the authority of the state. Being visual, real, and authoritative, handcuffs can be more persuasive than your strongest evidence. "The jurors are directed to ignore the shackles piled in the corner" has no effect.

Because sheriffs, bailiffs, clerks, and other courtroom personnel work for the state, many of them are hostile to criminal defendants and incarcerated witnesses. Sometimes this hostility is unconscious or unintended but nonetheless apparent. Sometimes it is not even intentional but just part of the job. You may have to stop the sheriff from hovering vigilantly near your client just before and after recesses.

In brief: Make sure that court personnel not only conceal handcuffs before coming into the room but also appear neutral at all times. A smirk, rolled eyes, or a suspicious look during testimony can influence jurors who believe that courtroom personnel know everything. Three sweating, trembling sheriffs, hands hovering over their pistols, will mar your defendant client's credibility.

---

3. You might also point out that "not guilty" does not mean "innocent." It merely means not proven guilty beyond reasonable doubt. This argument can be particularly useful when a defendant is unlikable.

JUROR ANARCHY

Regardless of the law and the evidence, juries can—and often do—vote however they please. Juries are free to say, "Yes, the defendant did it, but we disagree with the applicable law so our verdict is not guilty." They can even say, "Well, he probably didn't do it, but he's a rotten sort who ought to be in jail anyway, so: Guilty!" Civil juries do the equivalent. And it can happen to either side. ("Well, maybe the defendant company wasn't negligent, but the poor guy worked for them all those years, so now that he's crippled, the company has a responsibility to take care of him even if it was his own fault.")

No one can prove when nullification occurs because no juror need admit it. Since the judge has instructed the jury to render a verdict according to law, jurors who render instead according to sympathy or anarchistic conscience or talk radio or tea leaves are unlikely to tell anyone.

The public library has books intended for jurors to read before they serve. Usually these books are well worn. At least one emphasizes the prerogative of a juror to ignore law and facts, and that book is as well worn as any.[4] There is an organization that conducts lobbying activities, educates the public about a jury's right to acquit if it disagrees with the law, and even distributes leaflets outside courthouses.[5] The judge may instruct jurors that they must follow the law, but some jurors may have read or been told they don't have to. Whether they have been told that or not, if they feel strongly enough, they will nullify. It happened frequently during prohibition, it has been a common racist tool, it is touted today as a civil-rights strategy, and it can occur unpredictably in any case—including yours.

As a result, you should not ignore the possibility of jury nullification. This makes it important to portray your client as decent, well-meaning, and good, which you need to do anyway for other reasons. There is nothing to lose by emphasizing your client's decency and humanity, or by showing that *he or she did what any good or reasonable person would have done (or had the right to do) under the circumstances,* law or no law.

You should also remain alert for signs that your opponent might be encouraging jurors to nullify against you. For a variety of reasons, juror nullification is likely to be more and more common over the next few years. Don't let it sneak up on you.

---

4. *Jury Manual,* William R. Pabst, Metro Publishing, Houston, 1985.
5. FIJA: the Fully Informed Jury Association. 1-800-835-5879.

ASK QUESTIONS AFTERWARDS

Get someone to talk to your jurors after every trial.[6] Find out from jurors who are willing to talk (most will be) what they remember best, what they found most useful, what bored them or offended them, and what was most persuasive. Find out why they decided as they did. (See Application J, "Reading the Jurors" [Part V], p. 235.)

As in voir dire, open-ended questions yield more information, better-quality information, and information about a wider range of topics (including some you might not have anticipated) than do close-ended questions.

Writers and directors lurk in the theater lobby during intermissions and after the show to eavesdrop on the audience. This is because honest audience feedback (not your mother saying you were *wonderful!*) is the best way to know what worked and what did not. There is no better kind of preparation for your future trials.

---

6.   Don't do it yourself. Jurors are often reluctant to mention your weaknesses directly to you, yet that is what you most need to hear.

CHAPTER 5

YOUR PROPS: DEMONSTRATIVE AND REAL EVIDENCE

What is seen is more persuasive than what is heard. The word "weapon" carries less impact than a picture of the weapon, a model of the weapon, or the actual weapon. What is seen and heard at the same time is the most persuasive of all. This is the *raison d'etre* of plays and movies.

To be a professionally responsible persuader, you should use one effective visual presentation for every important point of your case. Think of each visual as the logo for that important point. The American Heritage Dictionary defines "logo" as a visual "*designed for easy and definite recognition.*" For example, testimony about a broken bone is more effective if the physician uses the x-ray to help him explain the break. Then, for the rest of trial, that x-ray can serve as a memory-jogging logo for the physician's testimony.

A good visual either clarifies better than words (a map is clearer than words) or persuades better than words (a hospital record blow-up is more convincing than testimony as to what it reveals). If it does either, it is also a strong reminder as trial progresses.

Visuals have such high impact that you should use them only for points that you want to emphasize.

OBJECTS

A victim describing a shooting has more impact if she holds the gun while she testifies. The gun underlines her words and vice-versa.

If a man has been injured in an accident caused by the use of the wrong-sized rivets, a co-worker's testimony can incorporate visual evidence:

COUNSEL Would you tell us what I have in my hand?
WITNESS Three rivets.
COUNSEL Have you seen rivets like this before?
WITNESS Yes, sir.
COUNSEL Where?
WITNESS They're the kind that broke.
COUNSEL Exactly this kind?
WITNESS Yes, sir.

COUNSEL	Please take them from me, and tell me if you've ever before seen these particular three.
WITNESS	I have, yes.
COUNSEL	Where?
WITNESS	They're the ones that broke. I picked them up right after the girder fell.
COUNSEL	Would you hold them up for the jury to see, please? Thank you. How do you know they're the same rivets?
WITNESS	The safety officer scratched her initials, see, here. I watched.
COUNSEL	How did she get these rivets?
WITNESS	I gave them to her.
COUNSEL	Why?
WITNESS	They were the wrong kind.
COUNSEL	How did you know they were the wrong kind?
WITNESS	I put the right kind in all day long. That's my job.

The impact will be even greater if your client, the man who was hurt, also holds the rivets. The jury will not easily forget it:

COUNSEL	Ever seen these before?
CLIENT	No, sir.
COUNSEL	Why not?
CLIENT	I don't have anything to do with rivets. I just climb after the boss says it's safe.

You can also pass the rivets into the jurors' hands, perhaps along with the right kind that should have been used. That way the jurors not only see but *feel* the difference.

Invariably, a witness is more memorable and authoritative when displaying real evidence.

PHOTOGRAPHS
YOUR PHOTOS:

Size. When displayed to the whole jury at once, 11 x 14 inches is large enough to convey information (though for some jurors it is barely visible), but too small to have impact. Not every juror sits front row center. Not every juror has the eyes of an eighteen-year-old. Doubling the photo's size quadruples the impact. Compare your 27-inch TV to your old 17-inch model.

In addition to having forceful impact, large photos can be seen by everyone at once. Thus, they allow all the jurors to share a powerfully reinforcing group response.

Cropping. Crop your photos tight (that is, blow them up in such a way as to eliminate the irrelevant outside portions of the image). When the relevant part of the image fills the entire frame, it is bigger, clearer, and carries more impact. For example, if the walls of the room are irrelevant, crop them out so that we see only the bed and torn sheets. (If the walls provide necessary context but still are not as important as the bloody sheets, you can highlight the sheets by other means such as key lighting. See below, p. 87, "Highlighting.")

Surface finish. Have your photographs finished flat,[1] not glossy. Gloss finish reflects light unpredictably, obscuring the image from unpredictable angles. Just because you don't see glare does not mean there is none from a juror's point of view. You have no hint of any reflection unless you are the one it is aimed at.

Scale. Unless the real size of the subject of your photo is obvious, tape an appropriately-scaled image alongside of it, or include something in the photograph that is instantly recognizable with respect to size (a pack of cigarettes, a human being, a car). Don't assume that jurors are familiar enough with a photo's subject to know its real-life size. Girders, for example, seem long and delicately slender when viewed from the ground, but they are two or three feet thick. That can make the difference between jurors seeing them as safe or dangerous.

Emphasize important visual elements. When shooting your photos or videos, use a portable light to highlight the part of the image that carries your message.

The thing you want to emphasize should be the first thing the juror's eye falls on. Don't settle for photos that force jurors to look all over the place to discern your point. Good photography pulls the viewer's eye directly to what is important. For example, a water tower photographed from directly below, with bright sky above, may be thrown into silhouette, obscuring the broken rivets. A portable spotlight will illuminate the rivets so that they are brighter than anything else in the picture. Thus, the juror's eye will see them immediately.

You can create visual emphasis by means of such other composition principles as camera angle, balance, color, color contrast, size contrast,

---

1. Some photo finishers call it textured or matte instead of flat.

mass contrast, framing, and texture. Film processing laboratories can also highlight the key sections of a photo.

THEIR PHOTOS:

Scale. If your opponent offers several photos of the same thing or the same place, note whether all the photos employ the same scale (such as one inch = five feet). If not, make sure the jury perceives the inconsistencies. Otherwise, distances and sizes from one photo to the other can be misleading. For example, a thirty-foot drop may appear to be only twelve feet if the photo, with a one inch = five feet scale, is placed alongside another photo with a one inch = two feet scale.

Lighting. Clever lighting can create misleading effects. A photograph may seem like objective reality but skilled lighting can give different, even contradictory, impressions. For example, an area can be made to look safe instead of dangerous, or vacant instead of crowded, or easy to traverse instead of treacherous. If the image gives a different impression than does the place itself, object.

Camera angle. Camera angles can create misleading effects. When Oliver North testified before Congress, observers in the room found him visually unimpressive and bland. But television audiences found him strong, heroic, and bold. The difference was the viewing angle. Observers in the room were all looking down at North, an angle that diminishes visual stature. But television cameras, located low and angled up, created a John Wayne image—the hero gazing resolutely up and out into the middle distance, nobly weathering the storm. The effect was so pronounced that afterward, cameras at the Judge Thomas-Professor Hill hearings were not permitted to employ that same heroic up-angle (except, of course, for the presiding Senators). So make sure your opponent's camera angles don't alter the visual impression. For example, if angled and lit cleverly, a treacherous jungle can seem a pleasant sylvan bower, or a dangerous city intersection can be made to look like a safe crossing, or vice versa.

Deceptive videotapes, films, and photos.[2] Videotape and film can be easily and subtly edited to diminish, exaggerate, distort, and even reverse reality. Often such alterations can be spotted only by viewing the outtakes. (Outtakes are shots removed during the editing process.) Ask to see *all* the unedited tape exactly as it came out of the camera, and compare its effect to the final edited version. If they reveal that the

---

2. See also Application M, p. 266, "Courtroom Technology" ("Photo Retouching Software").

edited version is misleading, either object or try to show the jury the outtakes.

CHARTS AND DOCUMENT BLOW-UPS

Size. Charts and document blow-ups should be large—2' x 3' is barely adequate; 3' x 5' is better. Visibility alone is not enough; you also need impact. As with photos, small is *never* okay because small never provides impact.

Print size. The print should be large and dark enough to be easily read by a nearsighted juror in the farthest seat. Go in early to make sure all your blow-ups can be read from the farthest seat.

Highlighting. Blow-ups of textual material are effective only insofar as the impact is visual. A 3' x 5' blow-up of a contract page is useful, but it is more effective if the relevant phrase is highlighted in advance with *yellow* translucent highlighter (other highlighter colors are opaque enough to obscure the words). Highlighting creates memorably visual emphasis on the relevant phrase. Highlighting also creates credibility by graphically showing the relevant passage in the context of its full-page document, such as a blood-pressure reading on a medical chart. Graphics designers can suggest even more effective ways of achieving the same thing.

Masking system. Devise a masking system that can reveal each portion of a document or chart a step at a time as you talk about it. When jurors read ahead they don't listen. Even if they do listen, you lose the developing impact of your succeeding points.

GUIDELINES FOR VISUALS

Frame. For emphasis and a sense of authority, charts, documents, and photos should have dark frames. Use thin, dark (black, brown, or dark blue) tape on all four edges.[3]

Mounting. Mount your displays on polystyrene board for easy handling and to avoid tearing.

One message at a time. Except for time lines and a few other exceptions, each visual display should make only one or two points. The key to visual design is "one message per image." Ask yourself what *single message* you want each visual display to carry. Then make sure the visual does not carry other messages that compete for attention.

Persuasive captions. The ethical use of photo, document, or chart captions is to distinguish one from another, but some ethical labels have more impact than others. You cannot label the photo of the accident's aftermath as "DREADFUL,

---

3. Not every graphics expert advises that you frame, but recent research indicates that dark framing is indeed effective.

GORY CATASTROPHE, westerly view," but you can label it "Aftermath" instead of "Photo #1."

New courtroom technology. Some new display devices are useful, effective, and inexpensive (particularly when the cost is spread over a number of cases). For example, during the busy days of trial, a video projection table saves valuable time in a number of ways, and adds effective, easily created visuals to every stage of your trial.

For a fuller discussion of courtroom technology, see Application M, p. 257, "Courtroom Technology: Tips & Caveats."

Day-in-the-life video. The more effective a day-in-the-life video is, the more vulnerable it may be to objections. If you are forced to delete persuasive material, edit in such a way that juror imagination will fill in the deletions. For example, if you are barred from showing the hypodermic piercing the skin, show the syringe being prepared.

There is something more insidious than selective editing: Easily available desktop software can alter photos, films, and videos in ways that are undetectable by any means. For example, a green car in a photo can be made pink or turned into a bus (or chicken) or flipped upside down or removed entirely. Such dexterous technology means that a witness needs a photographic memory to confidently assert that a given photograph fairly and accurately portrays what it purports to portray. Thus, a photograph is no more credible than its proponent because any photo can be easily and undetectably faked. Even though your opponent would never stoop to such deception, you never know what your opponent's client might do without your opponent's knowledge.[4]

The concern over undetectable video and sound retouching is just the beginning. New software allows the creation of, among other things, convincing but utterly false photos and moving images. Moreover, it will eventually be possible to inexpensively and quickly create a virtual reality by means of which jurors can experience any proposed reality for themselves—say, a car wreck, a surgical procedure, or even a rape or murder. It will be impossible to distinguish "real" representations from those that are retouched or utterly fabricated.

If you have reason to object to the admission of a photograph, film, or video, don't do it in the presence of the jury. Because people believe nonfiction film and video to be objective truth, jurors will assume that you want it barred because it helps prove your case wrong. You cannot convince jurors that film and video can be misleading unless you are prepared to spend most of the trial

---

4. Sound recording is just as unreliable. By means of new software, you can make a tape of anyone's voice saying *anything*. There is no way to detect the fabrication.

on that particular question (as did the defense in the first Rodney King case). So object in limine.[5]

GRAPHIC DESIGN

Graphic design is the choosing, coloring, and placing of letters, blocks of text, headings, drawings, photos, and diagrams so as to best achieve your goals. For documents, charts, or posters, a good graphic designer can maximize impact and sharpen emphasis. A poor graphic designer will waste your money and render your displays ineffective, so carefully investigate the candidates.

OPPONENT DISPLAYS: OUT OF SIGHT, OUT OF MIND

Regard your opponent's display as enemy artillery and get rid of it as soon as you can. If your opponent uses the easel or blackboard, remove or cover it at the first opportunity unless you plan to use it to prove the opposite point. (See p. 90, "Tit-for-Tat.")

Be just as careful regarding your opponent's published materials. If, after collecting them, the bailiff leaves them out and still visible, cover them with something. Don't leave enemy weapons lying around. They are visual land mines. The longer they are visible, the more harm they do.

Conversely, leave yours where they can be seen for as long as possible.

In the Jeffrey Dahmer trial, the fine defense attorney briefly showed a formidably persuasive graphic in his closing, but then missed (or chose not to use) the chance to have the jury stare at it throughout the judge's lengthy instructions. To show that Dahmer was insane, counsel displayed a circle representing Dahmer surrounded by multiple separate lines of print radiating outward from the center. Each line of print listed another of the mental pressures and disturbances in Dahmer's life. It focused into one image all the dark forces pressing on Dahmer. It persuasively summarized hours of psychiatric testimony. After closing, counsel leaned the chart against a stool at such an angle that the jury could no longer see the chart. Had he leaned it just a few inches differently the jury would have seen it throughout the judge's long instructions.

Because the judge was instructing the jurors how to go about deciding a man's sanity, a simultaneous viewing of the powerful poster might have been the weightiest persuasion of the trial. But instead of burning into their minds for sixty more minutes, the poster was out of sight and hence out of their minds during the complex, repetitive, boring instructions.

---

5. Every objection you make in front of the jury can seem to be a way of concealing harmful information. Concealment creates suspicion. Make as many of your objections as possible—no matter the topic—in limine, so that jurors don't think you are keeping anything from them. (See Chapter 9, p. 150, "Objections.")

No one can criticize Dahmer's counsel. He had a preposterously difficult task and did exemplary work. And local rules or his sense of fair play may have dictated how he placed the chart. But that trivial difference of placement angle, while it might not have altered the outcome of that particular case, could have won a closer one. Moral: Even such a trivial act as putting something down must be done with an eye to the jury's point of view.

TIT-FOR-TAT: THE BOOMERANG

Tit-for-tat is a powerful dramatic device. Audiences (and juries) love boomerang effects. When your opponent uses a chart, poster, photograph, or any such evidence, your best rebuttal is to use her own display to show how she is wrong. It hangs your opponent with her own rope. It is memorable. It is fun. It saves rope.

Just make sure it does not happen to you.

If each side scores equally well in a tit-for-tat exchange, the tie goes to whoever went second. This is because the impact lies in the "revenge" of the return attack. The revenger need not win, just match.

Boomerangs work not only with demonstrative evidence but with words and ideas as well. Whenever you can, use your opponent's words, arguments, stories, or her own witnesses' testimony to make your case.

Example: In a medical negligence case, a defense expert was devastatingly impeached when plaintiff's counsel asked her to take a defense-proffered anatomy chart and white out the anatomical structures that her area of specialty did *not* cover. Jurors watched in amazement as the poor witness whited out every anatomical structure relevant to the case. What was left had nothing to do with the case—and from then on, neither did that witness's testimony.

THE JUROR AS DEMONSTRATION

Use jurors whenever you can. For example, tell them, "If you run your finger along the back of your elbow, you'll feel the same bone that you see in this X-ray." Or, "If you tug hard on your shirt, you'll feel how one of these safety harnesses is supposed to pull firmly on your back."

You cannot say, "Run your tongue along your front teeth and imagine how you would like it if the defendant got up and smashed them." But you can say, "If you run your tongue over your front teeth, you'll feel how thin the incisors are and therefore how necessary it is that they be well protected."

THE FAMILY AS DEMONSTRATION

Family members add credibility and humanness to your client. Include family in the courtroom right from the beginning. During voir dire, introduce your client's mother, wife, sister, children, husband, father, or whoever else might reflect the kind of human being your client is. Introduce them by asking the jury, "Do any of you know Mr. Smith, my client's brother, who's sitting at the end of the third row?" This is particularly important with children. If you have no procedural reason for having the children there, the jury assumes you brought the children in solely to garner sympathy. It is better to use the children in voir dire to find out if jurors know them. Then send them home.

The way family members look and behave tells jurors a lot, especially with regard to decency and honesty. Jurors watch the family during testimony, so it is okay if Mom looks angry when someone is lying about her son. It is okay for Dad to grip Mom's hand when their daughter testifies how she felt when she awoke to find a strange man in her room. It is okay for the family to listen closely and feel good when they hear things in your opening statement that support your client.

Jurors sometimes see family members longer than they see even your most important witnesses, and make conclusions about your client based on the family's behavior and demeanor. Since your attention can rarely be directed behind you, have an assistant keep an eye on the family in court, in the hallways during recess, and even going to and from the courthouse. Jurors are always watching.[6]

Have your client with his family while jurors are filing into the room at the start of trial and at the end of recesses. It is hard for jurors to believe that a man is a vicious armed robber, an undeserving plaintiff, or a negligent landlord when they see real family things, such as a trusting child leaning half asleep on his shoulder.

Family members are often nervous and tense in court. Try to relax them so that they will behave naturally. Nerves and tension can make people seem angry, and jurors might misinterpret that. If jurors think that a husband is angry at (or uncomfortable with) his defendant wife, they will conclude that the husband knows she did it.

CLIENT AS VISUAL

There is one kind of visual effect that can destroy your case: a client who scowls at jurors—or glares, frowns, glowers, or looks at jurors in any way that makes them nervous. By glaring at jurors from under furtive or furious brows, a murder client may be arranging his own hanging. Because all clients—civil as well as criminal—are under intense emotional pressure, they often look at jurors in bad ways. Monitor your client regularly to be sure this is not happening.

---

6. And listening. Caution family members about talking in courthouse bathrooms. Who knows who is behind the door of the next stall? And keep that in mind yourself when you are in the bathroom.

VIDEO DEPOSITIONS

Video depositions are boring at best (talking heads are inevitably dreary), and at worst they make jurors suspicious (if the witness is honest, why didn't she show up?).

If you must use a video deposition, explain why the witness could not be in court.

Don't show video in the late afternoon. Due to physiological rhythms, many people get drowsy when watching video in the late afternoon. And almost everyone is borderline drowsy after lunch, so try not to show a video then unless you want less attention on it.

Have your witness videotaped in the best possible context: For example, a physician is more credible in her office than in a Holiday Inn conference room. Appropriate visual background behind the witness (books on shelves, diplomas, etc.) and the right stuff on the desk (authoritative-looking texts, family photos) can humanize and add interest and an air of reliability. A talking head on a blank background is 1) hard to trust because the situation seems artificial, and 2) boring unless it has a bee on its nose.

Have the video witness use visual evidence such as charts, objects, devices, etc. Take advantage of a video camera's portability and give the witness a reason to walk across her office or work area, to show, for example, how something works. A witness's work area adds interest and authority to the video.

During video testimony, make sure it is clear who is asking which question. Off-camera voices can sound alike to a jury.

DANGER: Because video depositions are boring, it is ineffective to use one to end your case. Whatever your opponent does next will automatically seem more interesting (unless she shows another video deposition).[7]

PROPS LIST

Theater stage managers and trial lawyers have to organize, track, and quickly locate many props, notes, charts, photos, documents, files, objects, and all manner of things. Nothing is worse than having to stop in mid-phrase looking like a disorganized amateur while you frantically search for something.

The solution is a props list: a carefully-organized, sequential itemization of everything you will need during trial. Do a periodic two-stage check of your props list:

---

7. For the same reason, don't come to the end of testimony and then bore everyone by introducing your remaining documents and exhibits. Get them in earlier so you can end your case with a bang (such as a great expert's ultimate conclusion), not a procedural whimper.

a) Check the props list at the start of each court day to make sure you have everything with you and that you know where everything is. You or an assistant should visually spot each item and check it off; make no assumptions. That way you know before you start if something is missing.

b) Check the props list again before you begin each new unit of trial. For example, before questioning a new witness, go over your props list to make sure everything you want to use with that witness is where you expect it to be. If a recess interrupts testimony, check the list again when the recess ends. Objects and pieces of paper have minds of their own; they scurry off and hide at every opportunity, cackling the whole time.

This sounds like idiot work—and it is. But better to do your idiot work in advance than to look like an idiot in front of the jury when you cannot find the murder weapon or a deposition for impeachment. This is particularly important for plaintiff's counsel in a negligence case. Why illustrate by personal example how easy it is to be negligent?

To show that you are a professional who is in control of your work and at home in the courtroom, you must be secure in the knowledge that you know where all your materials are. A football quarterback has to know where all his players are at any given moment. Once the ball is snapped and the play is underway, it is too late to yell, "Time out! Wait a minute, I can't find my pass receiver. I'm sorry, Mr. Referee, give me just a minute here."

PRACTICE WITH YOUR PROPS

You will look foolish and destroy the rhythm of your presentation if you have to wrestle with an unfamiliar easel and chart, or juggle bits and pieces of a scale model to move it or make it stand up. Practice in advance until you can handle everything automatically and without a hitch, and without being distracted from what you have to say. You want the jurors to pay attention to the information you are trying to convey, not to the clown who just knocked his easel onto the bailiff.

The world's best actors find it necessary to rehearse with props over and over. Hamlet cannot concentrate on "Alas, poor Yorick" with his thumb stuck in the skull's eye socket as if holding a macabre bowling ball.

EMERGENCY PROPS BOX

Have an emergency props box containing magic markers, highlighters, tape, chalk, bandages, tissues, spare glasses, cough drops, scissors, pens and pencils, comb, nail clipper, aspirin, hot fudge sundaes, staple remover, an extra pair of hose, a bottle of clear nail polish to stop a hosiery run, and anything else you might suddenly need during trial.

✠ CHAPTER 6 ✠

YOUR AUDIENCE COUPS: VISCERAL COMMUNICATION

A visceral is any communication that gets to jurors (or theater audiences or anyone else) on a gut level. Viscerals trigger strong emotional and sometimes near-physical reactions.

Finding viscerals throughout the raw materials of your case is particularly easy in "human" cases involving injuries or other personal concerns. But a practiced eye can find them even in the most abstract of contract and economic disputes.[1]

HOW VISCERALS WORK

Viscerals elicit a mental/emotional/physical reflex which occurs like a knee-jerk reaction—without the involvement of higher brain functions. Viscerals bypass the intellect to directly arouse emotional and near-physical reactions; there is no logic or thought. The process is a fundamental, involuntary survival mechanism. We can no more control our responses to viscerals than we can sneeze with our eyes open.

Evolution or God (or both) created this unsuppressible defense mechanism to make us seek or avoid such survival-determinative things as sex or violence, or to make us investigate such potentially life-threatening things as secrets can be, or—because reunions are visceral—to make us try to rescue lost or endangered members of the community. In today's sometimes civilized world, many viscerals (such as a fear of heights or the desire for revenge) may no longer be survival-determinative, but our visceral reactions to them have never evolved away. We are still equipped for the primitive jungle because our primal visceral reactions remain intact, vigilant, and ready to spring into action at any instant, *even when survival is not at stake.*

Some viscerals are inherent (sex) and some are acquired (fear of fire). Whether inherent or acquired, once something is a visceral it activates without the assistance of logic or any other thought process. If you are profoundly afraid of snakes, your fear is not only of ill-tempered, poisonous vipers; you can be equally scared of harmless, happy snakes who would not bite

---

1. See Application B, p. 189, "Humanizing Non-Human Cases."

you unless you tickled their feet. Like any visceral reaction, your snake fear acts as if logic did not exist.

Here is a sampling of other viscerals that arouse gut responses: Thunder and lightning. A good magic trick. Paper cuts on a tongue tip. An unexpected glimpse of a beautiful, strange face. A scuttling cockroach—or half of one, wriggling—on your pillow as you wake. Fingernails scraping a chalkboard. Scorpions, rats, bats, spiders, or the neighbor's kids. The sight of a sexy person. Sex. Love. First love. Blind jealousy. A dark swamp with something moving beneath. Reunions. Partings. Anything divine or satanic. Ritual. Anything obscene. Thoughts of distant travel. Thoughts of home. Homes destroyed. Anything funny. Carnage. Precarious situations. Anything repulsive. Great heights. Anything supernatural (if you believe it, and sometimes even if you don't).

Some viscerals are particularly useful in court: anything secret, such as gossip, hidden facts, conspiracy, and spying. Sudden change of any sort. Revenge. The unmasking of a liar. Confrontation and conflict, especially family conflict.

Because trials, as conflict, are by their nature visceral, no trial need bore a jury if you emphasize the conflict. Unfortunately, many lawyers allow attention to be deflected from conflict and from much else of potential visceral interest.

The list of viscerals could go on for a hundred pages. Some are minor and can bolster your moment-to-moment presentation or emphasize individual important points. Others are major and can guide your entire case presentation.

The nature and extent of reactions to particular viscerals vary among every culture, community, and group of individuals. Consequently, a specific visceral may be stronger or carry different import for some people than for others. For example, a cheap strip show arouses lust in the eager customer, outrage among the local decency committee, and inquisitiveness among the local kids. It pays to know your audience.

On the other hand, many viscerals have the same effect on almost everyone. (Cockroaches cut across a lot of demographic lines.) Observation and common sense will tell you which viscerals these are. You can also learn a lot by watching how audiences react to viscerals in movies, television shows, and theater.

USE OF VISCERALS IN COURT

To use viscerals in court, begin by finding a strong possible visceral on which to hang your entire case. Exploitation? Revenge? Deception? Infidelity? Manipulation? Blackmail? Familial conflict? You may need to look at your case from a variety of angles, but a visceral framework is almost always there to be found.

For example, because virtually everyone is brought up in the midst of familial conflicts, almost every great play has been written to center on the visceral of familial conflict. Similarly, structuring your case in terms of familial conflict will make it visceral. This does not mean that your case has to be about a family. You can present an employment case, say, in terms of management paternalistically dominating junior employees. Such a structural analogy gets jurors to relate their own life experiences to the events of the case.

Another example: Focus a case of industrial espionage on espionage, not on industry, science, or technology. You can bring in all the industrial science and technology you want, but structure it into the framework of your central visceral of espionage. Espionage is a wonderful, engrossing visceral. That is why it is the subject of so many spy books and movies.

Even in a contract dispute over something as dry as, say, a land easement, the dispute centers on a visceral you can find and build your case upon, such as greed, cheating, concealment, fraud, or abuse of power. It is hard to imagine a case without one.[2]

Often, the dominant visceral is found in the single outrageous wrong that you are fighting in court, such as the unforgivable instance of negligence or the outrageousness of the unfounded accusation.

Not only your case theory but every part of your case—every argument, every witness, every question, every demonstration—can center on viscerals. Even your phrasing. "It injured his arm" is information. "It slashed through his skin into a tendon" conveys the same information, but because it is a visceral (slashing skin and tendons), it arouses strong listener reaction. The former has little impact but the latter will be carried into deliberations.

You can present viscerals merely by talking about them. You need not actually scrape your nails down a chalkboard; just mention it and many listeners (or readers) cringe. You need not lick a cockroach to create a visceral effect. Just mention it. Similarly, in court you need not show someone actually engaged in the act of taking (the visceral of) revenge. Simply establishing why the perpetrator of violence wanted revenge will be viscerally persuasive. "Hamlet hated Claudius so he killed him" is mere assertion. Adding a visceral—revenge—turns assertion into persuasion: "Hamlet took revenge on Claudius for the murder of his father." This does not in itself constitute convincing proof, but it is fertile ground in which convincing proof takes root.[3]

To start using viscerals, begin simply. Find and employ one or two to get the feel of it. For example, select a visceral way of describing something.

---

2. See Application B, p. 189, "Humanizing Non-Human Cases."
3. See p. 99 below, "Revenge."

Instead of saying, "She did not tell her brother," say, "She *kept it secret* from her brother." "Secret" (hiding something) is a visceral, and by wording it as such you arouse juror responses. Those responses are not aroused as much when you merely say, "She did not tell."

You will soon get the feel of using such mini-viscerals. As you grow more comfortable with them, stack them: big ones around which you build your whole case, smaller ones with every new witness and topic, and mini-viscerals with every verbal description.

Shakespeare often has ten or twenty viscerals in effect at once. Read him so that you can imitate how he uses large viscerals for his main themes (such as revenge, familial conflict, spying and secrecy, infidelity, and many more) as well as smaller ones for everything else. Almost for this reason alone, Shakespeare is never boring except when a bad production downplays, misplays, or misplaces his viscerals.

FINDING VISCERALS

If Shakespeare is not your cup of tea, observe how any movie's major viscerals compose the themes and govern the structure of how the story is told. For example, the viscerals of violence, revenge, rescue, and reunion drive *Rambo* as well as countless other films. Movies contain such viscerals as deception, secrets, conflict, betrayal, and all the other ingredients of court cases. As you watch movies, keep viscerals in mind and note each one. You will quickly become adept at identifying them in your cases as well as in movies. This will allow you to structure your cases for maximum impact.

Watch whatever you like: movies, plays, TV, soap operas, comedies, mysteries, psychological dramas, zombie films, anything. You will easily spot many viscerals that will later be useful in your cases. It is like shopping without having to pay.

When watching plays, movies, TV, and real life, pay attention to what makes you react sharply, strongly, concretely. What makes you take notice? What makes someone behind you cry "Oh!" or "Eeee!" What makes you wince? What disturbs you, pleasures you, frightens you, sickens you? What makes your heart beat faster? What makes people grip their seats or lean forward? What makes the audience sit absolutely silent and still? What makes them hold their collective breath? Anything that gets to you, anything that creates a strong reaction, is a visceral.

Keep track of every newly-noted visceral for future case material. Catalog them. Then, with each new case, witness, and bit of evidence, consult your catalog to find the viscerals that match.

For example, after reading Shakespeare or watching a few movies, you'll know that "mystery" is an effective visceral. Thus, in your next case, instead of merely pointing out a discrepancy between hospital records and a nurse's testimony, you will introduce the discrepancy as a mystery (and, if possible, promise to "solve" it later). This emphasizes the discrepancy and makes it memorable. You have made a dry fact (the discrepancy) viscerally engrossing.

VISCERALS IN COURT: EXAMPLE

Most people are afraid of falling from a great height. It is a visceral. What can be more sickening than to feel the ground drop from under you when your "ground" is a construction platform thirty feet in the air?

If your client has suffered such a fall, without viscerals your questioning might go as follows:

COUNSEL   What happened then?

PLAINTIFF   I fell.

COUNSEL   And what happened after that?

PLAINTIFF   I blacked out.

COUNSEL   What's the next thing you remember?

PLAINTIFF   I was lying on the ground and everyone was running over . . . .

Not much impact. But if you recall from a play you read, or from Alfred Hitchcock's *Vertigo*, or from real life, that we all have an internal, visceral, inherent terror of falling, then you would not have rushed into line three. Sure, "What happened after that?" is the logical next question. But add viscerals (italicized):

COUNSEL   What happened then?

PLAINTIFF   I fell.

COUNSEL   How did you first know something was wrong?

PLAINTIFF   *I felt something move a little. I put my foot down and there was nothing there. It was like falling into a hole.*

COUNSEL   How *high off the ground* were you?

PLAINTIFF   Thirty feet.

COUNSEL   What did you do after you stepped down and *found nothing there?*

PLAINTIFF   *I stepped back with my other foot. There was nothing there either.*

COUNSEL   What did you do then?

PLAINTIFF   Nothing. There was nothing to do.

COUNSEL   Did you try?

PLAINTIFF   Yeah, *I grabbed, but I missed. I scraped my knuckles on the rail but I missed.*

COUNSEL   Anything else?

PLAINTIFF   I yelled.

COUNSEL   Why?

PLAINTIFF   I was scared.

COUNSEL   I'm sorry if it's frightening to think back on this, but what happened next?

PLAINTIFF   *I fell backwards.*

COUNSEL   And *there was nothing there?*

PLAINTIFF   Just air.

COUNSEL   *Did you look down?*

PLAINTIFF   No!

COUNSEL   What happened next?

PLAINTIFF   I blacked out.

COUNSEL   What's the next thing you remember?

PLAINTIFF   I was lying on the ground under the girder. Everyone was running over . . . .

This high-impact dialogue is built on viscerals—things that communicate on a gut level. Your witness does not have to (and must not) memorize anything; he just has to answer the right questions.

REVENGE

Revenge is so common a motive and so powerful a visceral that you should pay particular attention to how to handle it in court. It is often relevant and even central to civil as well as criminal cases.

Like every visceral, revenge grabs us because we are all deeply (viscerally) interested in it, even just watching it. We are programmed for it: by age five, any child with brothers or sisters has experienced repeated and intense desire for revenge. Anyone who was ever bullied in high school has not only hungered for revenge, but probably never had that desire fulfilled—which makes later sensitivity to it all the greater.

Hamlet is one of hundreds of revenge plays. And there are thousands of revenge movies. Two or three are playing right now, no matter when you are reading this.

If you happen to wander past a television and see the rotten bad guy do something rotten and bad to a good person (or squash a puppy with his boot heel), you can get caught there watching the dumb, predictable show all the way to its dumb, predictable end, commercials and all. You do it just for the visceral pleasure of seeing the bad guy get his just deserts even though you know in advance he is going to. You watch even if it is an awful show and even if you have seen it before. That is your hunger for viscerals at work. It is a familiar hunger that we all share. Thus, jurors feel it clearly and comprehend it precisely when you use it in court. They readily accept it when it is presented as a motive. They remember and talk about it during deliberations.

Suppose your client, Mr. Jobe, is suing for battery. Coming out of church, he was jumped from behind by Bruno. You don't have to show motive as an element of battery. Yet revenge is a visceral, so use it.

But don't jump directly to it. First, show the jury what created Bruno's desire for revenge: whatever your client originally did that lit the fires of rage in Bruno. The jurors will then come to their own conclusions about the ensuing revenge. You will barely need to mention it.

Your jurors will respond to revenge exactly as intensely as they feel that Bruno was wronged by your client. If you show that Bruno was mildly annoyed because his wife had lunch with your client, then the revenge's visceral impact on the jury is mild. If you show that Bruno was upset because your client took her to the mountains for the weekend, the visceral impact of the resulting revenge is stronger. Jealousy is a visceral in its own right, so jealous revenge has double impact.

The initiating wrong implies and impels revenge, so the more you focus on the initiating wrong, the stronger the jurors will viscerally feel the revenge. As long as you don't make Bruno seem justified, you can portray the revenge-inducing wrong as strongly as the truth allows. (If your client raped Bruno's wife, the jurors will want to beat up your client just like Bruno did. So be careful how far you go.)

If you emphasize Bruno's jealousy and his consequent thirst for revenge, jurors will believe and remember that Bruno (a) attacked your client and (b) hit him hard.

To use revenge as a visceral, present the specifics of the initiating wrong in graphic detail. The jury will take it from there.

But remember that revenge is just one of thousands of viscerals. You can find them in every case.

✠ CHAPTER 7 ✠

YOUR PLOT: TELLING YOUR STORY

Influencing what jurors want to do. The goal of storytelling is not merely to inform, but to make jurors want to do what you want them to do. This is the gold standard of all persuasion. It is best achieved by storytelling, because a story influences not only what jurors think, but what they feel. By influencing what jurors think and feel, you control what they want to do.

To shape your story, first decide what it is about your case that will make jurors want to do what you want them to do. Example: Your client's pain and disabilities will make jurors *want to help* by providing money, and the defendant's carelessness will make jurors *want to get that money from the defendant*.

Thus, such things (client pain and disability, and the defendant's carelessness) are the focus of your story. Some other things that can motivate juror behavior: juror identification with your client, what good financial compensation will do, and how well your side of the case appeals to the jurors' sense of fairness. Insofar as your story focuses on these things, it will motivate jurors to want to do what you want them to do. Insofar as your story strays into other topics, it will be less persuasive.

Consider each storytelling technique in this chapter as one more tool to help you achieve the gold standard of persuasion: motivating the jurors to want to do what you want them to do.

The love of stories. Our love—perhaps need—for stories is deep-seated. The difference between what we dream when we are still in the womb[1] and what we dream when we are a few years old is that our dreams take on story form.

The average American watches thirty hours of television stories every week, including hundreds of small stories in commercials. Americans love stories so much that they hear, see, and read thousands per year.

---

1. Yes, we do dream—almost continually—long before birth! The Stanford Sleep Laboratory, among others, has conducted extensive research in the area of dreams and has documented the rapid post-natal development of story content in dreams. (See William C. Dement's *Some Must Watch While Some Must Sleep*, a fascinating book on this research and its findings. The title, incidentally, is from *Hamlet*.)

The power of stories. Story is immeasurably more persuasive than explana-tion and argument. In fact, it is the most persuasive information-delivery system ever devised and our strongest nonviolent persuasive method. Every successful persuasive enterprise from the Bible to television commercials relies on story more than on all other kinds of communication devices put together.

Before looking at how to tell stories, it is useful to understand what makes them work. Most simply, storytelling gives its listeners pleasure (so they listen) and creates rapport between teller and listener. But there is a more complex foundation to how stories persuade. You can skip this next section and get right to technique (p. 110 below), but your storytelling skills will be better if you understand what follows:

Filling the gaps. Every means of oral communication leaves gaps: blank spaces that are not mentioned or that are not heard, and that each listener fills in his or her own individual way. Oral argument leaves the most gaps; oral explanation leaves nearly as many. As a result, listeners react in wildly varying and unpredictable ways to oral explanation and argument.

Stories leave the fewest gaps because they encourage the listener to fill the gaps in predictable ways.

Gaps can hurt your case even when they involve minor matters. Most gaps are caused when a juror fails to apprehend a relatively unimportant piece of information (for example, that your client was going 35 mph). The harm is done when a juror fills the gap with a case-pivotal misconception (say, that your client was going 85 mph). A minor fact is now a major fiction and the case is turned on its head.

In other words, gaps are your greatest enemy. Unfortunately, you cannot fill every gap by telling the jurors everything. The more you tell, the lower percentage the listener apprehends, because there are austere limits to the powers of attention and memory. In general, people hear only half of what is said to them, and remember even less. The result: gaps that they fill in their own ways.

The best way to deal with this dilemma is through storytelling. Storytelling controls how listeners fill in the gaps, elicits a *predictable* flow of emotional responses, and evokes the listeners' personal thoughts, memories, attitudes, opinions, and life experiences. For example, the failure to mention that the car was going 35 mph is unlikely to result in any juror thinking it was going 85 if a story makes the listener feel that the driver is a careful person—and from personal experience, each juror knows how careful people drive. Argu-ment and explanation cannot achieve the same thing as effectively because neither enlists the jurors' personal associations and emotions. Only story does.

Thus, by enlisting each listener's own personal thoughts, memories, atti-tudes, opinions, and life experiences, storytelling fills the gaps, and does so in the spirit intended by the storyteller. THIS BRINGS EACH LISTENER TO

THE SAME CONCLUSION AS EVERY OTHER LISTENER—even when every other listener's conclusion is based on dissimilar thoughts, memories, attitudes, opinions, feelings, and life experiences.

Had Shakespeare merely *explained* the facts of *Hamlet*, his audience would have fallen asleep. Had he *argued* that Hamlet did right (or wrong), some listeners would have agreed, some would have disagreed, and most would have fallen asleep. Instead of explaining or arguing, Shakespeare *told the story* of Hamlet, and almost everyone laughed, cried, got angry, and felt pity and fear in exactly the same places as everyone else. No matter who we are or what we are like, we all agree that Hamlet is good and the King is bad, despite Hamlet's having committed more and crueler crimes than the King! Everyone is glad when the King dies; everyone weeps when Hamlet dies. No explanation or argument on earth could achieve the same results.

By filling the gaps, storytelling gets a relatively uniform response from every listener, and puts an audience in unison with the teller.

How to tell stories. The basic structure for good storytelling has been well put by a storybook king:

Begin at the beginning,

the King said gravely,

and

go on

till you

come to the end.

Then stop. [2]

"Begin at the beginning, and go on till you come to the end. Then stop." The King left one thing out, the very thing monarchs often ignore: people. But he is right about the beginning, going on (the middle), and stopping (the ending).

1) A good beginning (involving people).

2) A progressing middle: getting the story's people step-by-step from the beginning to the ending.

3) A strong ending centered on people.

BEGINNING

A good beginning is just a sentence or two long and does three things:

—Focuses on people.

—Gets jurors listening.

2. *Alice's Adventures in Wonderland*, Chapter 12, Lewis Carroll.

—Arouses a sense of justice and fair play.

If you understand each separately, you will find it easy to do all three.

Focus on people. As a general rule, your story beginning should use the name or names of your main character(s).

Get jurors listening. Because people like stories, they will start listening as soon as you tell them you are going to tell a story. "I have a story to tell you about John Smith" is the basic generic beginning, and even so uncreative a start gets jurors listening. There are a million variants, but the embedded message is always, "I have a story to tell you about John Smith."[3]

Depending on the case, you can sometimes use a *teaser*—a startling, intriguing, or dramatic beginning that draws the attention of your jurors off of whatever it has just been on (such as voir dire or your opponent's opening) and on to whatever you are going to say. In a recent North Carolina murder case, a wonderfully skilled public defender, a diminutive and proper-looking woman who had just completed a rather quiet and polite voir dire, began her opening statement by exploding in the jury's face with, "*Motherfucker*! I'm going to *kill* you!" When the jurors came down from the ceiling, counsel calmly explained that those very words had terrified her client that night in the bar, making him believe he had to take lethal action to save his life. Those first six words told the jury that a story was coming up—and those words resonated throughout trial.

A teaser should relate directly to a main theme of your case. (In other words, don't scream "motherfucker" at the jury unless that word lies at the heart of your main contention.) In a recent case of a truck driver killed due to a railroad crossing's blocked sightlines, an extraordinary Kentucky lawyer named Gary C. Johnson began his opening by snapping his fingers twice at the jury. That got their attention: they looked at him as if he had gone crazy (as did the judge and bailiff)—until he explained that the two seconds between snaps was the length of time from the moment the train came into view until it killed the truck driver. The case rested heavily on that two-second gap, and the attention-grabbing teaser introduced it with prime focus. But if Johnson had simply snapped his fingers at the jury and then gone on to talk about something else, his teaser would have fallen flat. Moral: An attention-arresting teaser should express a main theme of the case.

You cannot find a highly dramatic teaser for every case, but anything that arrests the listener's attention and focuses it onto the story of your case is sufficient. Examples:

---

3. Some advisors timidly caution against using the word "story," as in "I have a story to tell," because they believe that "story" implies fiction. But "story" is widely used to mean a narrative that is true, such as in "The story of the Civil War" or Paul Harvey's "The rest of the story."

"It's November, 1988, and Jack Armstrong is a proud man—too proud. Pride leads a man to do dangerous things." (A cardinal rule of storytelling: use present tense. It creates immediacy and credibility, makes the narrative easier to follow, and gives the impression that "You are there!")

Or,

"It's December, 1990. Dahlia Drake is the richest woman in town. Her relatives cannot get this fact out of their heads."

Or,

"On June 4, 1991, Roderick Bradley thinks he's going out to mow his lawn. But his drunk neighbor has other ideas."

Or,

"It's the morning of January 21. Maria Townsend packs a lunch for Bobby, her twelve-year-old son. But because a driver's in a hurry to get to work, Bobby never gets to eat that lunch."

Each of those beginnings says, "I have a story to tell you." And each involves people.

There is one more component of an effective beginning:

Arouse a moral sense of justice and fair play. Because persuasion requires an effective appeal to the listener's moral sense, the beginning of your story should include a "moral marker" highlighting the wrong you are fighting. A moral marker arouses the jurors' sense of wrong, unfairness, or danger. It tells jurors why they should care.

If you are prosecution or plaintiff, the central wrong that requires a moral marker derives from what the defendant did. On defense, the central wrong is usually that your client is being unfairly accused.

The moral marker should not be about a subordinate issue. It must announce the moral heart of your case. Here are examples of story beginnings that employ a moral marker in combination with a focus on people:

—It's a July midnight. Joe Miller stops to help a man dying in the street. Today the State rewards Joe for being a good Samaritan by putting him on trial for his life.

—Celia Owens is afraid to let her grandchildren play in her own back yard. There are no monsters, no wild animals, no deep holes. But she has two neighbors, Norman and Nancy Jones, and no one who lives next door to them would be able to send their children or grandchildren out to play.

—March 23, 1995. Mary Smith rushes her son Billy to the Emergency Room with an asthma attack. Doctor Green does not read

Billy's medical file or listen to Mary's warning—so he gives Billy the wrong medicine. Ten minutes later, Billy is dead.

Or on the other side:

—March 23, 1995. Emergency room physician John Green struggles to save a child's life. He would have succeeded if the boy's mother had brought him in when she knew she should have. But instead she went grocery shopping, and now she's blaming the doctor.

To find out in advance if your planned beginning grabs attention, try it on friends. While you are at it, try the rest of the story on them, too.

You can get new ideas for ways to create effective beginnings if you pay attention to the starts of television shows and movies, note how jokes begin, and read many first pages of novels and short stories. Just remember that there are three—and only three—considerations for the beginning of a story:

1. Focus on people.

2. Get jurors listening.

3. Provide a moral marker.

Do nothing else or you will scatter juror attention instead of focus it.

MIDDLE

There are two repeating goals for the middle. Every single sentence should achieve one goal or the other—or both. With each sentence, either:

—move the people in your story forward (create *progress*),

and/or

—be interesting, involving, amusing, or engrossing.

Jurors will listen if you provide forward progress or say something strongly interesting. Being merely informative or argumentative (a forbidden ingredient of storytelling) is insufficient.[4]

What does moving forward mean? Let's watch a bear:

Once upon a time there was a big bad bear. One morning he wakes up hungry. So he heads into the forest to hunt. It's a sunny day and the temperature is sixty degrees. The bear comes upon a group of children having a picnic. He drags three of them back to his cave.

---

4. Anything that cannot be told either by forward-moving sentences or by something interesting should not be part of your story, but should be told some other way at a different time. For help with cases where finding interest seems difficult, see Application B, p. 189, "Humanizing Non-Human Cases." Also see Chapter 6, "Viscerals."

There he eats one of them and half of the second. He saves the rest
of the second and all of the third for dinner.[5]

Almost every sentence after the first moves the story forward:

1) Once upon a time there was a big bad bear.

2) One morning the *bear wakes up* hungry.

3) So *he heads into the forest* to hunt.

4) It's a sunny day and the temperature is sixty degrees.

5) The bear *comes upon a group of children* having a picnic.

6) He *drags three of them* back to his cave.

7) There *he eats one of them and half of the second.*

8) He *saves the rest* of the second and all of the third for dinner.

We don't merely get new facts. Except for sentences #1 and #4, every
sentence contains something that moves the bear forward. That's progress.

You can test whether a sentence moves ahead by deleting it. If deleting a
sentence leaves an action gap, the sentence was one that moved the story
ahead. For example, delete sentence 7:

He drags three of them back to his cave. [#7 deleted.] He saves the
rest of the second and all of the third for dinner.

There is an action gap: what happened to the first child and the first half
of the second? The deletion of sentence #7 caused a gap that is obvious even
if you have never heard the story before, so #7 must be a sentence that moves
the story forward.

If a sentence does not move the story forward (such as #4), deleting it
leaves no action gap:

The bear heads into the forest to hunt. [#4 deleted.] He comes upon
a group of children having a picnic.

We cannot tell #4 is gone—because #4 does nothing to move the story
forward. It contains information but no progress.

Practice telling stories in which every sentence moves your people forward, so that removing any sentence would create an action gap. As an
exercise, tell someone what you did yesterday from waking till going to sleep,
using only forward-moving sentences (and tell it in the present tense).

But that is only half the battle because court cases are full of information
and information contains no forward movement. Thus, you must go to the

---

5.   Compare how much less immediate the story is when told in the past tense: "Once upon a
time there was a big bad bear. One morning he woke up hungry. So he headed into the forest
to hunt. It was a sunny day and the temperature was sixty degrees. The bear came upon a group
of children having a picnic. He dragged three of them back to his cave. There he ate one of
them and half of the second. He saved the rest of the second and all of the third for dinner."

second alternative: Make anything with no forward movement extra-interesting. To understand how, look at the following additions (in italics) that do not move the bear story forward:

> Once upon a time there was a big bad bear.
>
> *He was born seven years ago, one of a litter of seven bear cubs, three of them male and four female, halfway up the side of the mountain he's on now, which is not the tallest mountain in that part of the country but still is too steep for people to climb.* (Note that the bear has not progressed since the previous sentence.)
>
> One morning the bear wakes up hungry.[6]
>
> *The normal diet for healthy bears is berries and the tender leaves of plants.*[7]
>
> So he heads into the forest to hunt.
>
> *It's a sunny day and the temperature is sixty degrees.*[8]
>
> He comes upon a group of children having a picnic.
>
> *All of the children live in the town of Fairview, a farming community of about twenty thousand.*[9]
>
> He drags three of them back to his cave . . . etc.

The italicized information may be important to your case, but it stops your forward movement. The bear does not progress, so juror attention will dwindle. You must find ways to make each non-forward-moving item interesting, involving, or engrossing. This can be achieved with viscerals (Chapter 6), forwards (final section of Chapter 7), and other techniques. You will get the idea by looking at the following italicized segments. Note how each adds interest to non-forward-moving information.

> Once upon a time there was a big bad bear. One morning he wakes up hungry. Usually he eats plant leaves, but sometimes *he dines on people* who wander into his part of the forest. *He's big enough to hunt for whatever he feels like eating,* because he's the largest of his litter of three males and four females born seven years ago. He has lived his whole life on this very mountain, which is not the tallest mountain in that part of the country but still is steep enough so that *climbing it every day has made his muscles grow strong and his claws grow sharp.* And now he heads into the forest to hunt. It's a sunny day and the temperature is sixty degrees—*ideal weather for children to be having a picnic in the woods.*

---

6. Waking up is progress: from being asleep to being awake.
7. This sentence has no forward action.
8. Ditto.
9. Ditto.

The information has been made interesting and even suspenseful by tying each piece of it directly to a visceral (danger). "Sunny day" is information so it is tied to a threat of danger: What will happen to the children at the picnic? Jurors will keep listening.

Jurors will pay attention to your story for as long as you continue to move it forward *or* make the non-forward-moving segments interesting, involving, amusing, or engrossing—i.e., visceral. But even with viscerals, don't go more than a sentence or two at a time without returning to forward movement. You want the jury to feel continuing movement toward a climax, which is how you end your story.

Building to a climax is like building to the strong ending of a song: you gather a head of steam. Your story's forward movement provides the head of steam, pulling your jurors to a *specific destination*. The jurors don't necessarily know the destination in advance, but your forward movement convinces them that you have one. That is why they keep listening.

When you run out of events that move your story's people forward, it is time for your story to end.

END

Climax. The end of a story is its emotional climax. In a movie it is the car chase, or the most violent scene, or the marriage, or the big fight with the bad guy. In Shakespeare it is sword fights, poison, and other mayhem, or a reunion and marriage. In court, the purpose of a climax is to carry jurors to the story's conclusion by focusing emphatically on the most terrible consequences of what your opponent party did: the catastrophic wreck, the filing of false charges, the moment of arrest, the loss of the inheritance, the devastating moment your innocent client was served notice of the outrageous lawsuit, or whatever termination point left no alternative but this trial.

Suppose, in an opening statement, you are trying to show your jury that your client's drinking had nothing to do with the terrible crash:

> And then the Sheriff follows Flash Wilson's Corvette around the bend, already going 95 miles an hour. Wilson is going even faster by the bottom of the hill when he smashes through the crowded school bus and cuts it in half. Five witnesses see it all. And Wilson's Corvette would have hit just as hard, caused the same explosion, and killed just as many children, even if Pop Jones, the school bus driver, had never tasted those few ounces of beer.

That is the end of your story. Stop. You have placed your message (that Pop's drinking had nothing to do with the accident) at the story's emotional high point.

Another example:

> Weak: "The house blew up and the Smith family was ripped to pieces."

Good: "The house blows up. And the Smith family is ripped to pieces *along with the defective gas monitor.*"

Tie your primary bone of contention (the defective gas monitor) to your climax (the destruction of the house and family). This leaves the jury with your central contention uppermost in mind instead of buried in a welter of details.[10]

CASE STORY

Case story is your total presentation. It is the sequential, building combination of every single thing you do or say, or cause to have done or said, from your first words in voir dire through to the last syllable of your closing argument. Your witnesses, questions, testimony, arguments, exhibits, and demonstrations all compose your full case story.

The principles of story also apply to case story: a clear start, a continuous sense of *forward movement* (or, via viscerals, high interest level), a strong and constant connection to *people*, and your case story's *climax* at the end of closing argument.

"Story" is your narrative of the events that led up to this case. "Case story" is the flow of events you create in the courtroom from beginning to end of trial that makes up your case presentation. Thinking of your overall case as a case story keeps you in your role as a storyteller throughout trial. It helps you avoid falling into the trap of considering yourself as a mere explainer or arguer.

Titles: *The Case of the* _____. Give your case story a title: *The Case of the Careless Homeowner*, or *The Case of the Jerk Who Turned His Back to Oncoming Traffic*, or *The Case of the Slimy Building Contractor*. No need to tell the jury; the title can be for your own private reference. It helps you structure every element of your overall case story to support, illustrate, or expand upon the central theme as expressed in your title.

Telegram. Trial skills coach Joshua Karton, a brilliant pioneer in adapting theater methods to the courtroom, advises attorneys to create a ten-word "telegram" of their case. Karton's method is now widely taught because attorneys find the telegram a key ingredient in planning and case presentation.

The telegram should communicate the heart of the case: the central situation, the wrong, and what you want the jury to do. That sounds like a lot to accomplish in ten words, but it can be done: "Derelict doctor prescribes wrong. Kills child. *Make doctor pay.*" Or, "Terrified community pressures cops. Wrong man arrested. *Let him go.*" Or, "Thief slashes waitress to death for ten dollars. *Hang him.*"

---

10. See p. 117 below for a further discussion of climax.

Your ten-word telegram guides and focuses your pretrial planning, introduces the jury to your case, and keeps you on track throughout trial.

SELECTION: WHAT TO INCLUDE, WHAT TO LEAVE OUT

You cannot ever tell the entire story of any event. If you try to relate every single element of even one person's single day, you will fill a dozen books. Every novelist, playwright, screenwriter, joke-teller, gossip, spinner of tall tales, lawyer, or liar *selects* what to include and what to leave out.

Length aside, you cannot bring in *every* fact or argument in your favor because sooner or later the persuasive value of each new item begins incrementally diminishing. Eventually, the next item is not worth the time to present it, thus diluting the jurors' attention and their ability to assimilate more important items. Consequently, you must exclude a lot. That requires careful selection.

Inclusion criteria:

a) VISCERAL considerations.[11] A ton of evidence with low visceral value weighs less than a few ounces of good viscerals.

b) CLARITY and SIMPLICITY. Select elements that jurors can digest and remember.

c) FAMILIARITY. Select material that is close to home for the jury. Even if the case concerns the other side of the moon, use analogies or other methods to bring it down to earth—preferably the earth in the jurors' own back yards. Because life experiences are so influential, street gangs scare city dwellers, not farmers—and droughts scare farmers, not city dwellers. Select the elements of your case that either most closely match your jurors' life experiences, or for which you can find analogies to make them do so. If you know your jurors, you will know what they will find most familiar.

d) COMMON VALUES and CONCERNS. Certain kinds of evidence and arguments have more appeal to some kinds of people than to others. Do your particular jurors have strong family values? Are your jurors business oriented? Are they more (or less) accepting of various community standards? Is education important to them? Find out where your jurors' values and concerns intersect with the materials of your case. Then focus on those intersections.

These inclusion considerations—visceral weight, clarity and simplicity, familiarity, common values and concerns—are important considerations of

---

11. See Chapter 6.

successful script writers. You rarely see work by writers who ignore them, because those writers lack audience appeal. And juries are audiences.

Exclusion criteria:

You need less than you may think.

a) Beware of bringing in so much that jurors will lose track of your major points. Less is more. There is no reason to show all 42 errors in the medical records if you can show that the doctor left his hat in the patient's lung.

b) Beware of bringing in so many supporting points that they drown out the points they are intended to support. Too much supporting material obscures your main points, trivializes your case, and bores the jury.

c) Make sure that everything you choose to say, do, or introduce proves or demonstrates what you want it to rather than something different or opposite. Analyze meticulously because potential harm does not always announce itself. Analyze dispassionately because something you desperately want to use might cost you the case. Analyze objectively because you may be too close to the case to easily see that jurors will respond to something differently than you do. For example, did the O.J. Simpson 911 tape (Simpson raging out of control in his wife's home) show, as intended, that he was dangerous—or did it show the opposite: that even when totally out of control, he did not attack anyone?

d) Make sure that everything you include is necessary to support a case-determinative point. You should be able to quickly outline the steps to get from each item to the case-determinative point it goes to prove. "I need to show A because it proves B, I need B because it proves C, and C is one of the points that proves my case-determinative contention."

SELECTING METHODS OF INTRODUCING EVIDENCE

A Broadway musical uses many methods to tell its story: song, dance, dramatic action, musical bridge, narrative, dialogue, solo, duet, soliloquy, chorus number, etc. The method chosen shapes how the information is perceived. A spoken soliloquy about love, a love song duet, and a love ballet all deal with the same subject, yet convey three different things at three different levels of emphasis.

You have the same potential variety in court. To make best use of that variety, suit your means of presentation to the impact you want the particular piece of evidence to carry.

Suppose you want the jury to know that your client fell forty-two feet from a construction tower. Say you have the following choices:

a) A model of the tower with a scale-model doll to show the drop with respect to the size of a person (visual information).

b) An expert witness with engineering drawings that illustrate her testimony, including cross-section diagrams of the tower with a readily-visible scale chart (logic).

c) Your client describing how it felt to fall so far (subjective emotion).

d) You, pointing to the back wall of the courtroom and telling the jury it is forty-two feet away (real comparison).

e) You, pointing out the courtroom window and saying that forty-two feet is twice as high as here to the ground, or as high as jumping off the three-story building across the street (juror identification).

Each possibility conveys the same fact but with different impact. Choose on the basis of desired impact, not convenience. Of course it is easier to point at a wall and say "forty-two feet" than to build a model, but convenience and ease are poor criteria.

Another consideration is *level of importance*. Don't give every piece of evidence its maximum possible impact. Jurors have a limited capacity for elements of maximum importance, so you should prioritize. Otherwise, items of lesser importance crowd your most important points out of the jurors' minds. So if the magnitude of forty-two feet is pivotal to your case, use a method of maximum impact: Get the jury to jump out the forty-two-foot-high window. But if it is just one of twenty moderately important statistics, use a less emphatic method (for example, just tell them the back wall is forty-two feet away).

RULES OF REPETITION

What evidence or arguments should you present more than once? Is a doctor's testimony enough or should you add the patient's testimony and the testimony of the mother who cares for him? Will a day-in-the-life video add or overload? Will multiple witnesses reinforce or undermine each other? Is there a danger of contradicting? There is always a danger of monotony.

Carefully measure the cost of saying anything more than once. It is true that repetition emphasizes, *but repetition teaches jurors that it is unnecessary to listen carefully to you.* They come to assume that no matter what you are saying, you will say it again . . . and again . . . and again . . . .

Playwrights suffer from the same disease. Half of every script's first draft is repetition. Like good lawyers, good playwrights eliminate it—whereas lesser lawyers and playwrights expand upon it! Did you like your mother telling you the same thing over and over? Do you think jurors like it?

When repetition for emphasis or clarity is desirable or necessary, there is a way to do it without being boring or annoying: You may repeat *anything*—evidence, testimony, argument, information, question, remark, demonstration, whatever the judge lets you get away with—as long as with each and every repetition you follow the two rules of repetition.

RULES OF REPETITION

1. DIFFERENT: Alter *how* the material is communicated (*different* words and organization, *different* medium, *different* visceral, or *different* point of view, etc.). For example, if a point is first made in direct testimony, bring it up the next time by means of a chart. Or use a strong verbal image to make the point again. To repeat a point from a video deposition, you might put a piece of real evidence into the hands of a witness. With strictly verbal repetitions (except for themes), vary the language. Every time, *alter* how the material is communicated.

2. STRONGER: Make certain that the importance, or intensity, or viscerality, or general impact of the repetition is *stronger* than the time before. Arrange your repetitions to progressively *increase in intensity or impact*.

Obey *both* Rules of Repetition with every repetition or you will bore the jury and undermine the effect of the thing you are repeating.

How many repetitions can you get away with? How many witnesses can you call for the same matter? How many exhibits can you use to illustrate the same thing? How many times can you reiterate the same argument or point? It is safe to repeat as long as you follow both rules: Each time must be *different in form* from every previous statement of the same material, and *better* (stronger) than the version immediately previous.

To practice this technique: whenever you hear anyone guilty of unmodified repetition, play the private mental game of thinking how to fix it.

STORY STRUCTURE

Once you have selected which elements to include, you are ready to structure them into your case story. Here are key organizational considerations (explained in the sections immediately following):

—Order of presentation.

—Climaxes: preparation and placement.

—Post-climax.

—Rhythm: varying the tempo, pacing, and degrees of relative intensity.

—Signposts: a technique of highlighting the relationship of your whole case story to each segment.

—Sub-stories.

—Progression: movement from one segment to the next.

—Backwards analysis: a method of dissecting and examining your case, and an effective persuader.

—Forwards: a technique of creating tension, suspense, and eagerness to hear what is coming later.

—Cliffhangers.

These structural considerations are covered below. After you read about them, start looking at plays and movies with an eye to spotting these structural considerations, and to see how they work, how they relate to each other, and how they affect the impact and persuasiveness of a story.

Because these devices and methods are used in films, some attorneys find it useful to reread this section as a refresher just before going to the movies.

The order of presentation. Order of presentation (what comes first, what comes second, what comes third, etc.) makes the difference between an attentive, sympathetic jury and a bored, hostile jury. An effective order of presentation requires (within the limitations of witness scheduling) the simultaneous consideration of four factors: clarity, context, and "build," covered in the following paragraphs, and rhythm, covered on p. 119, below.

Clarity. To achieve clarity, chronological order is almost always best. Listeners are accustomed to chronological order by virtue of movies, television, and real life. Chronological order is the habitually familiar framework into which jurors effortlessly place incoming information.

Nonetheless, some complicated cases are clearer when presented topic-by-topic instead of chronologically. But even in a topic-by-topic arrangement, maintain chronological order within each topic. Also make sure it is clear to jurors how all the topics relate to each other.

Moreover, creating effective context or build (both described below) can force you to break or suspend chronological order. And the vagaries of witness scheduling and of sequential discontinuity in testimony among witnesses can also interfere with chronological flow. Compensate by using such clarification devices as charts, time lines, and signposts[12] to help jurors keep track of the order of events.

In brief: Chronological order creates clarity. When context, build, witness scheduling, or anything else demands a chronological break, use a chart, time line, or series of signposts to bolster clarity.

Context. A juror's frame of mind at any given moment has been created by whatever he has just seen or heard in the moment previous. In turn, that

---

12. See p. 122 below, "Signposts."

frame of mind helps determine how he perceives the next thing he sees or hears.

For example, a pistol that seems mildly threatening turns terrifying if the jurors see it in the context of having just seen morgue photos of the victim's bullet holes. The context created by the photos intensifies the impact of the pistol.

Because context is a primary consideration for deciding on presentation order, ask yourself:

> 1. how each thing (witness, demonstration, etc.) might make jurors think and feel, and
>
> 2. how thinking and feeling that way will shape juror perceptions and reactions to the next thing you bring before them.

For *emphasis*, the jury must already possess the information that gives your new piece of evidence its fullest emotional impact. (Show the photos of the wound before you show the pistol.) For *de-emphasis*, introduce the piece of evidence before the jury has enough information to feel its full significance.[13] (Show the pistol before the wound photos.) Not only emphasis, but significance, relevance, memorability, clarity, and emotional impact are sharply affected by context.

"Here, ladies and gentlemen, is a photo of the *dog*!" means one thing if the jurors already know that the victim was bitten to death: they will see nothing but teeth. But it means something else if jurors don't yet know about the attack. They are just as likely to look at the wagging tail.

Context is a primary consideration for determining your order of presentation. It is crucial for every form of communication, especially when the purpose is to persuade. Just as the punch line of a joke is funny only in context of the joke's preceding narrative, so is the effectiveness of a piece of evidence, a witness, or an argument dependent upon what precedes it.

"*Build*," the third consideration for deciding on presentation order, is a progressively rising level of interest or importance (see also the following section, "Climax"). Jurors listen for as long as your case story builds. But they tend to stop listening when your build flags and starts to descend. *Descending* interest-level is the very device lullabies use to induce sleep.

Build your case story from low intensity up to final maximum impact. Use the same pattern of rising intensity within each separate segment of your trial presentation—each witness, each section of testimony, each story you tell in your opening, each argument, etc. Develop an instinct for build and an instinctive awareness for when build is missing.

---

13. This is one reason to introduce your case's liabilities during voir dire. See p. 62, "Introducing Weaknesses During Voir Dire."

If chronological order cannot provide an effective build, find a different order. But as with any break from chronology, make up for the consequent loss of clarity by using charts, times lines, signposts, and other clarity-enhancing devices.

Climax and Mini-climax. The *climax* is the build's conclusion: your peak of dramatic, emotional, or persuasive intensity. It is your concluding punch, the final payoff of your entire case story. It is almost the last thing in your closing argument.

Just as your overall case has a climax, the effectiveness of each line of testimony, each direct examination, each cross, and each address to the jury can benefit by a mini-climax. A mini-climax is the cap, the payoff, the punch of each segment.

Each successive mini-climax should be slightly stronger than the mini-climax of the section preceding it, so that your case is presented in a framework of progressively stronger mini-climaxes. This rising intensity holds the jury's attention.

A common error is to climax a section more than once. This can happen when a good response to your first climax tempts you to try for a second. Result: The effectiveness of your first climax is undermined, and your second seems forced and insincere.

Use only one mini-climax per section and only one climax for your final major conclusion. Smart performers leave 'em wanting more. Nothing should follow your climax except for your post-climax, as described in the next section.

Post-Climax (Let it sink in before you stop). Be careful about timing a mini-climax with respect to the start of a recess. Suppose you have timed things carefully: you finish a cross-examination by delivering your mini-climax just as the clock ticks to 12:30 p.m. and the judge declares luncheon recess:

COUNSEL   So you forged the check for money to pay your car loan?

SMITH   Yes, sir.

COUNSEL   Because you wanted to keep your old Chevy?

SMITH   Yes.

COUNSEL *(friendly, understanding)* That makes forging a check a little more understandable, doesn't it? Under the circumstances?

SMITH   I don't know.

COUNSEL   Mr. Smith, as much as you wanted to keep that old Chevy, *you want to win this case today even more.*

Good climax. But then:

COUNSEL   No more questions.

COURT   Let's recess for lunch until two-thirty.

The judge killed your climax! The jurors are starving. When the judge announces lunch, the jurors' mouths water and their stomachs forget your climax in favor of lunch.

To help your climax survive whatever real-life or courtroom events follow it, hold the jury in place for a moment or two after each climax. Don't say "No more questions" right away. Do something or ask something that will allow your climax a moment to settle in. Even a long pause helps. In theater, an internal mini-climax is often followed by a quieter moment or two. A play's final climax is often followed by a long, slow curtain or a gradual fade of the lights. Most playwrights use low-intensity dialogue right after the final climax so that the audience lives for a while with the power of the climax before getting involved in grabbing their coats, bumping past each other to get out, deciding where to eat, seeing that their car has been towed, getting chased by muggers, etc.

Here is the end of *Hamlet* the way a lesser playwright might have written the ending. Hamlet is wounded, Laertes dying, the Queen dead:

LAERTES   Hamlet, thou art slain . . . .

The King, the King's to blame.

HAMLET   The point envenomed, too?

Then, venom, to thy work!

Hamlet stabs King.

King dies.

Hamlet dies.

Laertes dies.

THE END.

But Shakespeare knew that his climax needed time to settle indelibly into the audience's emotional memory. So he wrote a hundred lines after the climax of Hamlet killing the King. And as you can do, he used his sustained post-climax to recap his strongest elements: ". . . carnal, bloody and unnatural acts . . . accidental judgments, casual slaughters . . . deaths put on by cunning and forced cause . . . purposes mistook, fallen on the inventors' heads." He reminds his audience of the play's strongest elements—right when audience attention is at its height. This reinforces the power of his climax and makes certain the audience leaves the theater with the essence of the play firmly in mind.

You can do the same thing. After your closing argument's final climax, recap your main persuasive points:

Over the past week you've heard about bad choices, dishonesty, revenge, and greed. You saw the shattered windows. You held the broken safety latch in your own hands. You heard what the neighbor said, you heard from the frightened repair man, and most of all, you listened to that poor little girl. Now there's only one way a story like this can end . . . .

Give each mini-climax time to sink in. And follow your final climax with a *brief* reminder of your best evidence so that jurors will recall it while they are still held in the emotional sway of your climax.

Rhythm. The attention-control techniques in this section are not easy to learn, but once mastered are among the easiest techniques to use. And because they can be deployed throughout trial, they are among the most useful and effective. Because rhythm-control techniques are not easy to learn, they are employed by few attorneys. If you take the trouble to master them, you will have a powerful courtroom tool that will rarely be matched—or even understood—by your opponents.

Human beings have a built-in mechanism that acts like an attention faucet. When rhythm is unchanging, the faucet turns off. When the rhythm changes, the faucet turns on and attention flows. If you control rhythm you control the courtroom, because rhythm control is a primal method of grabbing and holding attention.

Rhythm is inherent in everything that happens in court—such as words, the phrasing of questions, the sequence of witnesses and visual displays, the content of testimony and visual displays, and even your own intensity. When you control those rhythms, you control juror attention. When you let those rhythms take their own course, juror attention unpredictably and erratically waxes and wanes.

Not only does everything in court have rhythm, but so does everything in existence—from the life cycle of the universe down to the blink of an eye. Looking at some of these things will help you understand what rhythm is. For example, much popular music's rhythm is a regularly repeating alternation between hard and soft, such as a bass beat interspersed with regularly-occurring milder sounds that separate the beats. A clock's rhythm is tick—silence—tock.

The key to controlling rhythm is change. People pay no attention to a clock's sound because its rhythm never changes: tick - tock - tick - tock - tick - tock. Similarly, jurors pay no attention in court if your rhythm never changes (say, if you never vary the loudness, pitch, or pace of your speaking).

Rhythm's components that you can easily change include pacing, tempo, intensity, volume, and regularity of repetition. These change with respect to time. There are also spatial changes that apply to anything visual. Those which you can control include color, brightness, mass, contrast, texture, blend, and framing.

Whether aural or visual, the same rhythm used too long shuts down the attention faucet, as did those monotone teachers that droned us all to sleep in school. Our brains are dulled by sameness but powerfully aroused by change; if you hear a hundred people singing in chorus, you notice one wrong note more than you notice the ninety-nine right notes. If you are surrounded by hissing snakes, you pay attention to the one that rattles.

For an example of rhythm's controlling power, read any sentence aloud. Then reread it aloud exactly the same way, but pause before any word. This short pause is a rhythm break, and as such it emphasizes the next word or phrase because the pause is a . . . *change* in rhythm, and thus attracts attention. The emphasis accumulates onto the next . . . *phrase after the pause.* In court, you can use this simple rhythm-change device over and over because the pause is a break, a variation of the regular pattern (the rhythm) of your unbroken speech.[14]

If you combine the short pause with vocal emphasis on the desired word or phrase, you both clarify the point of your sentence . . . *and* you increase its impact. It is the commonest way actors and orators make audiences listen.

The pause and the pause-with-vocal-emphasis are easily mastered techniques. Now that you know what they are, you can do them. There are other rhythm-changing techniques that can focus juror attention onto anything in trial (such as a witness, a display, an argument, or a piece of testimony) as effectively as a pause-with-vocal-emphasis focuses attention onto the next . . . *word.*

To control attention with respect to larger elements of a presentation, Shakespeare alternates between quiet and loud, fast and slow, calm and busy, simple and complex, large (many characters) and small (two or three characters, or a soliloquy), important and trivial, frightening and comforting, city and rural, public and private, poetic and earthy, etc. This modulation rivets audience attention; each change rejuvenates that attention. You can hold juror attention with a similarly alternating modulation of, say, your sequence of witnesses (alternate male and female, young and old, expert and lay, loud and quiet, engaging and off-putting, similar to the jurors and different from them, rapid-speaking and slow, authoritative and shy, etc.). You can also alternatingly modulate the nature of the questions you ask them, the visuals you use, and every other case-story component. Intersperse witness testimony with charts, photos, or other demonstrative or real evidence.

Most important, *avoid adjacent similarities.* Create maximum change from one thing to the next. It is like planning six months of menus. You may love lobster, but lobster three times a day for twenty-six weeks will have you clawing the walls. Variety is the key to jury attention.

---

14. See Chapter One, p. 16, "Impact Point and Emphasis."

Pay particular attention to how you talk. When jurors doze off during the long afternoon, vary your tone to bring them back. That will not hold them long unless you soon say something that interests them, but if you don't change rhythm, they will be unlikely to hear what you say no matter how interesting it might be.

Human beings are sensitive to rhythm alteration even in their sleep! Lighthouse keepers sleep soundly through the racket of their rotating beacons but jerk instantly awake if the rhythm changes or stops. The brain is attuned to alteration but tunes out constancy. Thus, maintaining constant pitch, volume, inflection, or pace makes jurors feel as if they are counting dead sheep.

In brief: We note rhythm *change*, not *sameness*.[15]

VISUAL RHYTHM is similarly powerful. If there are six people on a stage—five standing together and one alone at a distance—the audience focuses on and remembers the one alone. This is because the brain notices uniqueness, not sameness (uniqueness is a kind of change). If ten actors wear scarlet and one wears dull gray, the audience watches and remembers the one in gray, even though scarlet is normally more noticeable. Visually as well as aurally, people notice difference; it is an inherent defense mechanism. If your Cro-Magnon ancestors had to examine every unmoving, vertical green vine one at a time before they happened to notice the slithering, horizontal, yellow mamba, they would be dead by now.

VISUAL DEMONSTRATION:

XXXXXXXXX O XXXXXXXXXXXXXXXXXX

You notice no individual internal X. You slightly notice the X's that begin and end each block (they differ from the others in that they are not surrounded by other X's). You strongly notice the O.

You notice an *italicized* word because italics are different—*unless the whole sentence is in italics, in which case you don't notice any particular word because when the whole sentence is in the same typestyle, none of the words are different.*

And though you don't notice the obvious correct spellings of every word, you kwickly spot obvious mispellings. (Half of them, anyway.) Obvious mis-spellings are changes from the expected: a rhythm break.

IN COURT, avoid adjacent similarities by alternating testimony with visual evidence. Never show video depositions back-to-back. Vary your kinds of demonstrative evidence: still photos, objects, drawings, computer anima-tions, charts, etc. And, easiest of all, get up out of your chair and move around!

---

15. I just employed rhythm change: paragraph lengths. The short paragraph stands out between the two long ones and is thus emphasized. Even a change in language style creates emphasis because it gets noticed. You can bet your skeptical little butt on it. (See?)

The visual rhythm of a person sitting in the same chair hour after hour has the energizing fascination of watching someone take a nap.

In some jurisdictions, you can get up and move around only if you have a reason to move. So give yourself plenty of allowable reasons. Go use the easel. Walk back to your table to get a pointer, then back to the easel, then back to the table for notes, then back to the easel again, and finally use the act of sitting down as punctuation for emphasis. (But never wander aimlessly. It distracts.)[16]

You can become an expert in rhythm change by going to the movies. Watch how their many short pieces—scenes, or sequences, or shots—are arranged to avoid adjacent similarities and provide alternating modulation: distance shot followed by close-up; chase followed by stillness; camera movement followed by camera still; loudness alternating with quiet; lots of dialogue/no dialogue; harmonious sound/jangling sound; character movement/stillness; dark/bright; funny/serious; colorful/monochromatic; quick edits/slow edits; wide-angle shots/narrow-angle. These elements and many others are worked back and forth and in combination with each other to create a film's rhythms. In brilliant films (such as Kurosawa's, Altman's, Hitchcock's, and Bradley's), the rhythmic effects are astonishing, but even lesser films and TV shows have rhythm elements you can easily spot to help you develop a feel for rhythm. This will enable you to know when your courtroom rhythm is working well and when it has fallen flat—and what to do about it. You will learn to sequence witnesses to create variety. You will know how to vary your vocal delivery. You will see that demonstrative evidence not only serves to illustrate testimony but also helps you win the constant battle of keeping the proceedings in fluid, shifting motion.

Choose your favorite art form (theater, music, dance, movies, painting, sculpture, pottery, poetry, literature, whatever you like) and study the rhythms involved. Everything you learn—be it visual, aural, or textual—will help you design, control, and execute the rhythms of your trial cases, and thereby control the attention of your jurors throughout trial.

Signposts.[17] This is the simplest technique drama can teach you, but its simplicity makes it no less useful: Be sure to repeatedly remind the jury how each element of your case story—each thing you introduce—fits into the overall picture. Don't wait for closing. During the presentation of each witness or testimony topic or demonstration or argument, frequently show its connection to the whole reason you are here in court. Show the connection via a signpost.

---

16. See Application M, p. 257, "Courtroom Technology," on the harmfulness of using remote controls for VCRs, TVs, etc.
17. See also Chapter 9, p. 143, "Demarcation."

No signpost: "Dr. Jones, what other conclusions did you draw?"

Signpost added: "Dr. Jones, what is *the third standard of care that was violated?*"

Jurors constantly come to intersections of a dozen roads to take. Even when you think the "right" direction is obvious, provide a signpost or they will get lost.

Sub-Stories. *Getting from piece to piece (Out to launch)*. Effectively linking the segments of your case creates continuity and a sense of inevitability to your flow of witnesses, demonstrations, arguments, etc. Don't link case story segments by the "and . . . and . . . and" or the "and then" method, or your case will seem to ramble.

Dramatists have a linking method: They make Scene 2, for example, the *result* of Scene 1. (Scene 1 causes or permits Scene 2.) Then Scene 2 causes or permits Scene 3, and so on. In other words, the purpose of each scene is to *launch* the next scene.

You can follow most movies or plays via scene launches. It is not just a matter of "Well, first this happened and then after that, well, that happened and then next this happened to happen and then . . . ." It is rather a series of *connected* events, each of which derives from a previous event and determines one coming up. The resulting sense of determination creates a train of inevitability: *truth*.

Disconnected events are easily doubted, but a connected string is easy to believe. This is drama's oldest principle and it works in court. Consider each piece of evidence, each witness, each argument, as a scene. Then link your "scenes" like falling dominoes, so that Scene 1 *causes* or *permits* Scene 2, Scene 2 causes or permits Scene 3, and so on.

For example, assume your client is the plaintiff in an automobile accident suit. Your case story elements (scenes) include:

1) A therapist to testify about the long recovery period and the hardest injuries to be rehabilitated.

2) A doctor to report on the diagnosis and treatment in the Emergency Room after the accident.

3) A witness who saw the defendant drinking heavily an hour before the wreck.

4) The victim's mother to describe the depression the victim is falling into more deeply as time goes by.

5) The police officer from the accident scene.

6) A day-in-the-life video of the difficulties the victim has getting through the day.

7) A witness who saw the defendant's car weaving and speeding.

Just placing the elements in chronological order (3-7-5-2-1-6-4) gives each element some sense of launch into the next. But if you point out how each element *causes, requires, or permits* the next one, then your jurors will better remember each element, give it greater weight, and have a firmer grasp on your overall case story. It is easy:

> The defendant's heavy drinking *causes* him to drive erratically and fast. Driving erratically and fast *causes* him to smash into your client's car, which *causes* injuries that *require* long rehabilitation and *cause* permanent damage; the permanent damage *causes* daily difficulty ever since, which in turn *causes* your client's descent into a morbid melancholic state.

It is obvious to you but not to the jury unless you make it so. Don't wait for closing to emphasize your launches. You want jurors to see the whole picture as you are presenting it, so that your case story seems logical and plausible.

If you are not working in chronological order, the task of emphasizing launches is more complex but even more essential. Jurors cannot follow random mosaics.

Backwards analysis. Backwards analysis is a powerful search-and-find technique. It shows you where to look for crucial evidence, and provides a convincing way to convey the soundness of your case to the jury.

Backwards analysis helps you find the flaws in your case before your opponent does it for you in front of the jury. And it can reveal flaws in your opponent's case, so you should backwards analyze both sides—*before* pretrial negotiations.

Consider the following plaintiff's scenario, similar to those that have been persuasive in thousands of damages cases:

> 1. A truck driven by a drunk careens through a curve and over the white line, smashing head-on into Sally Brown's compact car.
>
> 2. Sally, a 25-year-old research technician, is rushed to the emergency room and undergoes life-saving surgery. She painfully struggles through months of treatment and rehabilitation efforts.
>
> 3. Generally she heals, but ongoing headaches, muscular problems, and depression force her to continue physical therapy and medication, and she has trouble sleeping.
>
> 4. She manages to return to work, but as the months go on her job performance suffers; her thinking is blurred, she forgets easily, she is constantly fatigued, she does not work efficiently, and she seems unaware of many important things—like safety procedures.

5. As a result, she is fired. Due to her continuing difficulties, she cannot find another job. A medical expert will testify that she has improved as much as she ever will, and a job counselor will testify that her difficulties render her permanently unemployable.

In most cases, proving every such point to the jury's satisfaction results in substantial compensatory damages: past and future medical expenses, a lifetime of lost income, and a goodly sum for pain and suffering. There is a direct line from the wreck to Sally Brown's ruined life: Causation is clear.

But by applying *backwards analysis*, defense counsel has an excellent chance of discovering where to look for evidence that can vastly diminish, if not eliminate, one large area of damages.

The way backwards analysis can help the defense in Sally's case is revealed at the end of this section. The answer lies in facts already mentioned, not in something unmentioned such as a pre-existing condition. Don't skip to the answer; first read how backwards analysis works:

Years ago, first-grade teachers taught addition in this way: Add the top digit of a column of numbers to the digit below, then add their sum to the digit below that, and so on to the bottom. Then re-check by starting at the bottom and working upward. The theory: Two different approaches rarely reveal the same result unless there is no mistake either way.

When directors and actors analyze scripts, they employ a similar process. First they do the equivalent of adding the numbers down. They analyze the play from beginning to end to see how each event leads into or launches one following. Then they re-check their work by analyzing from back to front. They go *backwards*.

For trials as well as plays, analyzing backwards reveals whether you have every step in place. This is because there is a profound difference between tracing events forwards and tracing them backwards. Moving *forwards*, every event can give rise to an uncertain range of upcoming events—we can never predict for certain what will happen next. If a gun is fired into a crowd, anyone might be hit, or several people, or no one. Firing the gun does not preordain the next event.

Moving *backwards* is different. A gun being fired does not preordain that Joe Smith gets shot, but the fact that Joe Smith gets shot means that a gun was fired. It is beyond question. Going forwards leads to *many* possibilities but going backwards reveals just one: the one that occurred.

Because everything in real life progresses chronologically forwards, the brain acquires the habit of automatically accepting every real-life forward progression it perceives. We don't question the possibility or the logic of a perceived, forward sequence of events; after all, there it is, happening right in front of us. There is nothing to question. It happened and we accept that it happened. This is so ingrained as an automatic response that if we lack it, we are said to be out of touch with reality.

The brain's automatic acceptance of every real-life forward sequence tends to make us automatically accept even a *proposed* forward sequence. In a play, the proposed sequence of events is called the plot. In court, your proposed sequence (your "plot") is your case story. Though the apparent forward sequence of fictional (plot) or reported (case story) events may be flawed or impossible, our brains' automatic acceptance habit almost always accepts the progression without question. Thus, you easily miss flaws when you examine your case story going forward in time.

But the brain has no automatic acceptance habits for a backwards sequence. Thus, any flaws or omissions or errors are more apparent when examined backwards.

To use backwards analysis, examine each point to see how it is a result of some antecedent point. If there is no connecting link to some antecedent, you probably have a misstep in your case analysis. Things rarely crop up out of nowhere. If a point connects to nothing antecedent, it may be irrelevant, or you may have more work to do before you understand its significance, or your case theory may be inadequate or wrong because it does not encompass all the elements. Once you know this, you will not go into court with a flawed theory for your opponent to tear to shreds.

Even more useful, backwards analysis reveals new possibilities. From the viewpoint of each particular moment in your case story, look backwards in time to search for *every possible antecedent* that might have led to or caused the point you are on. Don't settle for the first potentially causative antecedent that you spot; look for more. (For example, from the viewpoint of Sally Brown's mental disabilities, look backwards to examine each antecedent—not just the obvious ones—to see what might have caused or led to her disabilities.)

If you can connect every element of your case by working backwards from the end to the beginning, if there are no gaps, and if no alternative and plausible causative antecedents pop up that can effectively undermine your contentions, then you likely have a firm grip on the case. But without backwards analysis, you may not notice blank spots, missteps, dead ends, unsuspected antecedents, and questionable assumptions. Instead, your opponent may find them. The jury may sense or even explicitly spot them. That can cost you the case.

In addition to being a powerful tool for analysis, backwards analysis is a useful presentational device. Presenting a backwards analysis of your case in closing argument bolsters your version of the facts. Show the jury how each important element derives from an antecedent that caused or permitted it. This creates a powerful sense of inevitability and truth.

Now return to the beginning of this section and look at Sally Brown's case point by point and *backwards*.

5. Sally Brown is fired and cannot find another job. She is permanently unemployable. Go backwards to:

4. Her job performance suffers; her thinking is blurred, she forgets easily, she is constantly fatigued, she does not work efficiently, and she seems unaware of many important things—like safety procedures. Go backwards to:

3. Generally she heals, but ongoing headaches, muscular problems, and depression force her to continue physical therapy and medication, and she has trouble sleeping. Go backwards to:

2. She is rushed to the emergency room and undergoes life-saving surgery. She struggles through months of treatment and rehabilitation efforts. Go backwards to:

1. A truck driven by a drunk careens through a curve and over the white line, smashing head-on into Sally Brown's compact car.

Now examine each point to see how it might be a result of every possible antecedent, not just the obvious antecedents. You will note that #5 (Sally is permanently unemployable) is a result of #4 (her job performance suffers). There is no other antecedent that could have led to her being permanently unemployable. The connection of #5 to #4 is obvious; we learned nothing by going backwards that was not obvious going forwards.

But examining every possible antecedent that might have led to Sally's problems in #4 (fatigue, poor thinking, etc.) reveals a possible link easily missed while going forwards: the possibility that Sally's mental and emotional problems stem not from antecedent #1 (the wreck)—but from antecedent #3 (her medication). This alternative antecedent should send defense counsel scurrying to a *Physician's Desk Reference* to see if the side effects of Sally's medicines match her problems as described in #4. If they match and if defense experts can find other medications without such side effects, jurors will have reason to think Sally can work again. This can save the defendant a million or two dollars in damages.

Not bad for a free-of-charge analytic technique.

Forwards creating tension (Hungry for next). As much as your case story needs clarity, it also needs tension. A story without tension is like a tightrope sagging to the ground: The performance dies. When your closing argument (or your opening or direct or anything you do) loses tension, you will feel as aimless as a tightrope performer on the ground. The Walking Wallendas cannot compete with the Flying ones.

Tension attracts the listener from the story's present moment into the story's future. Tension derives from the audience's hunger to hear or see what is going to happen next. You create that hunger by using *forwards*.

When a high-wire acrobat wobbles, the audience *tenses* (and thus pays attention) out of fear over what might happen next. When a movie heroine gets lost in the graveyard at midnight, the audience tenses over what might happen to her next. When your team trails by two in the bottom of the ninth with bases loaded, two outs, and the count three and two in the seventh game of the World Series, you are tense about what might happen next.

The previous section (on backwards analysis) warns that the unpredictability of going forwards is an uncertain way to analyze the relationship of events to each other. But that same unpredictability can be valuable if you use it to create tension by means of forwards. Forwards

　　　—create suspense;

　　　—create and hold audience attention;

　　　—focus attention where you want it.

A forward is anything that arouses an audience's strong desire to see or hear what is to come. A forward tells the audience that something visceral,[18] something extremely interesting, is coming up. Using a forward is like dangling a carrot.

> Forwards . . . maneuver into unison the attention-rhythms of many
> different sorts of people, despite individual variations in things like
> concentration span, interest, taste, understanding, emotional and
> intellectual involvement, physical comfort, attitudes, and mood.
> The playwright must seize *control* of audience attention.[19]

In good scripts and good case presentations, there will not be a moment without one or more—usually many more—forwards in effect. This is because it is desirable to have a state of forward tension *all the time*. Without it, neither audiences nor jurors pay much attention.

Don't confuse forwards with foreshadowing. Foreshadowing merely hints at what is to come; it does not necessarily make the audience eager for it. Foreshadowing says what is coming, but a forward *makes the audience want to see it* by telling them that it is going to be important or engrossing.

Foreshadowing: "Igor had a feeling that he was not over his sore throat." This hints that the sore throat will be around later. Wow. Can't wait, can you?

---

18. See Chapter 6.
19. *Backwards and Forwards* by David Ball. Southern Illinois University Press, 1983. I know it is self-serving for me to say that this text is indispensable for anyone who works in or is interested in theater. Sorry. I will do even worse and say it is useful for trial lawyers, too.

Forward: "Igor remembered that the only cure for his persistent sore throat was fresh human blood."

When there are no forwards in effect, jurors look forward to lunch more than to anything that has to do with the trial. So instead of saying, "You'll hear from my injured client," say,

> You'll hear from a man who'll tell you what it feels like to fall backwards forty-two feet onto a train track.

You have promised a firsthand narrative of terror (terror is a visceral) that your jurors will be eager to hear.

A voir dire forward: "Mr. Jones, if you're seated as a juror, you'll have to look at some photographs. They're candid and graphic. Will you try to look at them dispassionately enough to evaluate them fairly?" This is a weak question for gathering voir dire information (see Chapter 3), but it is a strong forward. Later in trial when you pick up those photos, every juror will be eager to see them. The forward also makes jurors aware from the beginning that you have credible high-impact evidence to support the contentions you will be making in the meantime. As a result, jurors will tend to attach greater credibility to those contentions even before the photographs are displayed.

Embedded in every forward is an additional bonus because a forward is a kind of personal invitation for the jurors to meet with you later in trial. This means that the jurors will anticipate a shared, important moment with you. By using a number of forwards you can dot the future landscape of the case with such upcoming meetings. Your opposition will only be able to watch, uninvited, from a distance.

Moreover, a forward not only makes jurors hungry for what is coming up, but it makes them pay more attention to it when it finally comes up. In the voir dire example of the graphic photos, the forward makes jurors pay heightened attention not just in advance but when you actually show the photos. And jurors will better remember the photos because they were thinking about those photos long before seeing them. In other words, a forward—like a narrow spotlight in a dark room—picks out and emphasizes whatever you point at.

Cliffhangers: the ultimate forward. *Cliffhanger:* The train roars toward the heroine tied to the tracks. She screams, the audience leans forward, and— today's episode ends! That old Saturday matinee trick always got the audience back the next week. In court:

> Later that night, Caroline gets home. The alarm indicator is green, so she *thinks*[20] everything is okay. She turns off the alarm

---

20. Emphasis on the word "thinks" is a forward in itself. It makes jurors listen carefully because they are eager to find out what was wrong.

system and checks the apartment. Everything *seems*[21] fine. She re-checks the locks on the windows and doors, re-sets the alarm system, undresses, and takes a hot shower. She gets into bed, drinks a cup of cocoa, reads a book, gets sleepy, turns out the light, and goes to sleep.

Two hours later she wakes in the dark. As she'll tell us,[22] lying there she knows her life is about to change forever. Because she realizes that someone—someone big, someone with a stocking mask—is seated on the edge of her bed.

Now let me tell you about the alarm system that the Never-Fear Company had installed just a few months before.

You have changed the subject to leave the jurors hanging in the terrifying darkness with Caroline. The longer they hang there, the longer they will taste Caroline's experience. That makes it harder for the NeverFear Alarm Company to defend itself.

A cliffhanger leaves jurors hanging. When people hang from cliffs they pay attention, and the experience lingers.

STORIES, NOT MAPS

Don't think of your opening statement as a "map of the case." Maps do not persuade. Instead, think of your opening statement as a story. Stories persuade better than anything else can.

Opening statement is the first time the jurors have nothing on their minds but paying attention to you. Take advantage of all that focus. Don't dissipate it by promising anything as boring as a map, or by such pointless disclaimers as, "Nothing I say is evidence." That may be a true statement, but its only effect is to persuade jurors not to listen. Think of your opening statement in these terms: "I'm going to tell you a story. When you have heard it, you will want to help my client."[23]

LARGER SIGNIFICANCE (GLOBALIZATION)

Every good play gives its characters and events significance beyond themselves. This makes the audience pay more attention and take everything more seriously. So near the end of opening, introduce a way for the jury to see the import of your case beyond itself. Otherwise, it may seem of little significance to anyone but the parties involved, and that is not enough to make jurors care.

---

21. Emphasis on "seems" makes it a forward.
22. The fact that *she* is going to tell it makes this an even more enticing forward.
23. See Application H, p. 221, "Opening Statement."

For example, no juror cares whether your multi-millionaire client, Mrs. DePockets, wins her case against the city. The city took a water-main easement on the corner of her twenty-two acre metropolitan estate. The only issue is whether the city will pay her the $12,000 they offered or the $175,000 she wants. Well, no juror gives a hoot! If I were on that jury, I would resent every wasted minute of my time.

You can make jurors care. Show them what is at stake over and above the concerns of Mrs. DePockets. In your opening, lay preliminary groundwork that you can build on in testimony and wrap up in your closing. Opening and testimony should pave the way for such closing arguments as:

—If the revenue office gets away with its treatment of Mrs. DePockets, it can do even worse to people who cannot so easily afford lawyers, surveyors, and appraisers to come to court to fight it out.

—Justice and government procedure have been violated. The issue is not just dollars for Mrs. DePockets, but the jury's importance in the ongoing process of protecting individuals from governmental abuse.

—The issues will have greater import in other circumstances. Perhaps the city is planning many more such sewer projects.

Effective persuasion requires you to show how the case is more important than itself. The defendant who caused the crash was not merely speeding; he was endangering everyone on the road.

Because it can be difficult to point out larger significance without arguing, much of this technique must wait until closing. But you can say, for example, *"The Tax Clerk will tell you* that her office does to everyone what it did to Mrs. DePockets." (You can quote almost anything in opening statement if you expect it to be admitted in testimony.)[24]

PLAYING THE EMOTIONAL CARD

Shoving emotions down jurors' throats is NEVER effective. It is a form of telling jurors what to think or feel, which is ineffective at any time but especially harmful in opening when jurors know little about you or your case. All they know is that some lawyer is trying to yank on their heartstrings. This annoys and alienates jurors and reinforces their suspicion of attorneys.

Look, for example, at this typical opening:

This is the case of how Sally Green's life was ruined forever. Her whole family who she loved so much died in a tragic wreck. Now every

---

24. Caveat: Prosecutors in many jurisdictions and everyone else in a few jurisdictions might cross ethical boundaries if they point out larger significance—such as, "If you free this defendant, none of us will be safe after dark again."

morning Sally wakes up crying, and every night she goes to bed crying. The horrible pain of her terrible loss will never go away.

"Ruined forever," "loved so much," "tragic wreck," "horrible pain," and "crying, crying, crying, crying, crying . . . "—overwrought phrases that express little and elicit less.

Emotion is a conclusion. As with every conclusion, you have to lead jurors to make it for themselves. You cannot simply announce your own conclusions and expect jurors to accept them.

To lead jurors to "conclude" the emotion you want, you must convey concretely, specifically, and exclusively—in story-narrative form—what happened and the results of what happened. If that does not arouse sympathy, *nothing* else you say can.

For example:

> On January 9, 1995, Sally Green is riding in the back seat of the family's Buick. Her husband, Jim, is driving. With Jim in front is their daughter Erica, 12. Beside Sally in back is Carol, 8 1/2. At two minutes after noon a drunk veers his Ford pickup head-on across the center line at 75 miles per hour. Jim is killed on impact. Thirty-eight minutes later in the ambulance Sally watches as Erica stops breathing. At 2:15 that afternoon a doctor comes out of surgery and says they could not save Carol.

By telling a narrative story of nothing but the facts—no conclusions, no abstractions, and barely a descriptive adjective—you have made Sally's loss more palpable to jurors than phrases such as "the awful pain of her terrible loss" could ever do. You have not said "tragic wreck" or "negligent driver." You have merely informed and allowed jurors to react.

You have aroused the jurors' feelings without trying to cheerlead jurors into feeling them. You have not said an emotional word. You have merely stated what happened and, thereby, *led* jurors to their *own* feelings and conclusions. You just opened their ears; their hearts automatically followed. Now when you point at the defendant and say, "There's the drunk," juror sympathy for Sally will transform to anger and revenge.

Caveat: Do not arouse juror sympathy unless you know what you want that emotion to impel jurors to do (i.e., don't make jurors feel sorry for someone their verdict cannot help, and don't arouse their anger unless it will drive the verdict in your direction). Unfocused emotions floating around the jury can have wildly unpredictable results.

Once you arouse juror emotions by means of a narrative story of what happened, you can later, if you wish, talk explicitly about the feeling itself. But it is no longer necessary to do so. You never need to say "tragic" or "sad" or "horrible." You never have to say how awful your client feels. You *showed* what happened to her, and that is a primary operating mechanism of plays and movies. There is no better way to tap juror feelings.

HUMANIZING

To *humanize* means to emphasize the human elements of a situation or person so that the jury can instantly and closely relate. Thus:

—*Use names.* Throughout trial, refer to your client in court by name, not as "my client." To *de*humanize your opponent party, say "the plaintiff" or some other name-neutral reference.

—*Eat.* On trial days, have lunch with your client at the restaurant where jurors eat. (This may not be wise if your client is accused of a violent crime.) Eating is a humanizing thing for jurors to see you and your client do, perhaps because eating is the most in-common human activity. Whatever the reason, the sight of it makes you both into real people.

—*Smile.* During trial, smile from time to time. It humanizes you, and humans persuade juries better than lawyers do. It also relaxes your witnesses—those you want relaxed on direct and the ones you want to mislead into letting down their guard on your cross.

—*Humanize people and issues.* Your client's injuries may mean he can no longer earn $25 an hour as a mason, but they may also mean he can no longer play baseball with his sons or sit down for a long Thanksgiving family dinner.

Humanizing means communicating in terms anyone can identify with, terms we all share. It is close: feelings, touch, children, love, buddies, intimacies. It is alive: celebrations, family events, the stuff of living a normal life. It is physical: shaving, unwrapping a new shirt, opening a beer or a great bottle of wine, watching the sun set while you hold someone's hand, giving your kid a puppy.

No matter how dry you think your case is—even if it is a dispute between the memory banks of two computers—the human computer operators and accountants involved have feelings and human connections.[25] There are human consequences to any dispute. *Somebody* had to get mad enough (or hurt or greedy or ambitious or . . .) to sue.

Juries don't care about record books. They care about what record books do to a *person.* Juries don't care about facts. They care about what facts can do to, or reveal about, a *person.* Juries care almost exclusively about people.

---

25. See Application B, p. 189, "Humanizing Non-Human Cases."

In a damages case, humanizing can be more persuasive than all your X-rays, financial statements, or accident and police reports. In fact, X-rays, financial statements, and accident reports are effective persuaders only insofar as they are also humanizers.

Humanize witnesses. There is all the difference in the world between, say, Western Service Corporation's internal accountant M.W. Wallace, Jr., and a guy named Marty Wallace who lives in Glenville with his family and has held the same job for eleven years. The corporate accountant is an abstraction; Marty is a person.

Humanizing communicates our common human experience. Humanizing is personal. It removes the formal barriers from between your client and the jury. If your steelworker client was crippled in a fall, ask him how he *feels* about not being able to get up high again. Maybe he loved it up there on top of the whole big, beautiful world. And now he cannot get up there any more. To point that out is to humanize his plight.

If you don't ask the right questions in advance, that big tough steelworker might never think to volunteer anything like that.

FAMILIARIZATION

Every well-presented case requires this technique to help jurors relate unfamiliar or complicated matters to things they understand and know well—that is, to their own life experiences. For example, many jurors are intimidated by corporate financial records. Before introducing such records, use familiarization to prepare the way. If you do not, some jurors will decide in advance that they will never understand. Consequently, they will not listen carefully when you get to that topic.

Familiarization means relating the unfamiliar to the familiar. Tell the jury that the financial records will seem dauntingly complex at first, but they are just an elaborate checking account register like our own personal checkbooks.

An example of effective humanizing and familiarization: A recent Michigan case concerned a now-defunct assisted-suicide law which included the element of *intent to cause death*. In March, 1996, Dr. Kevorkian's defense counsel, Geoffrey Fieger, argued that the doctor's intent had not been to cause death, but to end suffering. To many jurors, such an argument could seem a mere legal quibble because it relates to nothing in their life experiences; few jurors have put people to death. Thus, Fieger had a dilemma: His pivotal issue lay outside the jurors' life experiences, reducing his primary defense to an apparent attempt to hide his client behind a technicality of the law. This can be harmful not only because it is a limp defense, but because many jurors despise and reject attempts to hide behind legal quibbles or technicalities.

This is a typical dilemma: Counsel's case-determinative contention was alien to the experience of most jurors. So, in his powerful closing Fieger talked to jurors about taking a suffering pet to the veterinarian to be put to sleep. The owner's intent is not to kill; the intent is to end unbearable suffering. This close-to-home, logically understandable and emotionally bonding analogy bridged the gap between familiarity and legal technicality. It familiarized and humanized the distinction between intent to kill and intent to end suffering. Fieger had familiarized the heart of the case.[26]

HOW DO WE JUDGE CHARACTER?

Character consists of all the qualities, traits, and features that create the nature of a person and distinguish that person from all other people. Jurors draw conclusions about a person's character (and thus her credibility) based upon what that person *does*. How Sally acts in certain circumstances as opposed to how Jane acts in the same circumstances reveals differences in character. Thus, the more that jurors see of what a person *does*, the more they can (or believe they can) ascertain character.

Abstract character description is all but useless. "Sally is a generous lady" carries no persuasive weight. It is merely a conclusion, and jurors don't swallow conclusions. The only conclusions they believe are those they make for themselves. Your assertion "Sally is a generous lady" tells jurors what you want them to believe but does nothing to persuade them that you are right.

To describe your client as a good person, tell the jury what she *does* that a reasonable person would evaluate as good. Then you don't need to state the unpersuasive conclusion that she is good. The jury will see it. Saying "she's good" a dozen times is less convincing than telling us once that she volunteers to work Saturdays at the orphanage—or that she did until the accident.

When you describe a person by citing abstract qualities ("good," "clever," or "nasty") instead of actions, jurors cannot believe you. They know it is not only easy but expected for you to produce evidence of a person's *acts*. In theater and movies, characters are created by *actors*. That is because *actions* speak louder than words.

This principle is particularly crucial with character witnesses. Such witnesses as ministers, mothers, neighbors, and teachers can be persuasive when they talk about specific things your client has done. But assertions such as, "He's a good, good boy everybody likes" carry little weight.

CONCLUSION

Remember that the gold standard of persuasion is to make jurors want to do what you want them to do. The goal of this chapter's storytelling techniques is to achieve that standard.

---

26. Counsel Fieger won an acquittal.

✠ CHAPTER 8 ✠

YOUR CAMERA ANGLE: POINT OF VIEW

Point-of-view analysis is a problem-solving, research, and investigatory technique, as well as an indispensable reasoning procedure for drama and trial practice. It is the craft of examining events, behavior, and opinions through the eyes of each individual involved. It helps you spot everything important.

SEEING WHAT THEY SEE

In movie scripts, the letters POV stand for point-of-view. The screenwriter writes, for example:

DAY—INTERIOR—COURTROOM.

The jury, POV Judge Jones.

"POV Judge Jones" means that the screenwriter wants us to see the jury through the Judge's eyes, as if the camera were the Judge's eyes. The screenwriter might have written the reverse:

DAY—INTERIOR—COURTROOM.

Judge Jones, POV jury.

"POV jury" means that this time we see Judge Jones through the jurors' eyes. Both camera shots are in the same courtroom but each shows a different picture.

You can expand the concept of POV beyond mere camera angle. In real life, point of view is determined by everything that affects how a person perceives. This includes attitudes, opinions, wants, needs, hopes, expectations, personality traits, backgrounds, memories, emotions, associations, one's particular situation, one's particular relationship to what one is observing, the particular way one analyzes what is observed, how that analysis circularly affects the perceived nature of what is observed, and everything else that influences how each individual perceives and reacts. There are so many factors involved, and they interact so variously, that no two people see any situation exactly the same way. Anyone who takes information from witnesses knows this. It is a truth that perennially fascinates dramatists and drives countless parties to court.

Every party, witness, lawyer, and juror has his or her own individual point of view of what is going on at any given moment during trial, in the events leading up to the case, and regarding any possible consequences of the case. Keep yourself aware of the potential differences among each of these points of view, and of how each differs from your own. If the only point of view you know about is yours, the only person you can reliably persuade is you.

Juror point of view. To use point-of-view analysis to expand your understanding of a jury, view every detail of what is presented in court as the jurors see it: "What am 'I' [Mr. Juror] seeing and what does it mean to me?"

What you consider to be a sound argument or a witness's stunning revelation might be pointless to jurors. A sophisticated lawyer, familiar with and partial about the case, can miss seeing the gulf between the way she thinks and the way some jurors think about the same thing.

Some things jurors see that you might normally miss can be seen just by turning your head—*literally* turning your head—to notice what jurors are looking at. I once watched a plaintiff thoroughly impeached when his wife in the gallery hung her head in shame as he lied on the stand. Every juror was watching her and not the witness. But neither defense nor plaintiff counsel noticed where the jurors were looking, because neither ever looked at the jurors. If they had, they would have seen a dozen jurors noticing the wife in the gallery. Instead, defense counsel remained unaware of having won a major point and took no advantage of it. Plaintiff's counsel, equally unaware, did nothing to rehabilitate.

Spouses or other family members often react visibly. When a witness is in trouble, *the first place some jurors look is at you (to see your reaction), then at the spouse (to see his or her reaction).* This is because anyone who watches television knows instinctively that reaction shots are revealing. You may not have eyes in the back of your head to see when a spouse is having a visible reaction, but if you look at the jury, you can see what they are watching.

Look at your jurors often—several times a minute—to see what they are looking at and to monitor their reactions. If looking at jurors several times a minute seems odd or awkward to you, it means you have become unfortunately accustomed to keeping them outside the periphery of your attention. To be an effective persuader you must bring the jurors to the foreground of your attention and keep them there. The way to begin doing that is to look at them often. Not looking at jurors is like running through a china shop blindfolded.

Once you bring the jurors into your circle of awareness, the next step is to pay constant attention to their point of view both optically and analytically:

a) Optical: Know what each juror is watching. Don't assume that all the jurors are looking at the same thing as each other or as you. Much of the time they are not.

b) Analytic: Try to stand in the jurors' shoes to determine how those jurors are perceiving and reacting to everything. The only thing you can take for granted is that they usually react differently from the way you do. To determine the difference, factor in what you learned about them in voir dire: Ask yourself how each particular person on the jury might react to each important thing in the case.

For example, a shy and quiet juror who finds conflict unpleasant might take offense at a rudely aggressive cross-examination, whereas a different type of juror might like it. Or a juror unfamiliar with guns might find real evidence such as a .22 caliber pocket pistol too terrifying to hold, whereas a hunter might have trouble considering it lethal.

If plaintiff seeks a million dollars for injuries, you must understand and contend with how each juror looks at such a sum. Use what you learned in voir dire to help you see through their eyes. Each juror can have a different reason for thinking a million dollars is too much, and you have to contend with (or, on defense, reinforce) each of those reasons differently. A hard-working, lower-income juror might consider a million to be outlandish. Another juror might believe that there is a litigation crisis due to verdicts of that size. Another juror might have a sister with the same injuries as the plaintiff, but the sister never got any money. Another juror might have friends in the medical profession and would be embarrassed to be on a jury that decides on a million-dollar verdict against a doctor. Another juror might believe Matthew 7:1-2 ("Judge not, lest ye be judged. For with what measure ye judge, so shall ye be judged . . . .").[1] Each kind of resistance requires different treatment for plaintiff counsel to overcome or for defense to reinforce. But this requires that you know about them. You discover them by using point-of-view analysis.

Witness point of view (Impeachment).   To use point-of-view analysis during testimony, examine every step of what the participants say they did or saw exactly as they themselves did it or saw it at the time: "Why am 'I' doing what I'm doing at this particular instant?" See everything through the eyes of the witness and from that perspective critically evaluate what is being claimed. Take no step for granted.

Examine whether each detail makes sense when viewed through the witness's eyes. Don't just accept the statement that the witness found the money in the bushes. Ask yourself, "If I were the witness, would I have been in the bushes at that particular time?" Maybe it makes perfect sense. Maybe

---

1.   If, as plaintiff counsel, you suspect you have allowed such a juror to slip through voir dire, describe compensation not as a "judgment" but as a *balance* which removes the need for judgment. Point out that the jury's function is to balance a skewed situation, not to condemn.

not. By examining a witness's testimony through the witness's eyes, you sometimes find otherwise unnoticeable facts, discrepancies, and omissions. Ask yourself:

—why "I" (the witness) would have said or done each thing "I" claim,

—why "I" would have done or said it at that particular time and in that particular way,

—how "I" would or could have observed what "I" claim to have observed.

Are the answers:

—consistent with everything else "I" said, did, or observed?

—likely or even possible?

—consistent with the rest of "my" testimony?

—consistent with other witnesses' testimony?

Apply these questions to the testimony of your own witnesses as well as your opponent's. This will help you spot problems before your opponent (or a juror) does. Point-of-view analysis reveals facts and inconsistencies—or maybe just useful suspicions of inconsistencies—that are otherwise hard to find.

BACKWARDS ANALYSIS AND POINT-OF-VIEW ANALYSIS

A particularly valuable analytic tool is the combination of backwards analysis (see Chapter 7, p. 124) with point-of-view analysis. Examine an individual's behavior as viewed through her own eyes. From that perspective, trace her behavior backwards event by event and look for every possible alternative antecedent that might have caused her to do each thing she did. This process reveals omissions and helps you understand (and clarify to the jury) even the most complicated things people have done.

Point of view + backwards analysis: Example. In his book *And the Sea Will Tell*, defense counsel Vincent Bugliosi relates how a particular fact revealed his client's innocence. Weeks of effective prosecution were outweighed by the fact, and it provided the high point of his closing argument. It was a brilliant deduction but he could have found it without brilliance. He could simply have applied point-of-view plus backwards analysis.

The reason I don't reveal the crucial fact of Bugliosi's case is to get you to read his book. Because he writes technically and frankly, it is worth your time. And if you keep point-of-view plus backwards analysis in mind as you read, you will have the fun of spotting the pivotal fact I am referring to long before Bugliosi springs it. Simply look through each participant's eyes backwards from each important piece of evidence to see *how* and *if* it makes sense in the light of its apparent antecedents.

MEMORY

Point of view is heavily influenced by memory, and memory is a triple variable:

> 1) Memory modifies perception (what I remember will not be exactly what was).
>
> 2) Memory varies from instant to instant (how I remember something at one moment will be different from how I remember it at another moment).
>
> 3) Memory varies from person to person (how I remember something will be different from how other observers remember it).

In other words, a witness may be honest and certain but nonetheless mistaken. The fickle nature of memory plays havoc with what we think we perceived. This means that if you look hard enough, you will find inconsistencies among multiple witnesses. In a matter of even moderate complexity, if you find no inconsistencies among witnesses, they probably colluded to get their stories straight.

Memory is especially treacherous when it comes to eyewitnesses because jurors accept honest eyewitness testimony as 100 percent reliable. But due to the vagaries of perception and memory, eyewitness testimony is unreliable even from totally honest witnesses. Unless you can afford (and your jurisdiction permits) expert testimony on the unreliability of eyewitnesses, it may be impossible to convince jurors that the testimony of an honest and assured eyewitness is wrong. But at least you should know better so that you don't easily dismiss the possibility that the testimony is incorrect.

CHAPTER 9

TESTIMONY

When laypersons think of trials, they think of testimony. Many are not aware there is anything else. And because they have seen direct and cross on *Perry Mason* and *L.A. Law*, they have strong expectations.

Unfortunately, you have no scriptwriters creating snappy dialogue, forceful evidence, silver-tongued witnesses, convenient legal procedure, trenchant objections, or dramatic situations. You must do without the assistance of the Writers Guild of America.

But you can use their methods:

SELECTION OF WITNESSES

Which witnesses can best tell your case story? Careful selection of witnesses is as critical as the selection of characters for a play or movie. Aside from such obvious factors as credibility and relevance, consider the following:[1]

a) *Interest level*. How interesting a witness is can be as important as what she says. When you have prospective witnesses of equal informational value and authoritative weight, select the most interesting.

b) *Relationship to jurors*. Insofar as possible, delay final selection of witnesses until you can base your selections on what you learn in voir dire. For example, if your jury is composed of blue-collar workers who earn modest livings, think twice—if you have a choice—before calling a mildly impeachable witness who favors $1,000 suits. As far as possible, gauge the worth of each potential witness according to the characteristics of your particular jurors.

c) *Character type*. Although you don't offer every witness as an expert, jurors evaluate every witness's expertise. From your available pool of witnesses, choose those that your jurors will find the most "expert" on each particular topic. Among equally honest and interesting witnesses, evaluate the relationship between *character type* and *material to be presented*. Choose the witness who will seem

1. For selecting expert witnesses, see Application L, p. 249, "The Care and Feeding of Experts."

most reliable with that particular kind of evidence. On matters of driving, the retired taxi driver may be more persuasive than the bank president.

d) *Strong character type.* Certain kinds of people are particularly memorable: those who are extraordinarily positive or negative, lovable or detestable, rock-solid honest or slime-low liar, etc. Be alert to these and other strong character types. Don't underestimate their jury impact.

For example, Americans (particularly older ones) admire individuals who don't give up regardless of the odds against them. Even when there is nothing else good about someone, most Americans admire anyone who perseveres in the face of overwhelming adversity. That is why despicable villains like Bonnie and Clyde seem heroic. When jurors react that way to a witness, it colors how they hear and evaluate the witness's testimony.

AUDITIONING WITNESSES ("Casting")

The most important step in play production is casting. The human characteristics of the cast have a powerful effect on all that is communicated. The same is true in court.

It is difficult to predict which of a witness's human characteristics will emerge in court. The witness who was Rambo in your office can be Bozo on the stand, or vice-versa. A client with a story of woe and suffering might strike jurors as an unbearable whiner who deserves the pain. The witness who seemed frank and penitent in her jail cell may, on the stand, cover her nervousness with mannerisms that make her seem nasty and deceitful. The vulnerably gentle witness you interviewed in a living room might come across in court like an edgy presidential assassin. People are rarely the same on the stand as in real life.

How interesting a person is, as well as other factors such as clarity, warmth, and credibility, are as important as the information contained in testimony. You can reliably determine such factors only by "audition." Because audition-ing can reveal how a witness will do in court, you will know whom to choose, what remedial measures to take if you have no choice, and how to maximize the witness's positive characteristics.[2]

Auditioning requires different techniques and conditions than witness preparation or interviewing for information. For example, a good investigative interview requires relaxed and comfortable conditions, but an audition re-quires the opposite. Use the following guidelines:

a) Don't make your auditioning witnesses comfortable. Save that for court. Instead, make them *uncomfortable.* (It is best to use someone

---

2.   See Chapter 2, p. 26, "Witness Preparation."

other than yourself to do this, so that in court your witnesses will regard you as a source of security rather than pressure.) The goal is to see the impression a witness might make when nervous in the formal, intimidating environment of the courtroom.

b) Use a courtroom or a room of comparable size and formality. If possible, include people the witness does not know—a few mock jurors, preferably taking notes. Tell the witness that the jurors are there to help you evaluate. Witnesses get nervous in court largely because they feel they are being evaluated by the judge, jury, courtroom staff, and everyone in the gallery. This is your chance to see how a potential witness responds to that pressure.

c) Have someone cross-examine your auditionees the way you expect opposing counsel to cross-examine them during trial.[3] If you have never seen your opponent work, ask people who have.

d) Do not provide refreshments and do not allow smoking.

Auditioning is too elaborate a process to be used for every witness. But when you have a choice of witnesses on key matters, failure to audition can result in unnecessary surprises in court.

DEMARCATION

This book would be confusing and indecipherable without chapter divisions, section divisions, or headings—as if it were one unbroken 270-page paragraph. That is how court cases can seem to jurors if you don't provide explicit and frequent demarcations. The fact that you know which section of your outline you are on does not mean jurors know it. You have to tell them—often. Provide signposts. (See Chapter 7, p. 122, "Signposts.")

When you allow witness testimony to slide seamlessly from point to point, even attentive jurors get lost. "Why are we listening to this?" If you do not provide demarcation to quickly help them find their way, they stop paying attention.

Even the most dedicated jurors cannot pay attention all the time. Minds wander during long hours and days of testimony. Non-listening time is over 50 percent. This is probably higher than your own observations indicate, but that is because jurors can be daydreaming even when they seem to be hanging on your every word. It is a deception mastered in third grade.

Because juror attention waxes and wanes unpredictably and undetectably, you must constantly help jurors get their bearings when they return from their mental wanderings. You must also help the listening jurors to stay keenly aware

---

3. See footnote 1, p. 28 in Chapter 2 on the danger of you yourself conducting a practice cross-examination of your potential witness.

of what you are doing at each moment. It is rarely as obvious as you think it is. You must bluntly and repeatedly let the jury know the distinct purpose of what you are doing: "Officer Norton, you're here to tell us *about the fingerprints at the scene*, aren't you?"—and later, "Officer Norton, in preparing to come tell us *about the fingerprints at the scene*, did you look at . . . ?"

You should also keep the jury alert to the purpose of each grouping of questions: "Officer Norton, let's talk now about where the fingerprint was found . . ." and later, "Officer Norton, continuing with where the fingerprint was found . . ." Similarly, you should demarcate the sections of your opening statements and closing arguments.

To demarcate testimony, give each grouping of questions an explicitly labeled beginning, ending, and transition to the next grouping:

Beginning:

> Now, Miss Borden, I want to ask you about honing hatchet blades.

Ending and transition to next sequence:

> Thank you, Miss Borden, for explaining how to sharpen axes. Now let's look at how to swing them.

If testimony is interrupted by a recess, bench conference, or fire in the courthouse, remind your jurors what is going on when you resume:

> Now, Miss Borden, continuing with how you learned hatchet-swinging techniques, when did you . . . ?

When finished with a witness, remind us where we have been and put the witness's testimony into the context of your overall case story:

> Thank you, Miss Borden, for telling us what you did while everyone was sleeping that night.

Demarcation helps you increase the amount of information your jurors hear and retain. It also establishes and reinforces the relationship of each individual piece of testimony to your ultimate contentions. And providing demarcation helps you avoid the time-wasting trap of eliciting testimony irrelevant to your ultimate contentions.

Providing sufficient demarcation minimizes the number and depth of gaps in every juror's understanding of your case. (See Chapter 7, p. 102, "Filling the Gaps.") Without demarcation, jurors fill those gaps in arbitrary ways that often do not support your side. Thus, the presence or absence of demarcation can be pivotal to the outcome of any case.[4]

---

4.   Don't demarcate on cross if you are intentionally skipping from topic to topic to keep the witness off balance. But in closing, compensate by being extra clear about what the witness said.

LOOPING

For emphasis of an important point in an answer, use the witness's wording of that point in your next question.

MISS BORDEN: And that was the afternoon I lent the ax to the gardener.

COUNSEL: After you *lent the ax to the gardener*, did you ever see it again?

See Chapter 1, p. 19 for more examples of looping.

SUBORDINATE VERSUS MAIN POINTS

Help jurors keep track of how each subordinate point you elicit in testimony connects to the main point you want it to prove. For example, if you are trying to prove the main point that patient safety is compromised when blood pressure readings are taken too rarely, you may have a variety of subordinate supporting contentions: first, that a drop in blood pressure can signal the onset of shock; second, that a drop in pressure can signal a dangerous medication side effect; and third, that a rise in pressure can indicate the necessity of a treatment change. As you go about proving each of the three subordinate contentions, keep reminding the jury of the connection to your main point: *that each subordinate point shows that blood pressure readings must be taken at frequent intervals.* If jurors forget that connection even briefly, they miss the significance of both the subordinate point and the main point. As a result, they can go into deliberations unsure of what your main point might be.

Moreover, if your subordinate points are mistaken for main points, jurors might decide that you have failed to prove your case even if all you failed to prove was one of your subordinate points. The wording of most burden-of-proof instructions makes this a particular hazard on every issue for which the burden is yours.

Don't wait for closing to first clarify the connections between your supporting points and your main points. By then, jurors will have processed all the evidence without necessarily taking those connections into account. Errors will be inevitable.

Another example: Say that in a med mal case you need to show that the patient's injuries were (or, on defense, were not) serious enough to be a life-threatening emergency. But that fact is not case determinative; it is merely supporting. *It helps win the case only if it is linked in the jurors' minds with a standard of care violation (or, on defense, the lack of any such violation).* The connection must be made so strongly in opening, testimony, and closing that when the jurors hear "emergency" (or, on defense, "lack of emergency"), they automatically think of the specific standard of care that was violated (or met).

You must establish such automatic mental links between every subordinate point and the main contention it goes to prove.

In the med mal example, the main liability contentions are standard-of-care violations, causation, and consequent injuries. Everything else is subordinate support, and as such must be related directly, immediately, concretely, and repeatedly to one or more of those main contentions.

In any kind of case, first list each of your main (case determinative) issues ("What do I need the jury to believe?"). Then work backwards from each main issue to see what evidence and arguments you have to support it. Keep the distinctions between your two lists clear to yourself and to the jury throughout trial.

If you are tempted to slight this process, remember that jurors frequently go into deliberations unsure of what the main issues are. In the med mal example, even when jurors know what "standard of care" means or where the standards came from, they are often unsure of how the standards were supposedly violated (or upheld), or which particular standards are in question.

To guard against this, outline the following for the jury:

1) exactly what the standards of care are,

2) exactly what constitutes violation of each standard of care, and

3) how *each piece* of evidence shows (or, on defense, disproves) a specific standard-of-care violation.

A comparable outline can be made to connect the evidence (supporting items) to the main contentions in any kind of case.

When taking testimony, never go more than six minutes (the average TV-conditioned American's single-topic attention span) without reminding the jury how the evidence you are presenting at that moment supports a case-determinative matter.

This reminder can be achieved in a number of ways. In testimony, for example, it can be embedded in a question: "Doctor, you explained that a blood pressure drop can signal the onset of shock, and that shock can be lethal if undetected. Is that why the standard of care requires blood pressure to be taken and recorded?" This reminds jurors why you have been eliciting testimony about blood pressure. If you don't remind them at frequent intervals, they won't know why they are listening to what you are presenting—and they stop listening.

Remember that you are familiar enough with your case to know automatically which points are subordinate and which are main. Cases are lost when counsel does not take sufficient pains to make jurors equally aware of that distinction.

Character function. Make sure the jury understands your overall purpose in calling each witness. Clarify the relationship of each witness to your client and to your case.

Q In what capacity do you work with Joe Smith?
A I'm his boss.
Q For how long?
A Since four years before the wreck.
Q When did you stop being his boss?
A I'm still his boss.
Q So you can compare his work before the accident and after?
A Sure.

Now the jury knows why you have called this witness and what to listen for.

TRIAL TEAM BEHAVIOR

Make sure that everyone on your trial team—co-counsel, paralegals, your client—pays attention, looks interested, and appears satisfied with what is coming from the stand. This encourages your witness and sends good messages to the jury. When someone on your trial team stares into space, shuffles papers, or whispers during your witness's testimony, then jurors assume that the testimony is unimportant and pay less attention. If your paralegals react with horror to harmful testimony, they reinforce whatever harm it did.

UNAVOIDABLE MONOTONY

Some necessary testimony will have no effect on jurors but to bore them. For example, jurors who don't understand the necessity of laying a foundation will think you are wasting time. Let them know you have no choice. You can say, "Now, Officer Norton, I have to ask some background questions. Would you tell us how you learned to identify fingerprints?" In general, speed through the unpersuasive parts of necessary foundations and other such sequences. But slow down for the important stuff. (Added benefit: The change in rhythm will emphasize the important stuff.)[5]

"PLEASE TELL US . . . "

During testimony, establish and maintain two-way jury contact by referring to the jury as "we" or "us" in the wording of your questions:

"Please tell *us* . . . ."

"If *we* wanted to climb a steel column like you had to do, what safety equipment would *we* have to learn to use?"

---

5. For an effective and brief way to qualify expert witnesses without putting jurors to sleep, see Application L, p. 249, "The Care and Feeding of Experts."

"Did you mean for *us* to understand that the car was approaching at . . . ?"

This makes jurors feel more involved. They will then tend to listen more closely because they see you are seeking answers for their benefit.

TO CROSS OR NOT TO CROSS

When you fail to impeach or otherwise reduce the harm an opponent's witness has done, your failure emphasizes the harm. Aside from letting the witness repeat the harmful testimony,[6] you let the witness verify and reinforce it because she manages to stick to it even in the face of your skilled, hostile questions.

Worse, your failure tells jurors that whatever you thought you would find was not there: You were wrong about an element of the case! That makes jurors wonder what else you might be wrong about—including ultimate issues. (When you are on the other side of this circumstance, emphasize the cross-examiner's futile attempt. Present it to the jury as a measure of your case's strength: Despite your opponent's masterful cross-examining skills, your honest witness's accurate testimony was unshakable.)

Generally, you want to get a harmful opposition witness out of there as fast as possible. But not all opposition witnesses are harmful. Let an obnoxious or barely credible opposition witness babble on forever. The more some people talk, the worse they sound.

Such exceptions aside, think of cross as a process that costs you $100 per question. That will stop you as soon as you have what you want. Otherwise, you give the witness a chance to explain and possibly cancel the progress you have made. If a guy in a play kicks a dog, the audience assumes he is a bad guy—unless he gets to explain that the dog was biting him. So once you get what you are after on cross, stop. Let the witness explain on re-direct, when his explanation will have less impact.

CONTROLLING YOURSELF ON CROSS

When you are pressuring a witness under cross, don't turn the witness stand into a torture chamber unless you do so as a carefully (and infrequently) selected tactic. You will usually do better by gently gaining trust. Catch the witness off guard and *then* let him have it. But remember that jurors don't like watching torture. They may well side with a witness whom you, the professional, pressure too much.

Jurors despise cross-examiners who are arrogant, nasty, or harsh. This is truer in some parts of the country than others (North Carolina vs. Brooklyn),

---

6.   And it is a repetition that obeys the Rules of Repetition because it is cross instead of direct (*different*) and is hostile, which raises the visceral impact (*stronger*). This means that it is a highly persuasive repetition of that negative material.

but no matter where you are, carefully weigh cost vs. benefit of a harsh approach. Sometimes it is a good investment but often it is a self-indulgent expense that backfires.

Your attitude toward a witness on cross should mirror what you think the jury's attitude is, not what you would like it to be. First, get the witness to say things that will make the jury mad—and *then* display your own anger at the witness. Moreover, it is best if your mirroring of the emotion is slightly less intense than what you think the jury is feeling.

In other words, don't lead juror emotions; follow them. It is almost impossible to implant an emotion in the jury by displaying that emotion yourself. (See also Chapter 7, p. 131, "Playing the Emotional Card.")

IMPEACHING WITH VISCERALS

Viscerals can help you impeach.[7] They help jurors remember the impeachment in deliberations.

The following are samples of viscerals to attach to impeachments:

—A *generous show of kindness* on the part of one person for another in adversity. You can attach that visceral to yourself by the way you treat the witness you are impeaching. It is a visceral because the jury is moved by seeing that despite what you had to do, you proceeded gently and with kindness. Humanely and generously, you salvaged someone's dignity. You refrained from hurting a person even though you had every right to do so. Observers are moved by this; it is Clint Eastwood being gentle, John Wayne with a puppy, King Kong stroking the heroine's hair.

—*Entrapment* of a liar in public. This requires little more than emphasizing the moment the lie is revealed.

—*The boomerang.* Show, for example, that the witness who testified that your client hid the document was, in fact, the very one who hid the document himself. Boomerang impeachment is indelible.[8]

There are as many different viscerals for impeachment as there are reasons to doubt a witness. Viscerals are the strongest way to keep an impeachment active in your jurors' minds. Even if all you find is moderate bias, when a witness shades testimony because of a bias, the result is a kind of deception almost as visceral as lying. So point it out.

---

7. See Chapter 6, "Viscerals."
8. See Chapter 5, p. 90.

WITNESS CONDITIONING DURING DEPOSITION

Relaxed, mild questioning during a deposition can give the witness the wonderfully false impression that he need not fear you in court. This leaves him unprepared for how aggressively you come at him on the stand.

Or you might want to keep him nervous and shaky for weeks, maybe months, worrying about your getting him on the stand. In that case, pile it on during deposition. Corner him, embarrass him, tangle him up in every apparent uncertainty, confusion, lie, and ambiguity you can find. In an on-paper (as opposed to videotaped) deposition, you can run your torture chamber—you can be bullying, nasty, and generally monstrous—because a written deposition records only words, not your manner or tone. "I have one more question on that topic, please" seems polite on paper, but you can make it sound mean, threatening, bullying, sarcastic, or anything you want. This will put the witness in an advance panic.

DON'T DO THE EXPECTED

Your opponent has probably prepared her witnesses to withstand the kind of cross she thinks you will use. So do something else.

STAY HONEST

Don't let your tactics on cross show you to be a sneak. If jurors see you tricking a witness or being deceptive in any way, they will conclude that you trick and deceive juries, too.

OBJECTIONS

Objecting: the effect on jurors. Vigorous advocacy does not mean objecting to everything you can. It means weighing the effect on jurors of everything you do, including objecting. In the jury's eyes, some objections can redound to the discredit of the objector. Your objection may make jurors conclude that you believe the answer will hurt your case. You don't want jurors to think that you are using legal technicalities to try hiding the truth.

An objection creates a secret. Any information, no matter how irrelevant and boring, becomes viscerally interesting when it is withheld. (See Chapter 6, "Viscerals.") Secrets tantalize; they ignite juror curiosity to hear the answer. If your objection is overruled or your opponent finds an unobjectionable way to ask the question, jurors pay greater attention to the answer simply because you tried to bar it. Even if the answer is innocuous, jurors may assume it harms your case even though they don't see why. At a minimum they give the answer greater attention and weight.

If your objection is sustained and the answer never gets in, jurors assume that something exists which you are afraid to let them hear. That undermines your credibility and your case.

Any objection to form is often a blunder. If your objection to form is overruled, you look bad and the answer is emphasized. If your objection is sustained, the question is often acceptably reworded and the answer is emphasized.

Jurors resent losing time to evidentiary battles. They want to get on with hearing the case. If you object too often, they will start to roll their eyes every time you open your mouth. It is even worse when your objection results in sentencing the jurors to another half hour in the jury room.

Jurors resent being deprived of information, so don't be the one who does it. As far as possible, anticipate evidentiary problems in limine. Don't object in front of a jury unless you have a worthwhile, concretely tactical reason to do so—a reason that outweighs the objection's harmful effects.

In general, think of objections as medication with powerful side effects, and gauge whether the side effects might be worse than the malady.

Objecting: tone. There is nothing as silly as the joyful young (or not so young) lawyer who springs up triumphantly or peevishly bellowing "*Objection!!*" Jurors find it disrespectful, arrogant, and petty—no matter what your opponent has done. Remain professional. Taking pleasure in scoring an evidentiary point is amateurish and can make jurors decide that you are a jerk. All the world loves to see jerks go down to defeat, and jurors are in a position to make that happen to you.

When you object, do it without pleasure and triumph, but rather with a tone of regret that implies that your opponent is forcing you to intrude on the jury's hearing of the case. Jurors don't care who wins a battle of evidentiary skills. They resent lawyers who initiate such battles.

USELESS BATTLES

Don't risk your credibility by gambling that you can undermine a witness on an issue that makes no difference.

If the witness has testified about matters that make no difference, either ignore those topics or focus attention back to your case-determinative issues. For example, after the opposition expert on direct has babbled irrelevantly about the vagaries of varying blood pressures in a case where blood pressure made no difference, don't engage battle on that issue. Instead, refocus: "Doctor, no matter how high or low the blood pressure might have been, and no matter the meaning of high or low blood pressure, *the standard of care says that blood pressure and other vital signs should be recorded every half hour, right?*"

This restores the juror's attention to a case determinative issue. (See also Chapter 10, p. 160, "Useless Battles.")

CHAPTER 10

CLOSING

CONTENT

Jurors barely listen to closings. Many jurors—often most—think they have already made their decisions. Even those who are still deciding believe they have heard everything. The jurors are ready to deliberate and feel no need to hear anything more you might have to say.

Post-trial interviews reveal that the most common juror thought during closings is, "Why do we have to listen to all this again? These lawyers must think we're stupid." When you say, "Let's go back and look again at that fateful night of January 14, 1995," they say, "NO! NO! NO! Let's *not* do anything *again*. Please stop talking!" When you don't stop talking, they solve the problem their own way: they stop listening.

By the end of testimony, jurors want to get rid of you and on with deliberations. They don't want to listen.

Moreover, when your closing remarks confirm that you are just going to rehash what went on in testimony, you douse the last spark of interest. (Confess! You *have* said, "Let's look at the evidence again," or "Let's review what the police officer told us." Juror response: groan!)

Like school kids and law students, jurors can seem to be paying attention when they are actually taking a mental recess. They may not paint eyeballs on their eyelids in order to sneak an undetected nap, yet they still know how to fake attentiveness and frequently do so.

But don't throw in the towel and say to yourself, "I can't control whether or not they listen." You *can* control it if you remember that listening is a voluntary activity. Jurors listen if you a) give them reasons to want to do so, and b) avoid giving them reasons to want to ignore you.

NEW and USEFUL. Jurors listen to anything they think will be useful to their decision making or to their deliberations discussions. And they believe it can be useful only if they believe it will be new. Thus, the way to make jurors want to listen is to promise at the start of your closing that what you're going to say *has not already been said* (it's NEW), and that it will *help jurors to make their decision or to support their opinions in deliberations* (it's USEFUL).

Some jurors listen even when your closing is mainly repetition, but this does you little good. Juror opinions are rarely modified or solidified on the basis of repeated (i.e., "marshaled") evidence. You must build on what has gone before, not merely repeat it.

Of course, there will always be evidence that you have to review. The trick is to present that evidence as part of something new. ("I want us to look at whether the doctor's testimony was supported by what the patient said." This allows you to repeat both the doctor's and the patient's testimony, as long as the *relationship* between the doctor's testimony and the patient's is not old ground.)

In other words, *you can review facts and information in closing as long as you are doing something new with them or showing them in a new light.* Because it can be so difficult to figure out how to do this, and because closings come at the end of trial when you are exhausted, you may be tempted not to try. Succumbing to that temptation has one result: jurors don't listen.

Caveat: Don't wait until the middle of closing to promise that what you have to say will be new and useful. By then, jurors will already have tuned you down or out. Make your new-and-useful promise at the start of closing.

Obviously, there will be some things you need to say in closing that you cannot find new ways to present. But if they are the exception rather than the rule, jurors will know that *most* of your closing will consist of new ways of looking at the evidence. That is enough to make them listen.

Avoid statements that lessen juror attention. Even when you make your dual promise of new and useful, you should meticulously avoid statements that make jurors tune out. For example, "Nothing I have to say is evidence" not only makes jurors stop listening but makes them suspicious of what you are going to say—because they think, "If it's not evidence, there must be something wrong with it."

Other common phrases that teach jurors not to listen:

"I want to thank you all for listening so carefully." By implying that everything important is now said and done, this statement signals them that all that follows will be insignificant. Result: They listen less carefully. Solution: Save your thank-you for the end of closing and keep it brief (under ten words).

"You have now heard the evidence." They know they have heard the evidence.

"You have heard an awful lot of testimony during this trial." They know they heard an awful lot of testimony and they know they heard it during this trial.

"Some of the evidence was very technical." They know.

"Some of the evidence was conflicting . . . ." They *really* know.

"Some of the evidence was confusing . . . ."

Putting those apparently harmless phrases together is enough to make jurors wish they had earplugs: "I want to thank you all for listening so carefully. And my client wants to thank you, too. You have now heard all the evidence. There was an awful lot of it during this trial. Some of it was very technical, some of it was conflicting, and some was confusing . . . ."

Imagine the end of a TV newscast that said, "You have now heard the news. Thank you for listening. My producer thanks you, too, and so do the sponsors. There was an awful lot of news during this program that you just watched on your television. Some of the news was good. Some of it was bad. Some was easy to understand and some was not. Some . . . " By now, the entire world has changed channels.

Moral: Don't say things that make jurors stop listening. Jurors are all too eager to comply.

There are two other points to consider in order to avoid lessening juror attention to your closing. First: length. Some good practitioners advise that closing should be half the length of opening. Whether or not you agree, the underlying intention is accurate: brevity is usually desirable. Jurors are eager to go home. They don't want to hear a syllable more than necessary.[1] Second: tone. Discussing evidence as if the jury has never heard it before is another way to make jurors conclude that you think they are stupid. What's new is what you are saying *about* the evidence—but the evidence itself is not new, so try not to sound as if it is.

WHO ARE YOU TALKING TO?

You have three distinct audiences in closing: undecided jurors, adverse jurors, and favorable jurors. Because all three will deliberate, in closing you must speak to all three—and you must say different things to each.

You rarely know which juror is which (and some may fall between), but each group requires different measures. An effective closing interweaves the needs of all three.

Here are your primary goals:

1. For undecided jurors: Bring them closer to your side.

2. For adverse jurors: Open their minds for deliberations.

---

1. On the other hand, if your closing is too much shorter than your opponent's, it might seem to carry less weight. And in some circumstances, you will simply need longer than otherwise desirable because you have so much to cover. Especially in such a case, be sure to be as concise and unrepetitive as possible.

3. For favorable jurors: Motivate them to be firm and prepare them to argue for you in deliberations.[2]

Undecided jurors. Undecided jurors are the easiest to make listen, because (unlike those who think they have already decided) they are still looking for help in making up their minds. They want you to show them how the evidence can help them arrive at conclusions.

Undecided jurors often believe (sometimes wrongly) that emotional appeals will not help them to make a decision. And they are often suspicious of strenuous argument—even when it's convincing—because they know you are a professional arguer. Nonetheless, you should include emotion and strenuous argument in closings (for the reasons outlined below), but do so near the end so that undecided jurors do not stop listening before you have had a chance to move them in your direction (and so that adverse jurors do not stop listening before you have had a chance to open their minds). The first two-thirds of your closing should be focused on what the undecided jurors think they most need to hear: *clear and logical ways that the evidence can support a conclusion.*

Five steps will help you to do this:

STEP 1. First, highlight your pivotal evidence. (Supporting evidence, explanation, and argument come later.) As discussed above, first promise that your highlighting of the evidence will achieve something new; don't just rehash. Then *briefly* review your main points in such a way as to achieve whatever new thing you just promised. (As before: "I want us to look at whether the doctor's testimony was supported by what the patient said.")

Keep this section uncluttered, orderly, concise, and specific. Display a time line. (If you don't provide a time line, jurors will make one up themselves—with errors.)

STEP 2. Explain how each piece of case-pivotal evidence supports your side. Display a visual to support, reinforce, or illustrate each case-pivotal point. (Try to avoid using visuals for subordinate points except when you have no other way to establish the clarity of that subordinate point. Visuals lose effectiveness when you use too many.)

STEP 3. Explain how each piece of important *subordinate* evidence proves a specific case-pivotal point.

STEP 4. Emotion. Near the end of closing, humanize your client and his feelings (pain, suffering, fear, outrage, etc.). Make jurors understand and feel the human consequences of this case. This is the time to use powerful quotations from literature and songs, good analogies, and any other means to

---

2. When you have the opportunity to close both before and after your opponent, be sure to address all three groups both times. It is generally better to emphasize facts and logic in your first closing and save emotion for your second. For other suggestions concerning dual closings, see the last section of this chapter.

show the emotional impact of this case on your client. (Be careful not to make an overt bid for sympathy or pity. Jurors—even those who are on your side—will resent your overt tugging at their heartstrings.)

Although undecided jurors do not think they want an emotional appeal, they can be affected by hearing, late in closing, how your client has been emotionally affected. To this end, arousing jurors' emotions is useful if it helps the jury to empathize with your client's feelings.

Another use of emotion can be useful at this point in closing: juror *anger* at what your opponent party did that led to this case, or at the fact that they brought this case, or at how your opponent party and counsel have propounded and conducted their side of the case.

Caveat A: You cannot simply shove emotion down the jurors' throats. Instead, start by showing the facts that will elicit the emotion. Then gently nurture the elicited emotion until it becomes powerful enough to drive juror behavior.

Caveat B: Hopelessness is not a good emotion for plaintiff's counsel to elicit. Jurors do not like to put money into hopeless situations. It is more effective to arouse feelings of hope in the context of a tragic situation. (See p. 163 below on arguing damages.)

STEP 5. Immediately after step 4, use just a few words to connect your strongest evidence to your primary theme. ("The records were altered, so we know the doctor was careless," or, "Two eyewitnesses with no reason to lie saw him right where he had the opportunity and the motive to be.") This serves to connect the emotional impact of your case (which you have just established) with that primary factual contention.

There is more that needs to be done for undecided jurors, but those things overlap with what you need to do for decided jurors, as outlined below (p. 157).

Adverse jurors. Adverse jurors tend not to listen to you. This is because most of them think they have already made up their minds (so they don't need to listen to anyone say anything), and they also feel that you—of all people—have nothing to say that they want to hear. They are certainly not expecting you to provide ways that will help them argue their opinions in deliberations.

Thus, you must pay special attention to making adverse jurors listen to your closing, and you must take special pains not to say things ("Nothing I say is evidence.") that will reinforce their initial reluctance to listen.

Even if you get adverse jurors to listen to your closing, few minds change during closings. But *many minds change in deliberations*, because jurors yield more easily to each other than to counsels' arguments. Your favorable jurors are your best hope for winning over your adverse jurors.

In closing, help your favorable jurors by opening the minds of the adverse jurors. Logic and facts open minds better than can emotion and argumentative tones because jurors (like anyone else) tend to turn defensive or hostile when listening to emotion or strenuous argument with which they disagree.

A self-righteous tone especially creates resistance, not compliance. And you can harden adverse opinions beyond recall if you imply by word or tone that jurors who lean against you are wrong, stupid, unfair, or illogical.

To effectively deal with adverse jurors in closing, review your notes from voir dire to refresh your memory as to the kinds of negative attitudes that are represented on the jury. Try to address those attitudes in closing. For example, if voir dire revealed that you have five jurors who believe that there are too many lawsuits these days, as plaintiff you might decide to re-emphasize the differences between this lawsuit and the kind that the jurors think are too plentiful. On defense, do the opposite: Show how this one is just more of the same darned thing. (See Chapter 4, p. 69, "Bad Attitudes.")

With respect to adverse jurors, remember that the goal is not to change their minds, but *to open them up for deliberations* so that your favorable jurors can take over for you.

You can even appeal to adverse jurors' sense of fair play: "The hardest task of jurors is to keep an open mind about what other jurors say in deliberations. That's the only way the justice system can make sure that decisions are made by juries, not by judges or lawyers." Of course, jurors on your side are also hearing these same words. But that is okay if you talk effectively to your favorable jurors, as follows:

Favorable jurors. To make favorable jurors listen, make them understand that *what you have to say will help them argue their opinions in deliberations.* Otherwise, they think they have no further need of you.

Your favorable jurors are your troops. You must strengthen their resolve, arm them to fight for you, and convince them to fight tenaciously. Your primary goal in any trial is to train and motivate whoever your favorable jurors may turn out to be.

During opening and testimony, you create the weapons for your favorable jurors to use. In closing, you instruct your jurors how to use those weapons. You do this by translating the complexities of your case into terms and tools that jurors can readily use on your behalf in deliberations. Provide phrases, arguments, analogies, stories, comparisons, outlines, time lines, highlighted visuals, and anything else that will make it easy for them to help you.

For example, don't leave jurors with nothing but a complex of laws, arguments, and evidence which you hope shows that your client did not use excessive force defending himself by shooting the victim in the head. You must also provide phrasing that a normal juror can remember and use, such as,

"When you're attacked by three armed drunks, you can't take the time to aim carefully for their wrists."

Jurors on your side are better able than you are to persuade dissenting jurors. This is partly because dissenting jurors know that you have the strongest bias in the room. It is also because deliberations, unlike the rest of trial, involve *interchanges* of ideas and arguments.

It is not enough to give jurors tools with which they can argue on behalf of your contentions. You must also show them ways they can help other jurors see through your opponent's contentions. "If anyone thinks that the doctors did the best they could, just remind them that Dr. Smith said, 'They didn't do half what they should have.'" This helps to seal your favorable jurors' opinions in place and provides a way for them to work on adverse jurors.

Bonus: Jurors with tools (instead of just inarticulate agreement) to use on your behalf are more likely to speak up for you in deliberations, and will do so earlier. Not only does this help persuade neutral or dissenting jurors, but once jurors speak on your behalf, they are less likely to switch sides.

Motivation is equally important. Some jurors dislike or even fear confrontation and argument. Even if you provide tools, unless you motivate such jurors to use them, they will sit quietly and sooner or later cave in.

You motivate jurors via such means as humanizing your client and her plight, making jurors see and feel the emotional consequences of the case on your client, emphasizing the unfairness or dishonesty of the opposition case (appealing to fair play), showing jurors how this case provides a chance for the jurors to do something significant, and making sure that each of those jurors knows that his or her opinion is as important and legitimate as any other juror's—even when in the minority.

Cases are won by highly motivated jurors, and often in the face of early majority opposition.

PREPONDERANCE OF THE EVIDENCE

During closing, when jurors hear plaintiff's counsel explain preponderance of the evidence, they often think counsel is confessing that she has no case and cannot do what she promised to do. She has been promising since voir dire to *prove* her contentions: "We're not asking you to take our word for anything; we have *proof*." But now, she's saying the equivalent of, "Well, see, not quite proof, see, I meant just a little old *featherweight*, what I really meant was, uh, I didn't exactly mean I could *prove* anything, that's really hard, how could you expect me to do that?" (Because she promised she would.) "Well, I meant just *probably* prove; a featherweight is enough for the judge, so why shouldn't it be enough for you?" (Because the judge doesn't have to make the decision, that's why.) "Well, *more likely than not* it happened the way we said, so we win. Okay?"

No one is comfortable making important real-life decisions on the basis of a featherweight. Jurors don't transfer large sums of money from defendants to plaintiffs on the basis of featherweights or when counsel starts talking about how she can't keep her promise of proving her case.

When the burden of proof is yours, let the judge explain preponderance. If you must talk about it yourself, make it a voir dire issue or mention it in opening (if allowed). But bringing it up for the first time in closing is tantamount to confessing that your case is weak.

LEADERS DURING TRIAL

Over the course of trial, study your jurors. Watch them in the hallways and at lunch. Observe who makes decisions (such as where to eat lunch), who talks the most, and who is listened to. Then focus on those leaders in closing. (Don't exclude the others, but aim carefully at the leaders.) Consult your voir dire notes to help you tailor your arguments to those leaders. As the leaders go, so goes the rest of the jury.

CLIENT

The leading character in your closing is your client. Refer to her, include her, stand behind her chair at appropriate moments. A touch—a hand on a shoulder—can make jurors cry. Don't get so caught up in arguing your case that you forget whose case it is.

THE MAN WITH THREE ARMS

Examine the extended implications of your opponent's evidence, logic, and arguments, and you will often uncover contradictions and absurdities. This is a form of boomerang.[3] Defense counsel Roy Black did this in his brilliant closing to the William Kennedy Smith rape trial. Counsel Black showed that his client would have needed three or four arms to accomplish what the prosecution's principal witness claimed. Black's wonderfully ludicrous visceral image (a man with three arms) was extremely persuasive, as the rapid verdict may have indicated. *He extended the opposition's own evidence to a logically unavoidable conclusion that undermined it.* The prosecution could have countered only by denying the testimony of its own principal witness or by trapping Smith into waving at the jury with his third arm.

The man with three arms is a visceral by virtue of being comic and impossible: A man with three arms is a ridiculous distortion of a human being. It is also blatantly counter to what the jury can see: the defendant has only two arms. Counsel Black found an especially sharp-edged boomerang. You can think like him by exploring every logical extension of your opponent's

---

3. See Chapter 5, p. 90.

contentions. You never know when you will find something as striking as a three-armed man.

WORSE-CASE SCENARIO

Plaintiff's counsel should point out that the harm to his client was a *lucky* result of what happened. The defendant's level of negligence *could* have caused, say, the maiming and deaths of dozens of people, not just of your client. Perhaps the elevator fell only ten feet, but what would have happened if the same sub-standard cable and faulty fail-safe system had failed when the elevator was on the thirtieth floor instead of the second? (Be careful. In some jurisdictions this form of argument is improper.)

TONE

A common trap: allowing your anger at your opponent or your scorn for the opposition's point of view to turn into anger or a scornful tone directed at the jurors in closing. It is important to show your feelings, but it is also important not to yell at the jurors.

DISTRACTIONS

For closings (and openings, too), try to preclude courtroom distractions. Ask the judge to bar comings and goings on the part of gallery observers and courtroom staff.

If in your jurisdiction the court reporter does not automatically make a record of openings and closings, request that a record be made even if you anticipate no need for it. Otherwise, you may find yourself being upstaged by the court reporter fiddling with her equipment or sitting there paying no attention to you.

USELESS BATTLES

Don't automatically fight every contention your opponent makes. Sometimes you can turn it to your own use, and sometimes it is better to ignore it altogether.

Turning an opposition contention to your own use. Examine each opposition contention to see if it can be used to support your side. For example, your opponent contends that your client was already in critical condition when she arrived at the hospital, and, therefore, the doctors can't be blamed for what happened. Before you automatically leap to the adversarial position of trying to show that she wasn't in terrible shape, consider whether there might be an advantage to agreeing that she was in terrible shape. Perhaps you can then argue that the doctors, therefore, should have monitored her condition all the more thoroughly. Maybe your expert can say that the standard of care *required* more careful monitoring. It is extraordinarily effective—especially in closing—to prove your case via your opponent's assertions.

Ignoring the accuracy of an opposition contention. A common opposition tactic is to make an irrelevant contention: one that makes no difference to how the jurors will decide the case. The aim is to distract you and the jurors from your real points. An irrelevant contention can hurt you only if you take the trouble to fight it. Beyond showing that it is irrelevant, leave it alone.

If you take the trouble to fight it, especially in closing, you effectively persuade the jurors that it is not irrelevant. They will conclude that it must be important *even if they are unsure how or why.* Result: If they decide against you on that irrelevant contention, your case can be weakened.

On the other hand, if you ignore the contention's accuracy and merely show it to be irrelevant, the jury will probably give more thought to the shoddiness of your opponent's diversionary tactic than they will to the contention itself.

In a recent West Virginia collision case, the defense offered testimony that the road at the accident site was wet and the plaintiff's brakes were bad. Instead of arguing that road surface and brake condition were irrelevant because neither driver ever attempted to stop, plaintiff's counsel went to the trouble of eliciting testimony from two of his own witnesses that the road was dry and the brakes were good. Then in closing he argued those points emphatically.

Following a defense verdict, jurors in post-trial interviews said that they voted against the plaintiff because he failed to meet his burden of proof with respect to the condition of the brakes and the road. The judge had told them that the plaintiff had to meet the burden. Moreover, while none of the jurors could explain the relevance of the brakes or the road surface, most concluded that both must have been important *because plaintiff's counsel had made such a big deal about fighting them.* When it was pointed out that the brakes and road surface were irrelevant, one puzzled juror asked, "Then why'd [plaintiff's counsel] have that chart?"

Plaintiff lost the case partly because of issues that would have been harmless had counsel simply shown them to be irrelevant instead of fighting them.

Moral: Don't engage in battles that can only hurt you.

UNNECESSARY "MUST-BELIEVES"

Don't unnecessarily rest the fate of a case-pivotal point on whether or not the jury chooses to believe a subordinate point that you do not or cannot absolutely prove. It is dangerously easy to inadvertently convince jurors that they *must believe* some subordinate point in order for them to believe a main contention. If they fail to believe the subordinate point, you can lose the case.

For example, it can be dangerous to say, "The doctor read the X-ray too fast because, as we have seen, *he was tired and wanted to go home.*" That wording forces jurors to accept an unproven supporting point (that being tired and wanting to go home made the doctor read the X-ray too quickly), rather than just weigh it as a persuasive *possibility*. Result: If jurors don't believe he was tired, or if they don't believe he was tired enough to want to go home, or if they don't believe he wanted to go home badly enough to be careless in his work, then they could well reject the case-pivotal point about reading the X-ray too quickly.

When you raise an unproven probability to the level of must-believe, you confuse jurors and provide needless room for them to disagree with you. You can even make it impossible for them to side with you in deliberations.

Rule of thumb: The more effort you put into establishing any point, the more the jurors will think you regard the point as case-pivotal—even if it is not case-pivotal at all.

This does not force you to eliminate unprovable subordinate points. They are often valuable. But like fighting useless battles over points that make no difference (see previous section), it is usually a blunder—sometimes fatal—to set yourself unnecessary burdens by making case-pivotal points seem to be dependent upon unproven subordinate points.

Instead, offer such supporting points as *suggestions* rather than as must-believes.

For example, the point that the doctor was tired and wanted to go home is dangerous as a must-believe but useful as a suggestion: "Why did the doctor read the X-ray too fast? Maybe because he'd been up all night and wanted to go home. Or maybe because he'd accepted 27 cases that morning instead of his usual 15. Or maybe with that stack of paperwork on his desk he was trying to sign letters at the same time. Maybe it was because of all three. All we know for sure is that he read the X-ray too fast."

Note that this does not force jurors to choose which of your non-pivotal, unproven possibilities to believe. They can believe whichever ones they want, and in any combination. If they believe none, they can still believe your ultimate contention: that he read the X-ray too quickly.

You raise an unproven assertion to the level of a must-believe either verbally ("The doctor read the X-ray carelessly because he was tired and wanted to go home") or by emphasizing it so often throughout trial and arguing it so emphatically during closing that jurors can only conclude that it is case-pivotal rather than merely a suggested probability to be considered.

For example, in the O.J. Simpson criminal case the prosecution undermined a useful supporting assertion by presenting it as a must-believe instead of as a suggestion. The useful supporting assertion: Spousal abuse is a pattern of behavior that can—and in this case did—culminate in murder.

Many knowledgeable researchers give credence to the statistics and theory underlying such an assertion. But not everyone believes it, and common experience tells some jurors (or leaves them wanting to believe) that it is often untrue. Thus, without seeing proof, some jurors were bound to go into deliberations harboring reasonable doubts about it.

The strength with which such reasonable doubts attach to the ultimate issues of a case is directly proportional to the strength with which the proponent turns the suggestion into a must-believe.

If the Simpson prosecution had merely *suggested* that spousal abuse led to the murder, the suggestion may or may not have carried weight with some jurors—but regardless of how many jurors accepted it, none would have assumed that they *had* to accept it in order to convict. Thus, none would have felt forced to acquit simply for not accepting it.

But instead of offering it merely as a suggestion, the prosecution emphasized spousal abuse throughout trial and made it their closing argument's climax. This raised it to an unmistakable must-believe. Thereby the prosecution unnecessarily prevented jurors who doubted the unproven assertion from convicting. The last thing the jurors heard before going into deliberations was the unproven spousal abuse theory. The next thing they did was decide not guilty—in minutes.

Before you present any point in such a way as to make the jury think they have to accept it for you to win the case, be sure the point is a necessary link in the must-believe chain of your case. In closing, you naturally try to make everything sound as proven as possible. But don't let that lead you into needlessly promoting unproven subordinate points to must-believes. That trap can cost you an otherwise sound case.

DAMAGES

Both plaintiff and defense should consider *why jurors give (or withhold) money*. Jurors give money not for a prize but for a purpose. They want the money to have a use or uses they consider legitimate and desirable. For example, if the jury regards the plaintiff as a kind of person they do not want to help, they will minimize the size of the verdict even if they are fully convinced of the defendant's liability. That—and not merely attitudes about the "litigation crisis"—is why some injury verdicts, for example, are too small to cover even proven medical expenses.

The tendency of jurors (and judges, too) to award money mainly to accomplish something legitimate or desirable is so pronounced that *plaintiff lawyers should consider it pivotal in deciding whether to take the case*. It may be foolhardy to take a case unless you see a way to convince jurors that money will accomplish something that the jurors (not just you or your client) will find worthwhile or desirable.

This is not merely a question of how a jury thinks about damages. When jurors see no worthwhile or desirable purpose for awarding money, they tend to see all the evidence (liability as well as damages) in the best defense light. This can result in a defense verdict even when there is strong liability.

Conversely, when jurors see a strongly desirable or worthwhile purpose in awarding money, they tend to see all the evidence (liability as well as damages) in the best plaintiff's light. This sometimes results in a plaintiff's verdict even when there is weak liability.

Obviously, the ability of the jury to see worthwhile or desirable uses for an award is also a central negotiation and arbitration consideration, no matter which side you are on.

In trial, your themes of showing (or refuting) that money will go to a worthwhile or desirable purpose should normally be introduced in voir dire, detailed in opening, focused on whenever possible throughout testimony, and strongly emphasized in closing.

On defense, one of the strongest closing damages arguments is to show how money can do little or nothing to improve the situation. (Of course, if jurors are furious at the defendant, then the transfer of money accomplishes what the jurors regard as the worthwhile purpose of punishment. This can happen with or without a punitive instruction.)

Not every defense case can support the argument that money will accomplish nothing desirable or worthwhile, but when it is applicable, defense attorneys too rarely use it. Even in cases where money would accomplish something, the defense can still differentiate between an amount that would accomplish something and the greater amount requested by the plaintiff that would accomplish nothing more.

The mood of today's jurors is neither as anti-litigation as the plaintiff's bar believes nor as award-happy as insurance companies contend and the defense bar believes. Litigation crisis or no, jurors in most jurisdictions can be generous—but only when they are convinced that the money will do something that they consider worthwhile. Otherwise, they are often tightfisted.

For example, a jury that goes so far as to decide "Yes" on gross negligence might still decide on a verdict that does not cover medicals, much less pain and suffering or other elements of damage. One North Carolina jury recently did exactly that, reasoning that the medical bills had already been paid, the plaintiff was not a person who would do anything worthwhile with the money, and there was no worthwhile or desirable cause to punish the defendant because she was not going to do it again anyway.

In almost every case, jurors wonder, "Is it worthwhile?" "Is it palatable?" "Will the money do any good?" "Is it a good that needs to be done—*and do we want to do it?*"

Hope. Plaintiff lawyers should not paint an utterly hopeless picture of the client's (or survivors') situation. Jurors tend to put no money into situations lacking hope, because, logically enough, they find nothing worthwhile to support in a context of hopelessness. When possible, focus on the *hope* of the victim or of the survivors—and show how that hope would be enabled or enhanced by an influx of money.

On defense, show that whatever hope exists in the situation will not be aided by money.

Jurors generally find the following to be worthwhile: striving against the odds and refusing to lie down and quit, and survival in the face of adversity and enormous odds. They generally find the following not worth supporting: utter despair, giving up, pervasive whining and complaining, and total doom and gloom.

When it comes to damages, jurors act like everyone else doing anything else with money: they want to "spend" it to obtain some benefit.

Of course, jurors find it important to know how and how much someone or some entity might have been physically, emotionally, or financially hurt—but their ultimate decision about money attaches more directly to whether money will have effects they consider worthwhile or desirable. In arguing damages, plaintiff counsel must emphasize such worthwhile or desirable effects, and defense counsel must show that money can serve no such good purpose.

LANGUAGE

Plaintiff's counsel should not refer to money as an "award." "Award" means "prize," not compensation, and jurors don't like to give prizes. (On defense, of course, use the word "award" as often as you can.)

Finally, avoid the legalese of saying "damages" when you mean "money."

Plaintiff's attorney James J. Leonard, Jr. (Phoenix), whose oratorical skills are legendary, uses the phrase "money justice." Since he is as fine a teacher as he is an attorney, he would be happy for you to make use of that effective phrase.

OPENING CLOSINGS AND CLOSING CLOSINGS

When you have the opportunity to close both before and after your opponent, follow one cardinal rule: don't say the same things both times. Give each closing its own separate purpose, content, and tone.

In your second closing you may feel that because this is your last chance, you had better say everything all over again. ("And don't forget . . . and don't forget . . . and don't forget . . . .") But doing so makes you appear desperate and insecure about your case. Design your dual closings as a two-part, non-repetitive structure—and stick to your design.

In your first closing, fact and logic generally play better than emotion. Save your greatest emotional impact for the second closing.

Between your closings, your opponent will probably ask the jury to imagine what she would say in response to your second closing. This provides you with an opportunity to tell the jury in your final closing what *you* think she would have to say. You can make statements like, "What would she say about this issue? Nothing, because these is no evidence to support anything she would want you to hear. If there were, she'd have said plenty—but she did not." Don't play dirty pool; that offends jurors. But point out the weaknesses of what she would be likely to say to the points you make in your second closing. ("When I say that the driver was drunk, my opponent would want to tell you that it was the result of a cold medication. But cold medications don't blow 2.2 on the Breathalyzer.")

CHAPTER 11

CLE Courses and Law School

This chapter's suggestions are based on the wisdom of some of the nation's best theater-skills teachers. What they know about the process of acquiring skills can help law school students and CLE participants to learn and improve courtroom skills.

IS YOUR LAW SCHOOL OR CLE PROGRAM GOOD ENOUGH? (And what if it's not?)

For trial lawyers and for performers, mere education—the accumulation of information and comprehension—is only half the work. The rest is hands-on *training: skills acquisition* and *practice*. In addition to basic legal and execution skills, you have to shape and develop habits, your own ways of talking and thinking on your feet, and your own methods of drawing on and controlling your intellectual, physical, and emotional resources for every circumstance that might arise (predictably or unexpectedly) in front of a jury. This training is difficult because *you yourself* are the main tool of your job. You don't *use* a Stradivarius violin; you *are*—or must become—one.

CLE courses should provide either hands-on workshops or material that can apply immediately to your next case. Not all of them do. Law schools should offer practical trial skills workshops from day one through graduation. But because law school curricula cannot contain anywhere near enough practical classes, the jury system is delivered into the hands of undertrained lawyers. We would never trust a surgeon with so little practical training to remove even a wart, or a mechanic to change a water pump. Yet we entrust one of our most important civic processes—trial by jury—to novices with hardly any practical training. We call them counselors when they are still campers. And with such skimpy foundations, many never improve much, no matter how many cases they try and no matter how many CLE lectures they attend.

Most actors train full-time for years before entering their profession. Is trial law easier, simpler, and less important than acting? If not, then how can a few dozen hours of trial classes suffice?

You cannot change what your school or CLE program teaches. But if you use your law school or CLE program actively, instead of passively settling for what is handed to you, you can maximize its benefits. The guidelines below show you how.

If your school or CLE program is one of the few that gives training its full due, the following guidelines will help you get even more out of such unusually good conditions.

DO YOU WANT TO BE (OR REMAIN) A TRIAL LAWYER?

It beats heavy lifting, but it's *hard.*

Trial law may not be for you if you are a meticulously contemplative person who likes everything organized, safe, predictable, and neat. It is probably not for you if you like short (or even reasonable) working hours, privacy, regular schedules and routine, or insulation from the common masses.

But if you like to throw yourself 100 percent into your work, if you like placing yourself—your*self*, not just what you know—right on the line, if you enjoy exhaustive preparation for unpredictable and spontaneous confrontation, and if you like to profoundly affect the lives of the people you work for (and against), then trial law is a possibility. If you enjoy the process of persuasion and if the threat of *publicly* losing drives you that much harder to win, then maybe trial law is a good choice. If, in addition, you like working in front of people, if you can synthesize hard logic and raw emotion, if you enjoy enormous responsibility up to and including individuals and even groups placing their lives and fortunes in your hands, and if the thought of intense and public conflict waged passionately on behalf of a cause excites you, then trial law is for you.

You can also make a decent living. But if you divide the average trial lawyer's income by the average hours it takes to earn that money, you will find there are more profitable and reliable legal specialties.

Shy and Insecure? Good trial lawyers may seem to be among the most emotionally secure and confident people on earth. But many good ones—and most of the best—are surprisingly shy and insecure. The protoplasm of great trial lawyers is composed not of passion alone, but insecurity and fear as well—and therein lies their strength. It is why they drive themselves obsessively to master the learnable skills of persuasion and communications and to be extraordinarily prepared every time they walk into a courtroom, even after decades of cases. By these means, they carve out the one piece of the universe where they are in control: in front of a jury.

If you look inside the country's top three trial lawyers (whomever you think they are), you will see that two and a half of them are secretly as shy and insecure as anyone you know—including yourself. So don't count yourself out too soon.

On the other hand, being shy and insecure is not a prerequisite. The opposite is also useful: being comfortable and open with people and having confidence. But, of course, if you are confident, you don't need to be told that.

HOW TO EVALUATE A LAW SCHOOL

If you are the dean of a law school and wish to help the court system and the citizens it serves, consider whether your graduates are as ill-prepared for court as are the graduates of most other law schools.

If you are not yet a law student and know that trial law is what you want to do, evaluate your school choices carefully. You want a school that offers hands-on trial experience *regularly*, not just for a semester or two.

Don't be overly influenced by a school's general reputation. Top schools can be mediocre or miserly with respect to imparting trial skills and experience. This does not mean that trial teachers at such schools are bad, but that you get those teachers for too brief a time. So find out. Ask questions: how good are a school's recent graduates *in front of juries*?

Make sure a school's practical trial law offerings are a respected part of the curriculum. In some schools, such work is looked down upon. You are expected to listen, read, absorb, discuss, and write—but not to *do* anything. If you want to be a trial advocate, ask current students how much the school cares about practical courtroom skills. You want professors who relish helping each student become a fine trial practitioner. Skills-teaching requires enormous energy and personal commitment, not pedagogic dignity and aloofness. When it comes to trial practice, the paper chase must share time with the skills chase.

Moreover, make sure a traditionally good school has not changed. It might have trained its students brilliantly a decade ago. But faculties and programs change faster than reputations. Will they be there when you arrive?

This kind of investigation requires a good deal of time and trouble on your part. But since we are talking about your entire future, it might be the most important investment you can make.

WATCHING TRIALS

The best theater and film artists are good partly because they spent years going to every play and movie they could find. Trial lawyers-to-be (and trial lawyers-who-are) should see trials. There is no substitute for seeing, over and over, what you are trying to get better at doing. No matter how much you learn from classes, workshops, or books, your training is superficial unless you sit through dozens of trials you are not involved in, and you should continue doing so throughout your career.

Of course, that is difficult and takes a lot of time. Good. If it were otherwise, then every lazy good-for-nothing would do it. It is a good way to separate yourself from the pack.

Imagine how much you would know about persuasive trial methods if you had been watching several trials a year since you were ten years old! If law school is your museum, then the courtroom (or Court TV) is your theater. Watch trials. Talk to the lawyers. And after the verdict talk to the jurors. Find out why they voted as they did: what did they find persuasive, what did they think was a waste of time, what was confusing? And how do their comments compare to what you thought and what you would have done had you been counsel?

WATCHING OTHER STUDENTS AT WORK

Whether you are in law school or at a CLE program, you need extensive practice time on your feet *doing* things. But even in the best classes, only one or two students can do their thing at a time, while the other ten or twenty sit waiting their turns. A three-hour workshop might give you under ten minutes of actual work and just a few minutes of critique.

Look around next time you are in such a class. Not every student will be paying attention to others who are up and working. Even less attention is paid during a critique. "The teacher's criticizing someone else, not me. Why should I listen?" The room is full of vegetables.

Let them vegetate while you make your observation time as valuable as the time you spend on your feet working. Start by scrutinizing everything your classmates do when they are up and working. Keep careful, private notes as if you were going to be called on to do a critique. From the beginning of the course to the end, privately monitor each classmate's progress by tracking improvement, noting strengths and weaknesses, etc. Actively evaluate everyone's work at every moment.

Base your evaluations on what you learn from readings and classes, and make your evaluation notes concrete and specific. Mentally compare your private notes with what the instructor offers in open critique. (But never offer your comments unless specifically asked![1])

Mentally comparing your evaluations with the instructor's will help you learn better and give you more and better standards against which to measure your own work. In this way, you will benefit by the advice every other student receives.

---

1. One exception: Occasionally tell a classmate something about his or her work that you admired. "You really did your best work yet on that cross!" It is particularly good to do that for someone who has been struggling, because the encouragement can be a help. And you never know which of your classmates will, in twenty years, be running the wonderful firm you would love to work with. Chances are it will be the one you least expected. And whoever it is will remember your kindness.

When an instructor's critiques do not seem useful, you can still profit by the active mental work of doing your own evaluations. Even with no instructor critique at all, your mentally active observations will help you.

This transforms your sitting-down time into efficient learning time. Every hour of class will be a full hour of training for you, instead of your classmates' average of five or six minutes. You will end up with ten times the training they get. Moreover, you will provide yourself with hours of experience developing a valuable negotiating and communication skill: the ability to evaluate and to articulate your evaluation.

By taking this process seriously you will learn a lot even from the shallowest of trial courses and the worst of teachers. And the best of them will change your life.

READ!

Don't read only the assigned textbooks. There are hundreds of books by and about trial lawyers and their cases. There are biographies, fiction, and nonfiction. Get yourself inside the minds of the masters. You will synthesize guidance and wisdom from each as you create and expand your own approach.

DEVELOPING YOUR VOICE

This simple exercise is a miracle treatment for the quality of how you sound.

Read aloud at full speaking volume for ten minutes every day. Read *anything*—law books, newspapers, phone books, fiction, old love letters, whatever. Because your vocal system is muscular, reading aloud will have dramatic, rapid results. It is like push-ups for your voice. In a few months, you will sound more authoritative and more *present*. In a year or two, you will have a voice that takes control in court.

The improvement is not merely volume. A well-developed voice more fully communicates personality and feelings. It more directly conveys concepts and information, and with greater emphasis. It gives you confidence, gains you respect, and makes you credible.

Not bad for ten minutes a day. If only you could lose weight doing it! But no, alas. It just helps your voice.

FEAR OF FAILURE

In training (class, workshop, CLE), work at the cutting edge of what you know how to do. Take chances. Go *too far*. You will never stretch your limits if you don't challenge yourself.

Who cares if you get criticized? The more criticism you receive, the more you have to work on—and, thus, the more improvement you can show. The more you take chances by working to your limits, the more an instructor can help you improve. In school, the best way to get a professor's good recommendation is to show improvement at the very things she teaches you. And in CLE programs, when your colleagues see your great improvements, you earn their respect (and future referrals).

Most important: the more you work to the edge of your limits, the more your instructors will invest time and effort in you.

REHEARSE AS IF IT IS REAL

Treat your practice work in class and CLE workshops exactly as if it were real. *Maintain formal courtroom deportment at all times.* Don't relax, don't kid around, don't break your focus. This can be hard when the dominant mood—due mostly to student insecurity (or a lax instructor)—is informal. But don't let yourself be dragged down to the lowest common denominator. Work the way you know is best: as if you were in court.

The way you train and rehearse is the way you will do. Guaranteed. Let your foolish classmates relax and fool around while you use every moment to build the habit of implacably maintaining concentration under every sort of circumstance.

This is necessary because of a fact of human nature: When you are under stress or something unexpected happens, or when you are self-conscious because people are watching and evaluating what you are doing, you will automatically fall back on your most habitual pattern of behavior. If your habitual pattern of behavior is to break concentration, then that is what you will do. But if you use your class exercise time properly—by never allowing your concentration to break—then your instantaneously available *habit* (your default status) will be to maintain professional deportment.

For example, do not break your concentration when you make a silly mistake. If, say, instead of addressing a mock expert witness correctly as "Dr. Joad," you accidentally call him "Dr. Toad," behave as you would in court: Apologize good-naturedly for your silly gaffe and get on with what you were doing. Of course the mistake is funny and of course the class will have a good laugh, and you will want to, too. *Don't.* Use the opportunity to develop the habit of doing what you should do in court.

TAKING CRITICISM

Often, it is hard to accept in-class criticism of your work without becoming either self-conscious or defensive. Relax! *Listen* to what is being said, even if you are angered or embarrassed by it or think it is wrong. There is always something to be learned, and if you are busy explaining what you did, or wishing the instructor would shut up and leave you alone, you will miss it.

You are paying to learn, not to maintain your dignity or argue with the instructor. So detach your ego and listen dispassionately to your critique. If necessary, pretend to yourself that the critique is about someone else so that you can listen without ego or pride.

If it is a useful critique, say thank you. If it is useless, say thank you.

Demonstrate to your teachers that you are hungry for as much criticism as they have to offer. If you make them think you cannot or will not take it, they might go easy on you—and that is a disaster! You want them to be hard on you so that you can learn as much as possible.

Good skills instructors don't care whether you can argue with them. They *do* care whether you demonstrate your understanding of their critiques by the way you perform the next time. Learn to accept critiques without shutting down or arguing. If your teacher rips apart something you do in class, don't turn groveling, deferential, defensive, or closed off. Maintain a thoroughly professional manner. Bear in mind that the teacher's *job* is to tear you apart—or at least tell you what you did wrong or ineffectively. *And your job is to learn from it.* So just do your job.

In fact, encourage your teachers to do their job so you can better do your job. If they don't volunteer the information, ask, "What should I do differently next time?"

Never complain, never explain. Just listen. Then do it.

USE CHAPTER 1

Try to do everything in Chapter 1 of this book every time you do an in-class exercise. For example:

WORKING FROM NOTES

In law school, you will do much of your trial work from extensive notes because you will have had little time to prepare. Even after you graduate, if you are a prosecutor or public defender, you will have just as little time to prepare, and thus find yourself relying too heavily on extensive notes in court. Unfortunately, you will develop harmful habits by relying heavily on notes—including the habit of relying heavily on notes.

One of the worst things about using extensive notes is that it trains your mind to be active and spontaneous only during preparation, rather than when it should be most active: in front of a jury. *You cannot be a decent trial advocate if you don't train your mind to work best in front of a jury.* The overuse of notes trains your mind to rely passively on external assistance. Your brain's thinking circuits close down.

Using notes heavily is like grinding down a razor blade for fear you will cut yourself: It feels safer but the result is a dull, useless tool.

Starting in law school trial advocacy classes, and continuing in CLE and your practice, use only skeletal notes and use them sparingly. You will find that you don't need notes anywhere near as much as you think you do. Take a risk every so often: Get up and work with no notes at all. The scarier that sounds to you, the more important it is for you do it often. Notes are like cigarettes: They create their own need for themselves.

Chapter 1 (p. 2) details how to use notes without losing eye contact with listeners. In brief:

> NEVER LOOK AT A NOTE WHILE YOU ARE SPEAKING.

> NEVER LOOK AT A NOTE WHILE YOU ARE LISTENING.

While speaking or listening, don't even glance toward your notes. *Maintain eye contact with a human being—not with notes—whenever words are being exchanged.* Before you begin to speak to a witness or to the jury, first establish eye contact and *then* start talking. That will make jurors think of you as a human being talking to another human being.

When you know you need to glance at your notes before going on, *finish what you are saying AND STOP TALKING. Then* look down at your notes. Don't speak again until *after* you have looked back up from your notes to re-establish eye contact.

Develop the habit in classes to make it automatic by the time you are working. Otherwise, you will develop all the opposite habits and have a terrible time later trying to change.

LISTENING

As you already know, you should not look down at your notes for your next question while your witness is still answering your last. It gives the impression that you don't care about the witness's answer—and indeed that is the case because your attention is on getting your next question.

You do it for fear you will not have your next question ready when the current answer ends. But it is better to pause briefly after a witness's answer (the jurors will not notice) than to make the jury think you are uninterested in the answer. Besides, you *must* listen in order to ask the next question without sounding mechanical—or even downright stupid. For example:

COUNSEL   Please tell us your name.

WITNESS   Irving Irwin LeMur, III.

COUNSEL   And where do you reside, please?

WITNESS   I'm a plumber who lives at 571 Main Street in Durham.

COUNSEL   And please tell us what you do for a living.

WITNESS   Open your ears, meathead.

JUDGE   Yeah, open your ears, meathead.

JURY   Yeah.

Guess who was looking at notes while the witness was on line four.

After you ask a question, listen to the answer before looking down at your notes for your next question. If you listen carefully, you will rarely need your notes anyway. Try it a few times and you will see.

Good listening is harder than good talking. That is why students, not teachers, fall asleep in class.

CLASS EXERCISES

Keep your mind on your purpose. In workshops and classes, you are not there to show off what you can do; get out of that frame of mind or it will become habit and you will carry it into court with you. While doing your trial advocacy exercises, concentrate entirely on such purposes as the following:

—*getting testimony* from a witness the way you want it, or

—*creating a persuasive context* for a jury to hear the rest of your case, or

—swaying a jury to your side by bringing together the persuasive points of your case.

Don't think of yourself as on display. You succeed or fail not by what you do up there but *by what you get a witness or jury to do*. This gives you a realistic mental construct within which to work, and takes your attention off yourself and places it where it belongs: on your immediate goal.

MAKE OBJECTIONS DURING CLASS EXERCISES

During class exercises (if the instructor permits) get into the automatic habit of objecting when appropriate. Don't sit there shy and mute; say, "Objection." Even if you are not sure why it is objectionable, say it anyway. Who cares if you are wrong or cannot think of the reason?

If the instructor does not want observers to object, at least do so mentally.

Objecting, right or wrong, has several benefits:

—It gives you the experience of doing it and the repeated experience develops the courage to do it.

—It gives your classmates the experience of having to counter your objection and, thus, gives you practice contending with counters.

—Your constant vigilance to spot an opportunity to object keeps you actively part of everyone's work.

—It helps you internalize the rules of evidence and turn them into instantly available tools instead of nerve-wracking obstacles.

Establish a class pool: everyone antes five bucks. Then award half a buck out of the pool for every sustained objection. Nothing like a little cash incentive, is there?[2]

BEING OBJECTED TO IN EXERCISES

Learn the proper reaction for being objected to: nothing. Simply stop and wait until the judge rules or asks for your response. *Stay focused on what you had been trying to do before the objection.* Don't be distracted from your original point, and don't let jurors see you thrown or even disturbed. When someone in class objects, don't smack your forehead and apologize. Don't look foolish. Don't roll your eyes and grin or wish you were dead. Don't argue with the objector. Don't do anything. Stay professional. Practice this kind of control from the first time you are on your feet in class. You need to make it habit.

REHEARSE

Join forces with another student or colleague and cross-examine each other for a couple of hours each week. Deliver openings and closings to each other. Do this the whole time you are in law school and regularly once you are out and in practice. Chances are you will never be in court enough to get sufficient real experience.

GOALS

Don't let rules take over your life. In court, you must follow the rules but keep your mind on your ultimate goal: to persuade. Rules control how you are allowed to persuade, but you don't win just for following the rules. Laws, ethics, and rules of procedure and evidence are limitations, not goals.

Actors spend as much time learning to be plausible as you do learning rules. As a result, some acting students erroneously think that their goal is to be plausible. It is not. Being plausible is merely prerequisite to their real goal: to be interesting. The only thing less useful than a plausible actor who is uninteresting is a rules-following trial attorney who is unpersuasive.

In basketball you don't win for staying in bounds; that is just following a rule. The goal is the basket. In court, the goal is persuasion.

BOREDOM

You cannot persuade jurors if you don't interest them. When they are uninterested, they don't listen. Constantly remind yourself that the default state of jurors is boredom, and that they will continue to be bored until you do something to un-bore them. So when you are given a fact pattern, look first

---

2. Caveat: The intention here is to develop your ability to object—but when you are actually in court, object only when it is to your tactical advantage, which is rarely. See Chapter 9, p. 150.

for its *interesting* points. It is essential to do this first, while you are still sensitive to what might be interesting.[3]

Then choose how you will go about bringing a jury to your side *by relying centrally upon those interesting points.* Don't merely tack on the interesting stuff after you have prepared everything else. *Start* with what is interesting and build from there. Do this in your trial practice classes and workshops, and keep doing it for the length of your career.

MISCELLANEOUS STUDENT POINTS

—Never look at your opponent's notes.

—Keep your hair out of your face.

—Get your hands away from your face.

—Play to your audience. Your audience is your jury. *Don't ever let the jury see your back.* And look at your jury a lot. Jurors cannot feel rapport with you if you don't look at them.

—Do all your exercise work dressed for court. Even if your instructor does not require it, create in yourself an instinctive, habitual association between appropriate court clothing and your work as a trial attorney. That way you will be more comfortable in court, and the act of getting dressed for court will become a mental focusing activity to prepare you for your work.

—When it is your turn to act as a witness in an exercise, prepare diligently. This improves the exercise for other students and gives you valuable experience understanding how a witness thinks and feels. It also convinces your instructors and classmates that you are reliable and thorough.

DETAILS VS. GENERAL CONCLUSIONS: THE *SPECIFICITY* ASSIGNMENT

For opening statements, witness questions, or closing arguments—regardless of the particular purpose of the assignment you have been given—always add this *specificity* assignment: Never give a conclusion until you have first provided enough specifics for jurors to make the conclusion on their own.

In oral persuasion, a conclusion not preceded by specifics is not worth the air it takes to say it.

For example, don't say, "It was bad weather." Bite your tongue whenever such a general conclusion escapes your lips. Instead say, "It was 36 degrees, 100 percent overcast, and drizzling rain. It had been raining without break for two days. The sidewalks were slick and muddy, puddles every few feet. The wind

---

3. See Chapter 6, "Viscerals."

gusted up to 30 miles an hour all afternoon." Before you even say, "It was bad weather," the jurors will have already come to that conclusion on their own.

There is nothing easier to disagree with than a mere conclusion or generality. There is nothing easier to argue against and *nothing easier to forget.*

Conclusions and generalities do not persuade. Specifics do. Make every class exercise a specificity exercise so that you make specificity habitual.

DON'T ARGUE WITH YOUR INSTRUCTOR (Master *everything*)

Often, you will disagree with something you are taught. So what? There are eighty-eight ways to skin any cat. Try to master every approach your instructor gives you, no matter how it strikes you at first. You cannot validly evaluate it until you have mastered it.

Some approaches and ideas that at first seem dumb will turn out to be your strongest tools. Conversely, some that seem superb at first will turn out to be useless in your hands. For example, many authorities tell you never to let a witness explain on cross. Others swear that the best approach is to corner the witness and *make* him explain. Whichever way your instructor guides you, learn to do it superbly. Don't waste energy or class time arguing. Don't waste your time (or undermine your work) by doubting it. *Just learn it and do it the best way you possibly can.* Maybe it will work for you, maybe it never will. It is different for everyone. You cannot know how it fits you until you master it. How it sounds in advance is of no consequence.[4]

LIKING AND HATING TEACHERS

The fact that you like a particular teacher, or hate one, or are impressed or not impressed, is not relevant. Don't confuse the value or validity of the material with your reaction to the teacher. The most wonderful teachers in the world sometimes deliver rubbish. Similarly, the worst pedagogic clods give you a gem now and then—if you have not shut them out so completely that you don't notice it.

Assume that every teacher has something to teach you. Let your classmates ignore the lesser teachers. Keep your own ears open. Learning a little from several teachers is as good as learning a lot from one.

FATIGUE AND EXHAUSTION: THE REALITY OF THE PROFESSION

While you are still in law school, you can provide yourself with a realistic experience by occasionally presenting a trial practice exercise when you have had just a few hours' sleep for two or three nights running. Before getting to

---

4. The place to find out is in law school or at a CLE program where the consequences of your exploring cannot hurt anyone.

class, get coffee'd up and clean. And do your exercise so well that no one notices that you are worn out.

Pay attention to how this feels. Look for ways to prepare that you might use next time to bolster your work when you are totally exhausted. Take notes on how it all felt.

Trial law (if you are any good) is exhausting. Pre-dawn hours are spent preparing the day in court; evenings are spent reviewing the day. Even lunch is working time. Trial lawyers work under blitz conditions; once a trial starts, there is no breathing time. Law school is where to learn how to function on your feet, alertly executing a complicated, delicate task of jury persuasion—when, in fact, you are at the end of your endurance. You must do it well enough that no one but you knows how exhuasted you are, because jurors do not care that you might be tired. So in law school, when you drag yourself in after a seventy-two hour weekend party or three consecutive all-night study marathons, don't use it as an excuse. This is the morning to knock 'em dead.

If you find that you cannot work well when you are bone tired, then you will be a mediocre trial lawyer.

PASSION

Because law school and CLE exercises are brief and you spend only a few hours preparing for them, you don't gain the level of passion you would if the preparation took days, weeks, or months—like real cases. Thus, in law school and CLE workshops, you must make an extra effort to attack every class exercise as if its people and issues were truly important to you personally. You may feel foolish doing this when surrounded by blasé students monotoning their way through exercises. Let them—while you use your fullest emotional energies on everything you do. Make yourself care or you will develop the habit of being able to work without caring. The result is professional mediocrity.

"Passion" does not mean raging and raving. Passion can be—and usually is—quiet. But it has to be there. Your body language, vocal quality, rhythms, and a host of other factors make it clear when you don't care about your case. That is a hard stance from which to win.

Use every class exercise to practice generating a passion to drive your work—even when you don't feel like it. You will be practicing for reality. And you will not be habitualizing yourself to the world's least persuasive activity: passionless advocacy.

TRIAL PRACTICE JOURNAL: THE BEST TRIAL TEXTBOOK IN THE WORLD

Write down everything your trial practice instructors say to anyone, not just you. Many students write down little or nothing, not even what is said directly to and about them! It is no wonder they get into court and make every mistake in the book. They remember only five percent of what they were taught. You cannot blame your law school or CLE teachers if you forget what they taught you.

To maximize what your classes offer, *write everything down.* Don't wait for stuff to be handed to you on a silver platter. Grab it as it is thrown, no matter who throws it or at whom. Maintain a journal of everything said in class to every student. As you prepare each new class exercise, reread your journal to find *everything* appropriate for each new exercise. Thus reminded, you will practice it all every time it can be incorporated into any exercise.

Moreover, there is no better way to flatter and impress your instructors than to remember at the end of a course to do what they taught you (or someone else) at the beginning.

Your trial practice journal will be your most valuable book because it is the world's only book written just for you.

PERSONAL STYLE

Many branches of law require only knowledge. But trial law is personal—and the person is you. *You are your best asset.*

Starting even with your first class exercises, adapt every legal and persuasive skill you learn to your own personal strengths and natural style. The best service a teacher can offer is to help you find out what your own particular persuasive strengths and style might be. Most teachers—generally due to time constraints—do not volunteer such assistance, but will provide it if you ask.[5] Of course there are many techniques and a lot of law to learn. But just as performing artists assimilate a myriad of technical and aesthetic considerations into their work without submerging their personalities, so must you assimilate law and trial techniques into your personal persuasive self so that the result is you with skills, not skills without you. Remember who and what you are, why you are doing this, and which of your strengths are likely to become the foundation of all you do.

No two lawyers are alike, nor should they try to be. The time to start seeking your individuality is in your first trial class exercises, and it continues through decades of in-court practice and CLE exercises.

Some teachers say that you should learn technique first and bring your personality to bear later on. This is a naive and damaging view of how people learn skills. The assimilation process begins on day one. If you start out by trying to be like everyone else, you will—by definition—turn out to be average. Try instead to maximize the singular individual that is you.

---

5.   Watching real trials also helps you identify your own personal style because you will see a wide variety of personal approaches. You will see which approaches you identify with most closely, and you will spot new ways of relating your own personal characteristics to the legal and persuasive techniques you learn in class.

CHAPTER 12

And in Conclusion, Ladies and Gentlemen . . .

NERVE

Trial advocacy is a daring profession, and you cannot be daring if the possibility of failure or negative criticism cripples you. The only people who never fail are the people who never try anything worth doing.

You learn more from failure than from success. Civil engineers learn more from bridges that collapse than from those that stay up. So as bad as it feels to fail, when it happens don't blot it out of your memory. Scrutinize failures for every little thing you can learn. The result will often be among your most valuable lessons.

You need to be daring in order to have no fear of rules, local court practices, "the way it is usually done," objections, or anything else. If something seems like a good idea, try it. Decent judges do not take offense at carefully prepared, well argued motions. Don't timidly tiptoe up to customary limits and stop. Have the nerve to try to improve things. When necessary, it is your job to educate the judge and to help shape custom and practice. It is your job to respectfully and professionally question everything that gets in your way. Old ways are not always the best ways.

Don't break the rules and don't sneak around them. But give them a good, hard shake when they are in your way. Do so ethically, respectfully, and competently. Often, they will yield.

REPUTATION

Because so few cases come to court (and particularly if you are an effective negotiator), it is all too easy to gain the reputation of being an attorney who prefers to settle rather than go into battle. Don't let such a reputation attach to you. Instead, develop a reputation as a trial lawyer who *loves*, *above all things*, *to go to trial.* If your opponent sees how eager you are to confront her in front of a jury, it tips in your favor the scale of any offered settlement or plea bargain.

FUTURE BUSINESS

Do your best work every time you are in front of a jury. The fact that your opponent is an idiot, or that the case is a sure thing, or routine, or that you are busy with other tasks, does not excuse you from doing less than your absolute best.

This is not just an ethical responsibility. You are being scrutinized by jurors who are potential future clients or referrers. Every trial is a public window on your practice. There is no better billboard than your work in front of jurors. They will spread the word that you are a lazy jerk, if that is what they see—or a superb lawyer who is their first choice of counsel if they can be lucky enough to get you.

CURTAIN SPEECH

We are a proud lot, you lawyers, we players. We are the same lot. Even Hamlet seems to have known this. Late in the play, he takes up a skull out of an open grave. It is the skull he will soon discover to be his friend Yorick's, who, as the old king's *jester*, was one of our performing colleagues. Hamlet picks up the skull and asks, *Why, may not that be the skull of a lawyer?*

It is a close guess about this most famous skull in the world. Hamlet thought it was a lawyer and it turns out to be a player. It is almost the same thing.

PART TWO: APPLICATIONS

A, B, C, and E are adapted from articles published in 1995 and 1996 in *Around the State*, a publication of the North Carolina Academy of Trial Lawyers.

D, F, G, H, I, J, K, and L are adapted from monthly columns that appeared in *North Carolina Lawyers Weekly*, 1995 and 1996.

M is adapted from an article in *Trial Briefs* (Spring 1996), the journal of the North Carolina Academy of Trial Lawyers.

A: WORKING WITH CO-COUNSEL (Juror interpretation that hurts.)

There are few limits on how jurors interpret what they observe, so when working with co-counsel(s), be careful.

Equal importance: To begin with, arrange the division of labor (including voir dire) between you and your co-counsel in such a way that neither of you seems to be the lesser member of the team. If jurors think one of you is senior or dominant, they will assume that anything the other does is relatively unimportant. They will listen less closely to "lesser" counsel and assign lighter weight to testimony he or she elicits.

You can offset this by assigning important tasks early in trial to the junior member, such as a share of voir dire, or questioning an important witness.

Voir dire and rapport: Not every judge automatically allows voir dire to be shared with co-counsel (indeed, some will never have heard of such a practice), so prepare a motion to do so. Argue that it will save time, since you are each more familiar with different areas of the case and can thus more quickly pursue what you need to know in those separate areas.

Don't share by alternating questions. Change questioners only once or twice, and make the division by topic.

Though sharing voir dire is rarely done, it helps make co-counsel a fully effective member of the trial team. The kind of rapport that results from voir dire develops at no other time, because only in voir dire do jurors talk with you. This kind of rapport helps credibility—and you want your co-counsel to be as credible as you.

Allowing rapport to develop between the jury and only one member of the trial team marginalizes and thus diminishes the importance, credibility, and persuasive weight of the non-participating counsel and everything he or she does.

Respect: Treat your co-counsel not merely civilly, but with respect. Jurors who are or have been rudely treated as subservients in their own jobs can resent lawyers who treat junior colleagues as inferior. *The senior-junior behavior that may be appropriate in your office can sit badly with jurors in court.*

Each member of the trial team should treat every other member as his or her boss. Treat no one like an underling.

Paralegals and assistants: In the presence of the jury, be careful how you and your co-counsel treat your paralegals and assistants. Make requests of your staff as politely and deferentially as you would of your superiors.

Again, jurors who may have been badly treated as underlings at work can turn resentful if you behave like their offending bosses.

Moreover, make sure that both you and co-counsel treat staff *equally* well. When your co-counsel is deferential with the assistants that you order around like serving maids, you create a harmfully visible power-differential between you and co-counsel.

Bench conferences: Both you and your co-counsel should go to the bench for every conference so that jurors will see that you have equal stake and equal input. In jurors' minds, what goes on at the bench is mysterious and important. When co-counsel does not join you there, jurors conclude that he or she is not smart or important enough to deal with the mystery and importance of the judge.

Attentiveness: One common courtroom error is for senior counsel to fail to pay close attention when junior counsel is talking to jurors or questioning a witness. If one counsel studies the next witness's deposition while co-counsel questions the current witness, jurors conclude that neither the current witness nor her questioner is important.

Every member of the trial team should pay the same level of attention to your co-counsel's work as to your work. If your paralegal files papers or stares into space while your junior colleague questions a witness, and then turns raptly attentive when you take testimony, jurors infer that not even the paralegal respects junior counsel.

Monitoring: There are many ways you or your trial team might inadvertently undermine the position of your co-counsel in the jurors' eyes. Alert your trial team to the problem's potentially serious consequences. And stay alert to the problem yourself.

B: HUMANIZING NON-HUMAN CASES

CLEs and books that teach trial advocacy skills seem mostly geared for cases that involve such "human" elements as criminal behavior or the tragedy of personal injuries. What about cases such as contract and corporate disputes where the "people content" is apparently minimal?

Such cases are difficult because no matter how much you and your clients are concerned with, for example, Clause 3-B-vii, jurors don't give a darn. Jurors want to hear about the human expectations that led to the clause, and about the human behavior or human consequences that resulted from the clause or how it was executed. Jurors don't care whether Acme Corporation unfairly prospers, or was cheated by Barnes Corporation, or misinterpreted Clause 3-B-vii. But jurors do care about individual human choices that led to prospering, or to inter-corporate cheating, or to misinterpreting.

And they care intensely about how prospering, or intercorporate cheating, or misinterpreting may affect the lives of real human beings.

Human behavior is the jury's only common area of expertise. Jurors can figure it out, remember it, respond to it, evaluate it—and use it for making decisions.

Abstractions don't persuade. Everyday life does not include abstractions. The few abstractions that enter peoples' lives are communicated via concrete, humanizing methods (such as a preacher's story illustrating an abstract theological principle). So jurors do not readily deal with abstractions (such as Clause 3-B-vii), and are unenthusiastic about being asked to. They don't consciously use abstractions in their own lives to help make decisions, and they are not likely to do so in deliberations.

You deal well with abstractions because they fill your everyday life, and your personal stake in them endows them with human content for you. But not for jurors. Thus, you have to show jurors how the abstractions of your case relate to human elements.

To start with, you have to find the human elements. The first—and easier—way to seek human content is to examine *how the outcome of the case can affect individual human beings.* No matter how abstract a contention may be, the consequences of that contention's resolution will directly and indirectly affect people. (For example, a company's loss of funds can mean the loss of jobs.)

The second—and somewhat harder—way to look for human content is to find the *connections between the "inhuman" abstraction and the "human" elements* that led to the abstraction. What are the *human motivations* that caused the abstraction in question?

For example, what human motivations led to clause 3-B-vii? Everything a person does is driven by concrete human impulses and motivations. So find out and show what human motivations led one party to frame, interpret, or execute the clause as they did. And show the human motivations that drove the other party to interpret or execute the clause in a conflicting way.

Work backwards from each abstract issue of the case until you find the human motivations that shaped those abstractions.

Who created the clause? Why did she do it that way? It might be as simple as wanting to protect the company. It might be *ambition*: creating favorable contract clauses can lead to a promotion or raise. Or maybe she wanted to get done with the task quickly and go home. Such a motivation might have led to the carelessly ambiguous phrase now causing all the trouble.

Even in a case involving two numbers-crunching computers whose calculations disagree, *humans* programed those computers, and those *humans* had human concerns that influenced their work. Those concerns might be loyalty, pride in good work, morality, greed, dishonesty, ambition, fear, laziness, want-to-go-home-early, interworker competition, status and prestige, or any number of other *human* motivating factors.

For example: It is not enough to tell us why the software was wrong for the job. It is not even enough to explain the technical thinking behind its installation ("it was incorrectly thought to be innovatively efficient"). Find some human reasons (such as haste, pride, or greed). Or maybe a software engineer was trying too hard to make himself look good to his boss.

In other words, *add motive*. A motive is the initiating human impulse. Good criminal prosecutors show motive even when the law requires none. This makes the commission of an act seem plausible and provides a persuasive human component. While neither the crime nor the tort lies in the human motive, *the jury's ability to understand and believe the crime or the tort relies heavily on motive*.

So look at each abstract issue and trace backwards from the events that led to it until you come to a human being doing human things for human reasons.

Limitations on your own perceptiveness. Let me word this next observation as gently as I can. If you have difficulty humanizing cases, the problem may lie in what I am about to discuss. So ask yourself honestly whether this might apply to you:

Attorneys who work for years mostly with "non-human" cases sometimes find that their human response instincts become muted. They spend so much time with abstractions, figures, contracts, corporate matters—and clients whose concerns focus on the same things—that they lose some of their natural habits of perceiving situations and events in terms of human-content motivations.

If this has started to happen to you, there are cures.

Short range cures:

People-oriented aide. Go out and find the most people-oriented person you know; someone interested in how human beings behave. He or she need not be anything as sophisticated as a psychologist. A backyard gossip—of adequate intelligence—is just as good. Enlist this person's help: Run your case by him, tell him everything you can about the people involved, and ask him to make suggestions as to why each of the people did what they did. Even if his answers are not accurate, they can point the way to finding the human content in the case.

Tell your people-oriented person exactly what your problem is: that you are having trouble ferreting out the human side of your case. Ask him to brainstorm possible human connections: why so-and-so might have opted for a particular clause, or why someone in a corporation might have failed to do what the contract required. It is easy to generalize everything into corporate behavior, but a people person can help return you to human foundations. (Obviously, you must take precautions to ensure confidentiality.)

Focus group. Conduct a small, special-purpose focus group to explore what people-oriented folks think about the case. Bring together eight or ten people-oriented folks and give them the abstractions of the case. Have them brainstorm in "deliberations"—not to a verdict, but to try to determine why the people acted as they did.

Investigate. If you are not already in the habit of doing so, gather all the human information you can on the individuals involved in the case. Sometimes this consists simply of asking personal background questions in depositions such as family situations, personal matters, and other areas that you might not normally consider relevant. For larger cases it is worth hiring an investigator. Look for clues to personal, human motivations that might explain why, for example, a person might have opted to include (or violate) certain clauses in a contract. This might amount to digging up dirt—or admirable qualities. Either can provide motivating fuel.

It is not enough to know who at Acme Corporation refused delivery of an order, though that is where counsel's investigation usually stops. *Why* did he refuse delivery? Was he *trying to impress* his boss by taking the initiative about something? Was he *so overworked* that he just did not pay attention to what he was doing? "Trying to impress" and "overworked" provide human content to the abstractions of the case. Does he have a wife or a child or a parent who might be a high achiever? Could that be a clue as to whom he might have been trying to impress by the way he was conducting the business transaction in question?

Long range cures:

Go home. Spend more time with your family and friends. Become a better listener to them and maybe you will come into contact with something more human than you have taken the time to hear lately.

Go out. Start going to more plays and good movies—where you watch characters driven by human motivations. Occasional visits to art galleries would not hurt, either. (Concerts are less useful because music, particularly instrumental music, is almost entirely abstract.)

Go volunteer. Volunteer to do some hands-on *non-lawyer* work: Serve food at the local soup kitchen, for example, where you will come face to face with humanity and rekindle your human-content detector.

Whether you pursue the short-range or long-range solutions, you can improve the human content of your cases and the way you personally come across to juries. Such human elements, though peripheral to matters of law, have everything to do with the jurors' decision-making process.

C: THEME

Themes provide jurors with focal points around which to organize all the evidence and arguments. Themes are used in every form of communication in which the audience is not interactive—including music, theater, literature, good teaching, the visual arts, preaching, formal speaking, and even stand-up comedy. In every instance, theme serves as a logo or a billboard to announce, clarify, and constantly remind the audience of the purpose of what is being communicated.

In court, a theme is a main contention of your case. "This did not have to happen" is a theme for a medical negligence case. It helps keep jurors aware of the purpose of the evidence. The theme of "reasonable doubt" does the same.

Your themes are the contentions that you must make the jury believe if you are to win. If the jury does not believe that "this did not have to happen," you lose. If the jury does not believe your theme of "reasonable doubt," you lose.

"Should have known" is a products liability theme: The jurors must believe that the defendant *should have known* about the problem if they are to decide that the defendant wrongfully ignored something. "Could not see his face" is a criminal defense theme: The jury must believe that the witness could not see the defendant's face if they are to decide the identification was wrong.

"If it doesn't fit, you must acquit" was inspired by a bloody glove, but encompassed a defense response to most of the prosecution evidence.

Well-chosen and concisely-worded themes help the jurors organize the wide variety of evidence and arguments they hear during trial. Good themes also become the foundation of deliberations. For example, "If it doesn't fit, you must acquit" not only gives the jurors a way to gauge every piece of evidence (they will ask themselves, "*Does* it fit?"), but it also provides the context and terms in which they will argue about each piece of evidence that comes up in deliberations. Not every theme is broad enough to similarly encompass everything in the case, but you can be equally effective by providing separate themes for each major topic in your case. For example, "this did not have to happen," "ruined life," and "unacceptable care standards" might be the three themes of a med mal case.

Insofar as possible, introduce your themes in voir dire. Explain and develop them in opening. Emphasize them throughout testimony. And reemphasize them and tie them together in closing.

Don't repeat a theme merely for the sake of repeating it. That undermines its effectiveness. With the exception of closing, repeat a theme only and whenever you can show *how it relates to and is supported by each new piece of evidence and each argument you introduce*. For example, testimony that it was raining during an assault supports the "could-not-see-his-face" theme. Make that connection explicit at the time of the rain testimony:

Q. Was it raining hard enough to cut down on visibility?

A. Yes.

Q. So it was more difficult to see than if it had been a clear day?

A. Yes.

Q. So you could not see the driver's face?

A. Right.

Each time you use a theme, express it in the same words. Changing from "could not see his face" to "unable to make an identification" undermines its effectiveness.

Aside from words, themes can also be expressed and kept in front of the jury with visuals. (See Chapter 5, "Demonstrative and Real Evidence.")

Think of your primary theme as the title of your case ("this did not have to happen"), and each lesser theme as the heading of a different component of the case ("hasty diagnosis," "poor follow-up," "patient not kept informed," "no advise and consent," "patient has right to expect better care," etc.). This gives you a way to keep the main lines of the case separate and to show how they support each other.

A theme can—but need not—be cleverly or pithily worded. "If it doesn't fit, you must acquit" is snappy, whereas "this did not have to happen" is not. Yet each is effective because each provides a focal point for evidence and arguments, and gives your jurors a way to talk to opposition jurors in deliberations.

Some attorneys make the mistake of thinking that a theme *must* be cleverly worded. While a snappy or familiar phrase helps jurors remember, you cannot always find the perfect way to say it. Bad rhymes and limp punch lines hurt more than help.

Cliches can deaden your theme's impact—unless you speak the words as if they are brand new. "A bird in the hand is worth two in the bush" is hardly heard if you toss it off as a familiar old saying. But if you speak it as if it is a new and specific observation made for the purposes of this particular case, it will be effective.

The important thing is to provide concise and easily-memorable wording so that it sticks with jurors and they will say it themselves in deliberations. Often a quotation index can help you find something fitting from literature, and on-line help from the Internet can even provide a search of hundreds of song lyrics. (Caveat: If you use a biblical quote, be sure you are not inadvertently warping its meaning, using a controversial meaning, or appealing to one portion of the jury while possibly offending the others.)

D: FOCUS GROUPS, MOCK TRIALS

FOCUS GROUPS: Why, How, and How Much?

Driving home after a small focus group last year, the attorney I was working for said to me, "Thank God my opponent doesn't use focus groups!"

Why would one of the East Coast's preeminent trial lawyers make such a statement? Because a focus group is to trial practice as an X-ray is to surgery.

This essay outlines sixteen practical uses you can get out of every focus group or mock trial. If you have never done one, or if you want to improve the ones you do without going so far as to hire outside assistance, this section's step-by-step instructions will guide you as far as you can go on your own. This section also describes the use of outside assistance—consultants and market research services—to help you do better focus groups than you can manage on your own, and to assist you with larger cases when more resources are available, more information is needed, and maximum possible reliability and validity are essential.

If you are not interested in doing focus groups or mock trials, you are cheating your clients. This kind of research is the only way to test your case in front of jurors. Focusing a case is like test-driving a car or trying on shoes before you buy them.

Focusing a case is also a lot of fun. You get to see the only part of the case that is always hidden from you in a real trial: juror discussions.

If you happen to be the unfortunate opponent referred to in the first paragraph, you got blind-sided and needlessly hurt your client. You settled with us because you did not know what our focus research had shown us: that you would have murdered us in court. We were prepared to settle for a figure more favorable to your client by as much as tenfold. But you don't believe in focus groups, so you negotiated in the dark while we had the benefit of night vision.

Ineffective counsel? You can bet your client's bottom dollar you were.

WHAT CAN YOU LEARN FROM FOCUS RESEARCH?

1. You learn how the case plays in front of jurors. You can test how jurors respond to both sides' evidence, exhibits, explanations, contentions, people, issues, and methods of presentation, and how those responses affect the decision-making process.

2. You can find out how jurors react to *you* presenting this particular case.

3. You can see which issues are pivotal and which are less important.

4. You can spot unanticipated problems and weaknesses while you still have time before trial to do something about them. If they are

overwhelming, you can negotiate or plea bargain before your opponent finds out.

5. You discover unanticipated strengths and strategies while you still have time to figure out how to take best advantage of them.

6. You find out what you should do or say in trial that you had not planned on.

7. You find out what you should *not* do or say in trial that you *had* planned on.

8. You discover how well jurors *understand* and *remember* your evidence, issues, and arguments—so you can take advantage of strengths and fix problems.

9. You can learn how to select your jury—because you see which kinds of jurors take your side on key issues and which kinds take the other side. You learn what voir dire questions to ask in court, how to evaluate the answers, and how to tailor your case to the real jury you ultimately get. You can even anticipate, and thus better prepare for arguing, the kinds of challenges for cause you are likely to have the opportunity to pursue.

10. You hear the exact words, arguments, and images that jurors use in discussing your key issues. This provides effective ways for you to talk about your case when you get to court: the words, arguments, and images used by mock jurors represent the way jurors—not lawyers—are persuaded.

11. You learn how likely you are to win or lose—and why.

12. In civil cases, you see the range of damages that jurors are likely to award. And whether you are plaintiff or defense, you can test the efficacy of your damages arguments or decide whether to use a damages argument at all.

13. You can determine whether you are better off with a jury or bench trial (or some other form of resolution).

Not bad for so small an investment of time and money. And in addition to all you learn, there are three more benefits:

14. NEGOTIATION TOOL. If focus jurors favor your side, they will voice that favor in their deliberations—*and you will have it on video!* Later in negotiations, you can use video or transcript excerpts as powerful weapons. A video of mock jurors energetically concurring that "Millions isn't enough!" or "The plaintiff shouldn't get a cent, he should be run out of town!" or "I know it's only assault, but he should get life!"

or "Any jury that sends him to jail is deaf, dumb, and blind!" will bolster your bargaining position. (These are actual focus-group quotes.)

15. CLIENT PERSUASION. Have your client watch the focus deliberations. This will help persuade your client to go along with your advice about the wisdom of accepting (or rejecting) a settlement or plea offer.

16. ATTORNEY REHEARSAL. Presenting your case (and even doing a voir dire) in an abbreviated form to a mock jury of strangers gives you *practice*. Trial attorneys are the only "performers" who work with no practice or rehearsal. Actors, dancers, athletes, musicians, debaters, politicians, and even preachers engage in hours of practice for every hour of performance—because practice makes them immeasurably better. Practice does the same for trial lawyers.

Can you imagine a professional sporting event or drama for which the players do not practice? Is a trial less demanding?

If every lawyer engaged in case-specific practice before trial, the quality of American trial advocacy would improve beyond recognition. And while practice is invaluable for less-experienced attorneys, it is an odd fact that the more experienced and skilled an attorney is, the more she can profit by case-specific practice. *Focus group presentation provides the opportunity for this practice* at the same time that it provides all the other benefits mentioned above.

WHAT IT TAKES:

Focus research can cost anywhere from a few hundred dollars to tens of thousands. There are three basic options.

OPTION 1: Do it yourself. The final section of this article, below, describes how to do a mock trial on your own. When resources are limited, you can do a three-hour mock trial without outside assistance for a few hundred dollars and you will learn enough to test, strengthen, and adjust your negotiations, voir dire, and overall trial strategy. (Cost: $350–$700.)

OPTION 2: Do it with an expert guiding you through the planning, execution, and post-session analysis. An expert can show you how to get greater validity and reliability, and can help you analyze the results for use in negotiations and in trial. (Cost: $1,000–$3,500.)

OPTION 3: Do it with full research support. Trial consultants who also offer scientific market research resources can provide the services of Option 2 plus controlled participant-selection and recruitment procedures, multiple deliberating groups, state-of-the-art equipment and facilities, and management of all arrangements and logistics. (Cost: $7,500–$15,000 or more.)

ALTERNATIVE: not doing focus groups or mock trials at all. This alternative ensures that sooner or later one of your adversaries will gloat, "Thank God my opponent doesn't use focus groups."

If you are still skeptical, try Option 1 (doing it on your own). The steps below guide you through conducting an inexpensive session that will provide results useful enough to convince you that focus research works.

Caveat: Option 1 yields less information and greater uncertainty than focus research assisted by experts. But Option 1 is still valuable, as long as you remain alert to the range of uncertainty that results from doing it on your own.

HOW TO CONDUCT YOUR OWN:

1. FIND PARTICIPANTS. Ask the jury clerk for a list of 100 recent jurors. Use the following criteria:

> There should be no more than four jurors from any one trial.

> The 100 should come from an even mix of criminal and civil cases, and an even mix of verdicts.

> If possible, avoid jurors who served on cases similar to yours.

> Avoid venirepersons who were called but were not seated.

> In all other respects, the group should be selected randomly.

> These 100 will be a fairly representative cross-section, and having served recently, none can be called for service on your upcoming trial.

2. SEND A LETTER to everyone on the list. State that you are looking for ex-jurors to participate in an interesting jury research project for, say, $40 for three hours. (Depending on local economic conditions, less than $30 overweights your group with lower-income participants, and more than $50 wastes your money.)

The letter should direct those interested to call your paralegal by a specified cut-off date, no later than two weeks before your focus session.

3. SCREEN RESPONDENTS. When respondents call, your paralegal should screen them so that you can select a group of participants that roughly matches the demographic breakdown of real juries in your jurisdiction. Your paralegal should ask and log such information as age, occupation, family income range ($15,000-$25,000; $25,000-$40,000, etc.), marital status, number and ages of children, racial background, church affiliation and frequency of attendance, and clubs and social organizations. This information will allow you to select twelve respondents who make up a cross-section similar to that of an average jury in your jurisdiction.

Ask if they have been on focus groups or mock juries before. If they have, don't use them. If you do a lot of focus groups or mock trials, don't fall into the easy trap of using the same participants more than once. And if you employ a service to enlist your participants, don't let the service recruit from a pool of individuals who participate over and over. "Experienced" participants yield unreliable results.

When interviewing phone respondents, your paralegal should also make note of verbal dexterity. Does the respondent talk a lot? Is he or she relatively articulate?

4. SELECT AND NOTIFY PARTICIPANTS. After the cut-off date for response calls, use your paralegal's phone notes to select the twelve participants who, as a group, most closely mirror the demographic balance of the original pool of 100. Try to select participants whom your paralegal found to be talkative and articulate. Quiet participants are less useful in deliberations.

At this stage, your paralegal should question respondents to be sure they don't know any witnesses, attorneys, or parties in the case.

Your paralegal should get commitments from the selected twelve to attend.

Getting commitments from twelve respondents usually means eight or nine will actually show up. This is the minimum to give you a good chance of having varying viewpoints and useful deliberations. You can have more, but over eleven in one group tends to stifle full participation in deliberation discussions. You can have two deliberating groups—a measure that yields more information at a higher reliability. If you wish to do this, just double the numbers.

Your paralegal should also call the respondents you are not using. This courtesy prevents ill feelings. Explain to them that the necessity of balancing such factors as gender, age, and family income meant that you could not use everyone who responded, but you will call them next time.

5. ARRANGE LOCATION. If you use your own offices, be certain to do so in such a way that participants cannot figure out which side is sponsoring the session. Otherwise their desire to please will tilt their responses in your favor—and that undermines the validity of your results.

You need a room large enough to seat your participants around two sides and one end of a table. (You need two such rooms if you are going to have two simultaneously deliberating groups.)

Place a video camera on a tripod a few feet from the empty end, aimed to pick up every participant. Put a 360-degree table microphone at the center of the table, taped in place so it cannot accidentally be moved. Connect the camera to a video recorder and monitor in an adjacent room so you can observe deliberations and record at the same time.

If you have no video equipment, make sound recordings. You can buy a decent recorder and microphones for under $100. Video is far better because it lets you see who says what, and that provides useful information for voir dire. But sound alone is better than nothing.

6. GREET THE ARRIVING PARTICIPANTS. Give them *large* name tags so you can keep track of who says what. Provide modest refreshments (cold drinks, coffee, munchies). Gather them around the table.

7. PROVIDE A CONFIDENTIALITY FORM. Have them each sign one. Though such forms are hard to enforce, they add a useful note of formality and seriousness to the proceedings.

8. START VIDEOTAPING immediately, so that by the time jurors deliberate they will be oblivious to the camera.

9. EXPLAIN THE PURPOSE. Your paralegal should explain to the participants why they are here (to hear and respond to a real case) and *emphasize that their responses and deliberations will have a real effect on the lives of the parties involved.*

You, your colleagues, and your staff should avoid words such as "mock," "focus group," and any other way of conveying that these proceedings are not *real.* Don't say, "When this case *really* gets to court in front of *real* jurors . . ." or "If this were a *real* trial . . . ." Such references scuttle the participants' desire and ability to respond in a "real" way, and tend to prevent potential hold-out jurors from holding out. That means you will hear far less juror debate in deliberations.

10. STATE THE UNCONTESTED FACTS—briefly. Your paralegal should say, for example, "On January 23, 1993, a plumber named Sam Smith drove his truck into Sally Jones on her bicycle and broke her leg. Sally Jones, who is a telephone operator, claims that Sam Smith was speeding. Sam Smith denies speeding and says that Sally Jones rode out in front of him."

11. PRESENT THE INSTRUCTIONS. Your paralegal should read brief, clear instructions explaining any necessary legal concepts and *slowly read the questions to be decided.* Give each participant a written copy of the questions.

12. PRESENT THE CASE. Present each side of the case via a 15- to 20-minute "opening-statement-with-argument." *Focus exclusively on case-determinative issues in contention.*

Present your opponent's case *better* than you present your own so you can more safely rely on any favorable outcomes.

You can present both sides yourself, but it is better for a colleague to present one side and you the other. Perhaps you should make a $100 bet with your colleague as to which side "wins." This gets both of you to present your sides with passion, thus making it harder for participants to figure out who is sponsoring this research.

13. REREAD THE QUESTIONS. Have your paralegal reread the questions the "jury" is to decide.

14. EXPLAIN THE FOREPERSON'S FUNCTION. Have your paralegal instruct the participants to begin deliberations by electing a foreperson. Explain that the foreperson should enable and encourage all the participants to have their say. *Do not influence the choice of foreperson.* Save that sophisticated maneuver for trial.

15. LEAVE, closing the door securely.

16. MONITOR. From the next room, watch deliberations. Be quiet in there; voices carry.

17. DON'T INTERRUPT. For reasons having to do with the validity of the results, avoid the temptation to interrupt deliberations with new information, or "to set the record straight," or to point out anything for either side.

If you have progressed efficiently and limited each case presentation to 25 minutes, the participants will have 90 minutes for deliberations—the necessary minimum to get useful results if the two sides have been fairly and evenly presented. If the questions are answered before you run out of time, conduct a question-and-answer session with the participants *in which they do most of the talking, not you.*

18. CONCLUDE. Pay the participants, thank them, remind them that everything they heard is confidential, and send them home.

You have now accumulated a warehouse of information. You have test-driven your case.

19. LAST STEP. Write to your participants to thank them and to explain that the focus session was a normal part of your case preparation. Such a letter is not only a courtesy, but an excellent marketing device—because people understand and appreciate the value of painstaking preparation. Some of your best future cases may well come to you from focus research participants.

E: THE AWKWARDNESS OF VOIR DIRE

The beginning of voir dire can be the most awkward-feeling time for you in trial. This is because you have to shift almost instantly from being a lawyer battling over motions, to a people-person trying to make human contact with normal folks.

The transition is hard to make under the best of conditions, and even harder if your motions have fared badly.

> JUDGE: You cannot have either of your proposed experts. The pre-existing conditions can come in. So can the drug and spouse abuse charges. Now let's call in the jury panel.
>
> YOU: *Now?!?* Wait a minute, I'm in shock!

Anyone would have trouble getting into the right frame of mind to meet a jury. But you have no choice.

Compounding the problem: the jurors have been waiting around all day doing nothing. They were called at, say, 9:00 a.m. They showed up promptly, but without explanation were made to sit there like pre-Miranda prisoners. Maybe it is now 11:30 a.m. or even 3:30 p.m. Here is how they feel: They are no more eager to meet you than you are mentally set to deal with them. They are not eager to answer your questions.

To make matters worse, during motions you probably felt pressure to get quickly through whatever you had to say. This may have caused you to speak more quickly and tensely, which temporarily made you a poor listener. So when the jury panel files in, you talk to them as if you are a lawyer in a bad mood, in a hurry, uninterested in anything these folks might have to say, and unconcerned with their humanity and feelings.

Great start, eh? No wonder voir dire feels awkward and sometimes embarrassing. Your frame of mind after motions arguments is dead wrong for the upcoming task of voir dire because you are lugging motions baggage into voir dire. This triples the thickness of the ice you have to break.

What you need here is a MOMENT. Just before the jurors come in, or as soon after their arrival as possible, *sit down, shut out of your mind all that has gone before, and turn your thoughts and feelings around.*

One attorney I know takes an important-looking file from his briefcase, opens it, and peruses the contents. He is the only one who can see that it is a photo of his young daughter, and it is inscribed with crayon, "TO DADDY, WAY COOL!" He smiles every time. Such a courtroom aid makes it worth having kids, and it gets counsel ready for the human-centered task of voir dire.

Another attorney I know shuts her eyes and mentally sips a glass of wine (cold beer works, too). Another gets a mental shoulder massage. Some attorneys sing (mentally) a favorite mood-changing song. Simply find something that makes you feel warm and sociable, and that helps you replace your arguing-motions self with your people-oriented self. Let it take you over as the jurors file in for voir dire. You will feel more comfortable and the jurors will be more open both to your questioning and to you.

You should do this even when you go second in voir dire. You will listen better to the human content of the answers your opponent elicits, and you will be more prepared when it is your turn to question.

Actors use transitional moments when they go from the paraphernalia and technician-laden bustle of backstage into the very different world in front of the lights. Doctors often use such a moment as they go from the dark concentration of an operating room to the socially-demanding interchange of talking with anxious relatives in the waiting room. Presidents of nations use such a moment to go from spatting with spouses to international TV press conferences.

The uniqueness of voir dire. Even without the distraction of in limine matters, voir dire can feel awkward to you because it is a unique trial activity. It demands skills and a manner of behavior that you use nowhere else in trial and hardly anywhere else in your practice.

An easy solution: *practice.* A night or two before trial, gather seven or eight people you don't know, pay them $10 or $15, and voir dire them for two hours. Use the same questions you will use in court. Do this a day before your real voir dire in court because such last-minute rehearsal gets you primed for the real task. It will have you up and running—and comfortable as well as effective—right at the start of your real voir dire the next day.

Caveat: Jurors are more forthcoming in practice voir dires than in court. Because the trappings of the courtroom tend to intimidate jurors into silence, you will need to make more persistent use of open-ended questions and follow-ups (see next section, "Conducting Voir Dire") in court than in the practice session.

A final trick to help make voir dire a more comfortable and successful experience: Watch other attorneys' voir dires. Chances are you will think you do voir dire just as well, and that will give you a comforting confidence next time out. And when the attorneys you watch are better than you, you will learn from them.

F: CONDUCTING VOIR DIRE

If you walk into any courtroom during juror voir dire, you can quickly determine whether or not counsel is doing a good job. Just listen to who is doing most of the talking. Badly run voir dires consist of ninety percent counsel talking and ten percent jurors talking. A well run voir dire is the opposite: counsel says little and jurors do most of the talking. Counsel merely asks and listens.

It is almost an absolute principle: The more talking you do, the worse your voir dire. You may wish to educate or indoctrinate, but if you don't get prospective jurors talking before you tell them what to think, they will not reveal the biases and attitudes you need to uncover in order to exercise worthwhile strikes and successful challenges.

Lecturing jurors does little good. Insofar as you can educate or indoctrinate in voir dire, it is best done by asking questions that will lead jurors to say the things you want the rest of the jurors to hear. (See also Chapter 3, p. 59, "Educating Jurors.") Jurors believe each other more readily than they believe you. So don't indoctrinate by asking, for example, "Do all of you agree that home repairmen should be held responsible for the quality of their work?" Such a question persuades no one, and the answers (or lack of them) reveal little, if anything, about any juror.

Instead, ask a bias-seeking question that also educates: "Mr. Smith, when you hire someone to repair something in your home, what do you think you have a right to expect?" Either Mr. Smith or some other juror will respond with what you want the jury to hear: honest pricing, a repair job that stays fixed, decent materials, etc. Keep going until you get what you want. Then ask other jurors if they agree—and why. And be sure to ask what experiences they have had that might have led to their opinions.

This kind of questioning allows jurors to feel that the standards by which they will judge this case come from their own sense of right and wrong, not a lawyer's.

Lecturing jurors in voir dire or asking thinly-disguised indoctrination questions is not only improper, but almost never persuades. Whatever you want the jury to know, if you cannot get it onto the floor via a bias-seeking question or through the answers such a question can elicit, then save it for opening when you can support it by reference to evidence.

Lecturing during voir dire also diminishes the jurors' only opportunity to talk with you. When jurors talk with you, they are bonding with you. Bonding creates rapport and makes jurors want to do what you want them to do.

In brief:

—Get jurors talking so that you know whom to strike, how to challenge for cause, and who your audience is.

—Educate by having jurors teach themselves as they respond to your bias-seeking questions.

—Remember that when jurors talk, they are building rapport with you.

—Don't cross-examine jurors. Listen to them.

—Encourage jurors to debate with each other. (See Chapter 3, p. 50, "Voir Dire Deliberations.")

Test yourself. Tape record your next voir dire and count the words. Is it ninety percent juror talk and ten percent you? Or is it the other way around? If you are talking more than ten percent of the time, here are three ways to improve:

TECHNIQUE #1: ASK OPEN-ENDED QUESTIONS.

Open-ended questions are *non*-leading questions. They suggest no particular answer and cannot be answered in a word or two or even in a phrase or two. (See Chapter 3, p. 47, "Open-ended vs. Close-ended Questions.")

Begin voir dire with open-ended questions that jurors can answer easily and confidently. Ask the jurors about themselves: the things they do, their families, their neighborhoods, and their jobs. "Tell me about your children," "Would you please describe your neighborhood?" or "What do you do on weekends?" starts the conversational ball rolling. Once that happens, you can go on to ask open-ended questions on other topics, and the jurors will continue talking to you.

Close-ended questions are useful only for introducing new topics ("Has anyone ever signed a contract?") or when pursuing a challenge for cause ("You've been afraid of doctors ever since they cut off your leg instead of your arm, haven't you?") Otherwise, avoid them.

Close-ended questions are particularly harmful at the start of your voir dire when they will teach jurors that you expect and want single-word answers. But when your initial questions are open-ended, jurors comprehend and more readily accept that their role is to talk a lot.

TECHNIQUE #2: WATCH and LISTEN.

Watching and actively listening to juror responses not only helps you pick up every possible clue-providing nuance. It also means that you are behaving in a way that encourages fuller responses. *Nod* as a juror answers your question. People continue talking when you nod because they feel you approve of the fact that they are talking and of what they are saying.

Encouraging juror response by how you watch and listen is particularly important when a juror is saying something you don't want to hear. If a juror thinks you don't want to hear something she has to say, she shuts up. But if it is something that seems counter to your case, you need to hear it. When a prospective juror starts revealing an attitude that could hurt you, don't argue, scowl, or shut her off. Listen intently, watch closely, nod, and encourage her to keep talking. Encourage the fact that she is talking, even if you cannot encourage the content.

Don't worry that she will poison the other jurors. If she is expressing a harmful opinion now, she will express it in deliberations, too—so you want to know about it while you can still do something about it, and while you can see which other jurors might agree with or be affected by her. And if she or others who agree with her end up on the jury, you want to know about their harmful opinions so you can deal with them over the course of trial. (See Chapter 4, p. 69, "Bad Attitudes.")

Whatever you do, *don't* turn off a responding juror by exhibiting disapproval or scorn for an answer.

For example, juror Winston might say, "Anyone who drinks even half a beer and then drives a car should be whipped and jailed!" Now, just because you are on defense in this DWI case, don't fight that answer. Don't say, "But Mr. Winston, you'll be able to put aside how you feel and decide this case according to the law, won't you?" That is a pointless close-ended question that shows Winston that you find his answer "wrong," thus stopping him from further revealing how he feels. It usually gets you only the answer that Winston thinks you want to hear ("Sure"), not the answer that might be true. It shuts Winston up and ends any possibility of a challenge for cause.

Instead of resisting what he is saying, encourage Winston to continue talking. Don't make him defensive. Respond as if he is expressing an interesting, intelligent, and legitimate attitude. This will help you get him to explain why he believes what he believes (often by revealing an influential life experience that has created an immutable attitude), how long he has believed it, and *whether he is likely to change his mind in the next few days.*

By pursuing such questioning, you learn about the juror and you increase your odds of a successful challenge for cause—because you have gotten Winston to state, restate, and reinforce his strong feelings, possibly to relate them to his life experiences, and to insist he is not about to have different feelings during the upcoming trial.

TECHNIQUE #3: ASK FOLLOW-UP QUESTIONS.

The point of Technique #2, *watching and listening*, is not only to gather information. Careful, active watching and listening also helps you know what to ask next. For example: "And what about you, Mr. Mason? You looked like you were disagreeing with Mrs. Smith. Tell me about that." Now encourage Mr. Mason as he answers—all the while keeping an eye out for other jurors who might be exhibiting visible signs of having thoughts or feelings about this topic.

If a juror exhibits no sign that he has anything to say, try, "Mr. Jones, I can see you have something to say about this, don't you?" Half the time, he will say no. But the other half of the time, he will indeed have been thinking something—and now you get him talking about it.

As a prospective juror answers a question, find something in his response on which to base a new question that will keep him (or someone else on the panel) talking. If the answer to an occupation question is "I'm a plumber," follow up with, "How did you learn your trade?" If he again answers briefly ("In trade school"), ask him what his favorite or most valuable courses were and why he liked them. Then ask how he found that learning valuable in his life outside of work. Keep trying to get him talking, and he will soon understand that you are not going to be satisfied with short answers. That will usually get him talking more than briefly.

Then ask another juror, "Mr. Turner, Mr. Jones learned to be a computer programmer by going to technical school. How did you learn to be a truck driver?"

(If you are stopped because your question is not relevant, find an area that you can justify by reference to the issues of the case. If an issue is safety, don't just ask about how Mr. Turner learned his job; ask about the kinds of safety measures involved in the job and how he learned them.)

Careful watching and listening for clues to help you formulate follow-up questions is a crucial interviewing skill, yet it is really nothing more than being a decent conversationalist. But it requires you to formulate questions on the spur of the moment—questions that you can justify as bias-seeking. For example, you have to be able to quickly formulate a question such as, "How did you learn to be a software designer?" and be able to explain (if necessary) how it is bias-seeking. (Perhaps the issues in your case make it necessary for you to be wary of jurors who believe that it is easy to learn how to do new things.)

Because you cannot plan follow-up questions in advance, you must spontaneously create questions that both seek bias and do whatever else you want the question to do: educate, create rapport, get a juror talking, etc. To develop this skill, *practice outside of court*. As you are driving to work, think of open-ended questions you might ask jurors. Then justify these questions as bias-seeking. Practice daily on ten or fifteen questions, and soon you will be able to do it instantly and automatically.

(If you have trouble asking open-ended questions, start with "Why," "How," "What," "Tell me about . . . " or "Please explain . . . . " For further guidance, see Chapter 3, p. 47.)

The result of your practice will be a valuable courtroom arsenal: you will be capable of extemporaneously creating questions that seek bias while at the same time designing them to condition, educate, inoculate, create rapport, undermine your opponent's case, test peripheral juror attitudes, etc. And there will be almost no question you cannot figure out a way to ask.

For example: "Mr. Dillon, some people think it's wrong to keep a loaded gun in the house. How do you feel about that—and why?" Your "educational" intention may be to get jurors discussing necessary gun-safety precautions because your case rests on the fact that the defendant observed none. But the question to Mr. Dillon also seeks bias: some people believe there should be no gun rules at all, whereas others believe that no one should keep guns, with or without precautions. You need to know if Mr. Dillon has any such bias and how it might affect his thinking with respect to the issues and people in this case.

USING THE JUDGE.

In addition to the three basic techniques to get jurors talking (asking open-ended questions, watching and listening, and asking follow-up questions), you can also enlist the judge to help. Urge the judge to introduce voir dire by telling prospective jurors that a) there are no wrong answers, and b) the court needs and expects jurors to be forthcoming and to express themselves fully and freely.

CLOTHING.

A final hint: *Dress down* for voir dire. Wear lighter colors, jackets, and slacks rather than suits. Wear looser-flowing skirts and blouses rather than severe fits and lines. Wear clothing that does not distance you from or intimidate jurors. Unbutton your jacket, relax, and talk to these people. Don't make speeches, don't try to impress them, and don't hide your own nervousness behind courtroom formality.

PRACTICE.

If you have not tried this approach to voir dire before, your next step is to practice before you actually go to court. (See Application E, p. 203, on voir dire rehearsal.) Arrange such a practice session the night before every case; it provides a dress rehearsal that allows you to start your case in court much more sure of yourself.

If you know someone who already knows how to do voir dire using the methods described above, have her watch and critique your practice voir dire.

Many trial lawyers have little love for voir dire because voir dire is hard to predict and prepare. But the difficulty diminishes if you think of voir dire as a group conversation. Open-ended questions, good watching and listening, and follow-up questions are the central skills of conducting a group conversation. Develop these techniques through practice and by observing how others apply them. If you learn to run voir dire as a group conversation, jurors will converse.

Bonus: In the future, when one of those jurors needs a lawyer or has to recommend one, she will not choose your opponent who in voir dire talked *at* them and barked cross-examination questions. She will choose you because you came across as a good listener, an intelligent questioner, and—the inevitable conclusion when such qualities are evident—a personable, effective, and honest attorney.

G: PEREMPTORY & CAUSE CHALLENGES: MAKING CHOICES

There is a methodical way to determine what information to seek in voir dire and how to use that information to decide whom to strike. Even your best-run voir dires are useless if you have not carefully planned what to look for or what to do with it when you find it.

The method suggested below derives from social science research, observation of jurors, post-trial juror interviews, and extensive courtroom experience. In every kind of case, it helps you achieve intelligent and productive voir dires that are comfortable for both you and the jurors.

And because voir dire interlocks with everything else, this method leaves you with a juror-based perspective of your case that will be invaluable from pretrial motions through closing.

I. General technique.

This method is a systematic way of 1) identifying important factors in your case that will elicit differing responses from different jurors, and then 2) identifying those jurors who respond the most unfavorably to those factors.

The method is based on the fact that jurors rarely start out by being for or against your case as a whole. Instead, they are for or against particular parts of your case. The way they feel about those particular parts dramatically influences how they perceive everything else in the case.

For example, many jurors believe that anyone arrested is probably guilty. Such a juror does not decide guilt at the outset but honestly thinks she has an open mind. Yet her belief (that anyone arrested is probably guilty) tends to influence her to see every piece of evidence in the best possible light for the prosecution. As a result, she eventually arrives at an "honest" guilty verdict.

You can rarely discover in voir dire how a juror feels about your whole case, but you can find out how jurors respond to individual key matters.

Applying this method diligently enough to rely on the results requires painstaking preparation. But once you have used this method a few times, it will be second nature to you and help you in so many other areas of trial that it will ultimately save you time.

In addition, because this method immerses you in every important individual factor that connects the jurors to your case, it maximizes the sensitivity and accuracy of your jury-selecting instincts. Brilliance is one percent instinct and inspiration, and ninety-nine percent perspiration. This method is mostly perspiration—but it helps you get the most out of your instincts.

II. Selection profile.

The goal of voir dire preparation is to develop a selection profile. A selection profile lists potential juror characteristics (such as opinions, beliefs, attitudes, fears, likes and dislikes, biases, life situations, and life experiences) that can influence how a juror will think and feel about (and thus react to) the laws, principles, people, evidence, and arguments in your case.

Example: a juror who has the characteristic of fearing that the courts are soft on crime will settle for a lower burden of proof than will a prospective juror who has been unjustly fired from her job. Thus, the juror's opinion that the courts are soft on crime influences how the juror interacts with an important factor in the case (burden of proof). A juror with a different characteristic (having been unjustly fired) will have a higher burden-of-proof expectation.

The unequal expectations of each of these two jurors do not only attach to burden of proof but also determine how each juror will interpret and assign weight to every piece of evidence throughout trial. The juror who believes the courts are soft on crime will tend to assign greater weight to every piece of prosecution evidence and less weight to defense evidence, and may even turn some defense-supporting evidence into prosecution-supporting evidence. The unjustly-fired worker will do the opposite.

In other words, *the factors that direct the decision-making process are primarily the juror's characteristics, not the content of the case.*

Juror characteristics determine how jurors will think and feel about every separate thing in the case. By using voir dire to discover those charac-teristics—the characteristics on your selection profile—you can anticipate how each juror is likely to regard your case.

III. Creating a selection profile.

Creating a selection profile requires a careful analysis of your case, as follows:

LIST 1: LAWS AND PRINCIPLES

First, list the important elements of every law, principle, policy, doctrine, and guideline that will be involved in the case. "Self-defense," for example, is too general unless you list its separate elements: "reasonable or necessary force," "no other escape," etc.

Include every element of such applicable laws as negligence, damages, respondeat superior, burden of proof, arson, assault, etc., and such principles as "reasonable person," "standard of care," "good faith," *and whatever else the jury must understand in order to render a verdict.*

Thoroughness is important; carelessly leaving out an element can cost you the case.

LIST 2: CHARACTERS

List every party and important witness (both sides), and indicate the salient characteristics of each. Salient characteristics include but are not limited to race, profession, education, status and social class, age, gender, background, personality type, demeanor, physical appearance, and similarity to the jurors.

LIST 3: FACTS AND TESTIMONY

Make a witness-by-witness list (both sides) of the important points each witness will make and of other important evidence such as documents and texts.

LIST 4: ARGUMENT

List every important contention and argument likely to be made by each side.

LIST 5: VARIABLES

From the items on the first four lists, create a fifth list of *everything that can elicit differing responses from different jurors*.

Items that will elicit *identical* responses from every prospective juror will not help you select. They need not (and should not) be dealt with in voir dire, so they don't belong on your list of variables.

The hard part is to distinguish variables from nonvariables. This requires careful analysis and can also benefit from such means as focus groups, post-trial juror interviews from similar cases, speaking with other attorneys who have conducted similar cases, and drawing on the research skills and experience of jury consultants.

Here are examples of the kinds of variables you will be looking for:

SAMPLE VARIABLES from LIST 1 (Laws and Principles)

Respondeat superior will elicit differing responses from different jurors. Not every juror considers the doctrine fair. Thus, it belongs on your list of variables.

On the other hand, most elements of, say, larceny laws elicit identical responses from all jurors, so those elements don't belong on your list of variables. But do include any elements that might elicit differing responses—such as intent or dollar value.

Another example: By talking to jurors in voir dire or post-trial interviews, you may have discovered that the seriousness with which various jurors regard "standard of care" often depends upon each juror's own particular background. Some jurors believe that standards of care are sacred and should be absolutely obeyed. Others regard standards of care as mere guidelines of varying importance depending on particular circumstances. Thus, "standard of care" belongs on your list of variables.

SAMPLE VARIABLES from LIST 2 (Characters)

Policemen and firemen: Various jurors have differing responses to policemen, so police witnesses on list two should be on your list of variables. On the other hand, firemen rarely belong on your list of variables because everyone regards firemen in the same way. (Except in Los Angeles after the riots when different people regarded firemen in different ways. When such differences exist, firemen should be on your list of variables.)

Physicians: A prospective juror whose close friends include doctors will not want to be on a jury that might award millions of dollars against a doctor. So if such a juror is seated, he is likely to make sure that the jury does not, in fact, become one that awards millions against a doctor. This is not because the juror necessarily favors doctors, but rather because he knows he will have to face his doctor acquaintances long after this trial is history. He will not necessarily vote dishonestly, but he will subconsciously tend to see each piece of evidence in the best light for the doctor. No plaintiff's med mal case can withstand such a viewing of the evidence. Thus, because some jurors have doctors as friends and other jurors do not, include on your list of variables the fact that the defendant is a doctor.

Occupation is not the only character consideration. A witness who is 87 years old will be accorded differing levels of credibility by different jurors. A witness with a foreign accent will be given widely differing levels of respect by different jurors. A witness who stutters will be regarded by some jurors—but not all—as foolish.

SAMPLE VARIABLES from LIST 3 (Facts and Testimony)

Guns: Different jurors will have differing responses to the fact that the defendant kept a loaded rifle in his closet. Some jurors will disapprove; others will think it is a good idea. Since it is capable of eliciting disparate responses, the rifle on list three should be placed on your variables list.

Locked doors: On the other hand, every juror will have similar responses to the fact that the defendant locked his front door before going to sleep. It should not be on your variables list.

Weather: The fact that the weather was bad at the time of the auto wreck elicits juror responses that differ in accordance with each juror's own bad-weather driving experiences, so it goes on your variables list. But evidence that the sun was shining does not go on the variables list, because every juror will respond to that information in the same way.

Money: Arguments concerning the different elements of damages will elicit differing responses from different jurors. For example, different jurors will respond differently to your lost-wages argument if you are seeking money for your client's widow. Jurors who are heavily dependent on a spouse's income might think she should be awarded the full total of the wages your client would have earned if he had lived. But other jurors may decide that because some of those wages would have supported your deceased client, the widow is not entitled to the full amount. Others will decide that since the widow can remarry, she is entitled to little or none of the lost future wages. Since there may be such differences about replacing future lost wages, "lost wages" should be on your variables list. But there will probably be no differences about medical and burial expenses, so those expenses do not belong on your variables list.

SAMPLE VARIABLES from LIST 4 (Arguments)

Complex arguments that persuade some jurors (the smart ones) will merely confuse others (the less-smart ones). Thus, complex arguments from list four should be placed on your variables list.

Arguments that rely on ethical considerations can also elicit differing responses from different jurors; the variable is each juror's own sense of morality. ("If she valued life, she would not have had an abortion.") Thus, ethical arguments, like complex arguments, should be on your list of variables.

On the other hand, jurors will all respond the same way to your argument that a person who volunteered for work at the soup kitchen must care about people. It does not belong on the variables list.

(The items you have left off of the variables list are not necessarily unimportant. You are not eliminating them from the case. You are merely eliminating them as matters to be considered during voir dire, because they will not help you sort favorable jurors from unfavorable.)

ASSEMBLING THE SELECTION PROFILE

Your selection profile is a listing of every likely juror characteristic (including opinions, beliefs, attitudes, fears, likes and dislikes, biases, life situations, and life experiences) that might affect how a juror will think and feel about the items on your variables list.

You can determine these juror characteristics by analysis, common sense, brainstorming with colleagues, interviews with jurors who have been on similar trials, jury research tools including focus groups and jury simulations, and the advice of experienced jury experts. Some attorneys rely heavily on statistical surveys, but experience and research evidence shows this to be a frequently ineffective and always expensive tool. Analysis, discussion, and advice, as well as good focus groups and a common-sense understanding of human behavior, provide better results.

When creating your selection profile, it is essential for you to give the lawyer part of you a day off. Enlist the part of you that is not a lawyer to create your selection profile. Shed your legal mindset and apply instead your best knowledge of real-life human behavior and reactions. If this seems like an utterly alien assignment to you, find a colleague to do it with you. It is often the most important single task in the whole case.

Separating the Good from the Bad.

Selection profile items fall into one of two categories. The first category includes juror characteristics that are likely to interact with items on your variables list in ways that are *good for your case*. For example, the characteristic that a juror is close to doctors will interact positively with the variables list item that your med mal defendant client is a physician.

The second category includes characteristics that are likely to interact with variables-list items in ways that are *bad for your case*. For example, the characteristic that a young juror has four elderly grandparents who are in advanced states of senility may interact negatively with the variables list item that your key witness is 87 years old.

Weighting the profile.

As voir dire progresses, your task is to seek the characteristics that are on your selection profile. With each such characteristic you find in any juror, give it one of four possible weights: *absolute, high, medium,* or *low*. A characteristic's weight indicates how heavily the characteristic can influence that juror's decision. A characteristic that cannot affect a juror's decision has zero weight and, as such, does not belong on your list of juror characteristics.

With each individual juror, a characteristic's weight is determined by gauging two things. First, consider how important the characteristic is to the case (hating alcohol use is usually more important to a DWI case than is believing some cops to be dishonest). Second, consider how strongly the juror holds the characteristic (having a father and two brothers who are doctors is a more strongly held "knows doctors" characteristic than is merely having a friend who is a doctor).

By noting the weight of each of a juror's characteristics, you can quickly rate that juror. An "absolute" (such as a physician on a med mal jury) against you means *get rid of that juror*. Any scattering of lower weights (for such characteristics as, say, sharing particular background traits with your client, not trusting foreign accents, or disapproving of guns in the home) makes you consider dropping that juror and gives you a quantitative way to compare him with other jurors.

This method also helps you to avoid dangerous temptation: If a juror you like has, say, three "highs" against you, she can doom your case despite the dozen "mediums" about her that are in your favor and that make you like her.

Some attorneys and consultants assign a number value to each weight—4 for absolute, 3 for high, 2 for medium, and 1 for low—so that a juror's relative worth can be mathematically computed and compared to other jurors. This is useful as long as you do not let apparent mathematical "certainty" overwhelm your judgment and instincts. Nothing is certain.

Example of using a selection profile: If you are counsel for a med mal permanently damaged juvenile plaintiff seeking a sufficient verdict to pay for home care, you may be tempted to retain a juror who is generous (medium weight in your favor), loves children (medium weight in your favor), is absolutely certain that money is a fair compensation for pain and suffering (high weight in your favor), believes that children belong in their own home (high) and is pretty sure that there is no litigation crisis (medium or low).

You may really want that juror. But your selection profile will spotlight her potentially harmful characteristics: She and her family rely for their health care solely on the agency hospital (high weight against you), she is grateful to doctors for having saved her son's life (medium weight against you), thinks that maybe high medical verdicts—even though deserved—cause health care costs to rise (medium weight against you), and has a handicapped child of her own (medium to high weight against you because she has never received compensation to help her child).

This is a comparative process. Unless there is an "absolute" weighting (for example, if the woman in the preceding example is a nurse), it does not tell you outright to strike any particular juror. Rather, it helps you place that juror on a comparative hierarchy from good to bad.

Caveat: The fewer challenges you are allotted and the less time the judge allows for voir dire, the higher in importance (and thus the fewer) must be your selection profile items.

Other advantages: Your selection profile has the added advantage of being a check list. You can easily keep track of whether you have asked each juror about every item that you have determined in advance to be of importance.

Your selection profile also saves voir dire time because it helps you determine which areas to cover with each particular juror. You needn't ask every juror every possible question. Just select those particular items that are potentially relevant to each juror.

Is that all there is to it?

No. There are two other considerations: *leaders* and *instinct*.

LEADERS

You need to identify which jurors have leadership qualities. A leader carries more than one juror's worth of influence in deliberations. A single leader can—and often does—turn a jury around.

For this reason, you cannot afford to have a leader whose selection profile characteristics are high negatives or even medium negatives. But you need at least one leader with high or medium positives.

Identifying leaders.

You can identify leaders partly by the way they talk in voir dire: do they talk a lot or do they hang back and wait for others to take the lead? Do they offer their own opinions or just agree with others? Do they express themselves clearly, articulately, and persuasively? Do others seem to agree with them, to like them, and to defer to them?

You can spot leaders by such factors as background and occupation. (For example, doctors and teachers are accustomed to telling other people what to do, and people are accustomed to being told what to do by doctors and teachers.) You can also ask jurors to tell you the circumstances in their lives in which they are regarded as leaders. (For guidance in identifying leaders and understanding their influence, see Chapter 3, pp. 54-55.)

Leaders you don't want.

Leaders with negative selection profile characteristics should be put at the top of your list of jurors to challenge. Get them talking as much as possible because, sooner or later, they may become extreme enough in expressing their negative characteristics to give you grounds for a challenge for cause. For this reason (among others), it is always a mistake to cut off discussion with negative jurors.

Moreover, the more negative their remarks, the more likely it is that other jurors will begin to disagree. The ensuing juror remarks can turn into a kind of inter-juror argument, revealing how these jurors think and interact with each other and which of them might be leaders.

Keeping leaders you want.

Though you cannot control whom your opponent challenges, there are some techniques that may help you "hide" leaders you like from your opponent's challenges.

One way to protect a favorable leader is to question non-leaders (or leaders with mixed positive and negative characteristics) in such a way as to elicit so great a flood of positive attributes for your side that your opponent gets nervous enough to challenge. This leaves your opponent with fewer challenges, reducing the chances that he will challenge your leader.

This method of protecting a favorable leader depends on how the numbers work out. It also forces you to risk losing followers who might be good for your side. But you must weigh that cost against the benefit of having the leader you need to bring the jury to the verdict you want.

Don't try to "hide" a positive leader by curtailing your questioning once you discover her strong positive characteristics. Only by thorough questioning can you be sure that this leader does not also have strong negative characteristics. It is safer to risk losing a possibly favorable leader than it is to gamble on accepting a leader who may not be on your side after all.

INSTINCT

Another tool with which to decide who to challenge is *instinct*. You probably already use instinct. Raleigh attorney John R. Edwards simply asks himself whether he wants to spend time with the juror in question. By asking himself that question, he finds he can put together the whole conglomeration of information he has found out about that juror during voir dire. Raleigh attorney Joseph B. Cheshire V thinks about whether he would want to sit down for dinner with that juror and whether he and the juror would like each other.

Some attorneys just ask themselves if they want to walk into the courtroom every day and see that juror.

To make best use of your instincts, consider how well you and the juror seem to get along with each other. Are you comfortable talking with each other? Is there awkwardness or discomfort between you? Are the channels of communication and trust open or shut?

Such methods of bringing your instincts into play will combine the benefits of your instincts with the value of your selection profile and the information you gather in voir dire. This combination can turn weak instincts strong and make strong instincts extraordinarily reliable.

FINAL CAVEAT:

NEVER DO VOIR DIRE ALONE! No matter how small the case, you need someone *other than you* to take notes. If you have no paralegal or secretary who can take notes, hire an office temp.

You cannot learn about jurors if you don't look at them, and you cannot look at them if you are busy taking notes. Every instant your eyes are not on the jury, you are missing an opportunity to gather valuable information. Your momentary glance at what you are writing is often the very moment that a juror does something revealing.

Moreover, you cannot generate good rapport if you keep looking down to write notes. Note-taking interrupts and can even reverse the rapport-building process. Moreover, jurors are less candid when you sit there like some sort of high inquisitor, writing down everything they say.

So bring someone to voir dire to take notes.

In addition to using a note taker, it is also valuable to use another attorney or a consultant to help monitor jurors and participate in your decisions. If you are a one-person firm and the case is too small for a consultant, call in a favor from an attorney friend and bring him along. Return the favor in kind some other time. When questioning a juror, you need someone to monitor the other jurors as they listen. Their visible reactions can be as revealing as anything they say or do when you are questioning them.

It is important for the jury to see you consult your client about selection decisions. But clients are rarely objective or knowledgeable. They may know if a juror dislikes them, or if they instinctively dislike a juror. But clients rarely have your comprehensive overview of the case and you are the one who has to deal with the jurors—so consult with your client but don't lose control of selection.

These voir dire techniques constitute a methodical way of examining how the important matters in your case might relate to individual prospective jurors. You will eventually want to adapt and tailor these techniques to your own style, but first, master them as given. Before you start altering them, see by experience why each step is important.

H: OPENING STATEMENT

Opening is the first time that jurors have nothing to concentrate on but you. Ended are their worries about answering voir dire questions and they are no longer wondering if they are going to have to interrupt their lives for jury service. By opening, their only concern is finding out what you want.

Tell them.

Real estate's three key words are "location, location, location." For openings, they are "structure, structure, structure." There are many good ways to structure openings. The one that follows illustrates general structural principles which you can adapt to a wide variety of cases.

But first, no matter which side you are on or what kind of case it is, there are some things you should never do.

A. NEVER say, "Nothing I say is evidence." It may be a true statement, but why lessen juror attention? Do comedians begin by saying, "Nothing I say is funny"?

B. NEVER speechify. Talk informally and "real," just as you would to friends at lunch. Great persuaders make listeners feel as if they are listening to personal dialogue, not formal oratory.

C. NEVER read your opening (or anything else) from prepared writing. Don't write out complete sentences or phrases. It is fine to work from a skeletal outline or a series of brief notes—but don't have your eyes on it when words are coming out of your mouth. You have to *see* your jurors to convey credibility and create rapport. (See Chapter 1, p. 2 on working from notes.) You have to watch jurors *as you talk* in order to know if you have made your point, if you need to explain further, or if you need to put it another way.

D. NEVER forgo opening. Some attorneys think you cannot do an effective opening before you know your opponent's case. But you know your own case. Not sharing it with jurors at the beginning is like starting a movie with the audience still in the lobby. The advantageous position in closing you may get for forgoing opening is rarely worth it. Jurors tend to continue believing whatever they believe first. Why give up the chance to be first believed?

E. NEVER use legalese. "Pursuant." "Vehicle." "Plaintiff." "Damages." "Compensatory." ". . . have occasion to." Etcetera. Legalese—especially in opening—hurts your persuasive skills and often alienates jurors.

F. NEVER omit using visual aids in your opening. Charts, photos, a piece of real evidence, maps, document blow-ups, etc., are essential in opening. Rule of thumb: Use one visual to support each case-determinative point you make in opening, plus—without fail!—a time line.[1]

These "Nevers" apply to every opening.

The particular opening structure that follows is primarily for personal injury cases, but you can add, delete, and rearrange steps to meet the needs of any kind of case and to make the most of your own personal style and communication strengths.

Opening statement structure:

1. Grabber

2. Case Capsulation

3. Crucial Terms and Concepts

4. Story

5. Catastrophe

6. Aftermath

7. Damages

8. Who You Are Suing (or prosecuting, or defending from) and Why?

9. Undermining the Opposition

10. How Do You Know?

11. Empowerment of Jurors and Larger Significance

The effectiveness of each section depends largely on where you put it, because placement determines context (see Chapter 7, p. 115, "Context"). In an opening, each section creates the context for the next section. As you adapt the following structural sequence to your own particular kind of case, make your adjustments with a constant eye toward creating effective context.

1. GRABBER.

When you start your opening, the jurors' minds are not yet on you or your case. They may still be thinking about voir dire, or their real-life concerns, or your opponent's opening, or any of a number of things other than your case. Thus, they will not hear what you say as well as you might hope. To make them listen carefully, you need to begin your opening by forcefully drawing their attention to what you have to say about your case.

To do this, begin your opening with an attention grabber that startlingly introduces your most case-determinative theme.

In 1994, a courageous public defender screamed at a North Carolina jury, "*MOTHERFUCKER, I'M GOING TO KILL YOU!*" (See Chapter 7, p. 104.)

---

1. For more on time lines, see Chapter 5, p. 83, "Demonstrative and Real Evidence"; Application I, p. 233, "Use time lines," and Application M, p. 261, "Time lines.")

The words startled the jurors out of their seats. They were the words that had been yelled at the defendant on the night in question by a violent drunk. They terrified the defendant into shooting the drunk to protect himself. That opening grabber seared the main defense contention into the jury's consciousness.

Not every beginning can (or should) be that dramatic. But every beginning should be concise (under 25 words) and attention grabbing. Examples:

> "John White will never walk again. Why not? Because Harold Thompson wanted to get to *Forrest Gump* on time."

> "There's the drunk driver. And here's the family with no mother."

> "Acme Corporation did not spend $2 for a safety switch. So Allen Black sits here with no right arm."

2. CASE CAPSULATION.

The context: Once you have grabbed the jurors' attention, it is time to briefly describe the case. But don't do it until now. If you describe the case before you seize juror attention (i.e., before the grabber), jurors' minds will still be on their immediately previous concerns (what happened in voir dire) as well as on real-life concerns (such as what might be happening back at work, who will pick up the kids after school, etc.) Unless you start with a grabber, jurors will not register all you have to say in your case capsulation.

A case capsulation is a brief (under 125 words) narrative overview of the case. For example, "On April 3, 1991, John Smith drives his truck through a highway barricade of orange barrels at 85 miles an hour and slams head-on into Allison Bufort's Honda. He cripples her for life and causes permanent brain damage. An hour before the wreck, he'd had five 16-ounce beers." Say no more. You will fill them in later.

Capsulation provides a necessary context for all that follows, because listeners more easily grasp and remember a story's specifics if they are first told the story's general overview. (When listening to *Little Red Riding Hood*, you particularly notice and remember details about the wolf's teeth if you already have the overview that this is a story about a wolf who tried to eat grandma.)

USE ADJECTIVES AND ADVERBS SPARINGLY. Use strong verbs (such as "slam") a lot, but use modifiers infrequently (don't say "poor Allison"). Let nouns, verbs, and concrete facts tell the story graphically enough to lead jurors to their own conclusions. This is important throughout opening, and especially for your case capsulation.

Rather than an assertion such as, "The weather was bad," say, "It was sleeting, 29 degrees, and the wind was blowing 30 mph." Jurors will draw the right conclusion—and because it is their own conclusion, not force-fed by you, your opponent will have a hard time making them see it another way.

Avoid conclusions and verbal modifiers throughout opening and for the rest of trial. Simply feed jurors the actions and facts from which they can draw your desired conclusions.

3. INTRODUCTION OF CRUCIAL TERMS AND CONCEPTS.

The context: Once the jurors know what the case is about, they are ready to hear an explanation of important technical terms and concepts (standard of care, negligence, emergency reaction time, reasonable person, etc.). But if you explain such terms and concepts before jurors know what the case is about (i.e., before the capsulation), they will have no reason to pay attention. Even if they do pay attention, the information will be abstract because they have no context for it. For example, the definition of "standard of care" is meaningless—and therefore forgettable—until they know something about your case. That is why your explanation of terms and concepts follows your case capsulation.

The explanation of terms and concepts is important because jurors cannot act on what they don't understand. If allowed, explain terms such as "standard of care," "compensatory," "punitive," "notice," etc. Civil plaintiff lawyers often feel it necessary to explain "preponderance of the evidence," but consider carefully how to tell the jury that you need not fully prove your case. (See Chapter 10, p. 158, "Preponderance of the Evidence.")

Defining terms and concepts allows you to persuade as well as inform. For example, explaining "reasonable person" both instructs *and* persuades that citizens are legally expected to exercise reasonable care and attention.

Caveat: Jurors remember concepts, not technical words. If you define "compensatory" in opening, its meaning will stay in jurors' minds all the way through trial, but the term itself will have to be briefly redefined when you use it later.

4. STORY.

The context: By now you have established a context of three things: attention, awareness of the case's overview, and awareness of terms and concepts on which the case turns. Now the jurors are primed to hear your story of the case in all its necessary detail. If you had tried telling the full story before establishing this context, jurors would pay less attention and much of the story would make no sense to them.

Moreover, if jurors know basic concepts in advance they will draw their own conclusions about who is right or wrong without your having to tell them. If they understand the concept of "standard of care" as they hear your full story, they will conclude for themselves that a standard of care was violated. This is a more effective way to persuade than just telling them what you want them to believe.

The full story of what happened should be told in three parts. Do not refer to the catastrophe itself until you finish with these three:

First, describe your client's day leading up to the catastrophe.

Second, go back in time. Leave the jury hanging on the verge of the catastrophe while you go back to tell about your client's life over the days and months before the catastrophe.

Third, describe the defendant's actions in the last moments leading up to the catastrophe. This section of opening ends just before the catastrophe. (The catstrophe is part 5 of your opening.)

These three story parts are described in detail below. In each, you will be a better storyteller if you tell the story in the present tense and through your client's eyes (see Chapter 8, p. 136, "Point of View"), and humanize your client (see Chapter 7, p. 133, "Humanizing" and the sections following it). It is also crucial to use visual aids for your main points: real evidence, charts, maps, photos, document blow-ups, etc.

FIRST, tell the story of your client's day up to but not including the catastrophe. Tell it from your client's point of view: What did she see, feel, hear, taste, smell, think, want? Include what she had been planning in the minutes and hours before the catastrophe. For example, when your client got dressed that morning, what was she dressing to do that she never got to do because of the catastrophe?

Humanize your client: What did she eat and wear? To whom did she talk? What were her immediate plans? Use details that portray a human being with whom jurors can identify.

Tell about things she did that day that she can no longer do (such as mowing her lawn or putting on her clothes). Don't yet say that she cannot do those things anymore; that step comes later.

If there is a question of shared negligence due to anything she did leading up to the catastrophe, describe her actions in a way that makes clear that she did nothing wrong. But draw no conclusions (don't say, "she did nothing wrong"). Let her actions speak for themselves.

Use present-tense verbs, not past. Present tense lends immediacy: "By 8 a.m. on April 3, 1991, the sun is shining and Allison Bufort, in her old ripped jeans and straw hat, is working in her yard. She mows her lawn, then plants two rows of corn where they will get plenty of sun alongside the garage. At 11 a.m. she goes inside, drinks a glass of iced tea, then showers, puts on her blue skirt, white blouse, and brown leather shoes. She's getting ready to take her boss to lunch. She's planning to tell him she's resigning as chief teller at the bank because she's been hired to be branch manager at another bank."

Continue step by step until just before the catastrophe. If it is a car wreck, continue up to the last moment when she is driving along with nothing wrong.

Then STOP. It is time for the next part of the story:

SECOND, go back in time. Shifting to past tense, describe your client's life during the days and months before the wreck. Use a signpost (see Chapter 7, p. 122, "Signposts") so the jurors can easily stay with you: "Now let me tell you about Allison's life before that moment. Let's look at a typical day. Every morning for years, Allison made biscuits from scratch, then ran upstairs to roust her two kids from bed . . . ." Don't yet say how the catastrophe changed things; just describe how things used to be.

Then come back to the moment just before the catastrophe, and continue from where you left off before: "We're back now to early afternoon, April 3. Allison is slowing down to take the Eastway exit up ahead. In the oncoming lane is a white pick-up truck a hundred yards away. The gap between them is closing at a combined speed of 135 miles an hour—Allison at 50, the truck at 85. *Now let's go back and see how that white truck got there and why it was going so fast.*"

THIRD, go back in time as far as necessary to show what the defendant did that led to the catastrophe. For example, "John Smith stops at the 7-11 to buy his daily six-pack of Budweiser tall cans." Note that the correct placement of such information sways the case before you even describe the wreck. Use present tense again, avoid conclusions, and take us to the verge of the catastrophe.

5. CATASTROPHE.

The context: Once the jurors have a complete picture of all that has led up to the catastrophe, they are primed to hear about the catastrophe. They understand the background situation, they know why it happened, they comprehend the legal concepts involved, and they have emotional connections to the people involved. If you had delivered the catastrophe before having established all this, the catastrophe's emotional impact would have been an *uninformed* emotional impact and would thus be an unreliable motivator of juror belief and behavior. Jurors would remember the horrible thing that happened to your client but they would not be motivated to do what you want them to do. So tell the full story first, and then the catastrophe.

Be sure to dwell on the catastrophe even if nothing about it is in contention, because it is a prime motivator of the jurors' decision-making process. This is true even in criminal cases. If jurors ultimately decide that the real catastrophe was the crime, then the defendant is in trouble. But if they think that the catastrophe of this case was the arrest of a person who might have done nothing wrong, then the state's case is in trouble. A criminal case revolves around the jurors' ultimate decision as to which is the real catastrophe.

The same principle operates with respect to civil defense. Is the real catastrophe what the plaintiff claims it to be—or is it the circumstances that led to someone filing outrageous contentions against your client? In criminal or civil cases, your task in this section of your opening is to etch onto the jurors' memories and emotions the catastrophe *as understood from your client's point of view.*

To do this, describe the catastrophe in present tense the same way you have been telling the story. But shift gears. Until now, your story has been like a movie: narrative motion-picture scenes that cover a period of time during which people were engaged in doing things (planting corn, driving to work, buying beer, etc.). But when you get to the catastrophe, stop the movie camera. Describe the catastrophe by means of still photos: strobe shots that are like stop-action bites or flash-frozen instants. These frozen instants make the catastrophe clear and visceral, rendering it more important than everything else.

One frame at a time, state what your client sees, hears, feels:

"Allison sees the truck cross the line, smashing two yellow pylons." (pause)

"The truck is in front of her, yards away." (pause)

"Allison swerves hard right toward the gray barricade." (pause)

"She sees the truck driver looking down at the seat beside him." (pause)

"Allison hears a shriek of metal against the concrete barricade." (pause)

"Her car wrenches under her as the concrete barricade bounces her like a billiard ball." (pause)

"She hears her brakes screeching." (pause)

"She hears the brakes from the car behind her." (pause)

"She sees the truck driver still looking down at his seat. She does not know he's looking for a bag of pretzels." (pause)

"The impact catapults her head into the steering wheel." (pause)

"Her head breaks the wheel." (pause)

"The impact cracks her skull." (pause)

"Her chest is crushed forward into the steering column, breaking all her ribs." (pause)

"Her head snaps back but her body is wedged in place by the seat." (pause)

And so forth.

The pauses should be split-second brief but distinct. They help emblazon your stop-action "photos" onto the jury's consciousness. The opposition will not easily overcome those pictures.

As you narrate, use charts, diagrams, photos, and maps as appropriate (and as allowed). For example, point at the barricade when you say that Allison swerves into it.

If there is a question of shared negligence, include in your stop-action narrative the right things she did (drove at 50 mph, blew her horn, swerved). If she did anything wrong (such as hitting her brakes too hard and losing control of the car), first show the preceding emergent event(s) that caused her to lose her ability to make reasonable judgments. In other words, don't just show that she hit the brakes hard; make that action the result of the sudden appearance of the truck headed right for her.

6. AFTERMATH (plaintiffs only).

First describe the nature and extent of the specific injuries. Then describe the *effect* of those injuries: How did the injuries resolve, and how have they disabled her?

Don't mix those two descriptions. First describe the nature and extent of each injury; then go back and describe the effects of each injury. The separation lets you cash in on the details you used in Part 4 (describing your client's life leading up to the catastrophe) to help you describe the effects. Contrast what she could do before with what she can*not* do now; specific activities such as working in her yard, mowing the lawn, taking a shower, working as a bank teller, etc. ("She can no longer stand at the stove and make biscuits or stand at a bank counter and conduct transactions.") A before-and-after theme bolsters every plaintiff's injury case.

Avoid medical explanations when first describing injuries. Prematurely explaining medical matters confuses the jury and dissipates the impact of hearing about the injuries. Wait until you have described the injuries and their effects. Then offer underlying medical explanations (for example, explain medical reasons why she cannot move, communicate, or breathe comfortably).

Visual support is invaluable: medical reports, X-rays, prescription forms, etc.

Finish this section by describing prognosis and degree of permanence.

7. DAMAGES.

What has this cost and what is it going to cost? Use general figures ("Her medical expenses so far have gone over $300,000 and she'll need $3,000,000 more to take care of her from now on"). Include "in-kind" costs: for example, the value of her spouse's time caring for her after the catastrophe. (Be careful with such in-kind values: You don't want to make it seem as if her husband is actually charging to take care of her.)

Point out that the worst of her losses goes beyond tangibles and includes her permanent pain as well as the mental anguish caused by her pain and disabilities.

8. WHO YOU ARE SUING (OR PROSECUTING, OR DEFENDING FROM), AND WHY.

Plaintiffs or prosecutors should describe the defendant(s). Be explicit about a) who they are, b) what they did that caused the catastrophe, and c) their legal and moral transgressions and responsibilities.

Defense should describe the opponent party(-ies). Be explicit about who they are and why they are wrong in bringing this case.

9. UNDERMINING THE OPPOSITION.[2]

Don't leave a tree standing. Not even a bush. Make rubble of every case-pivotal point that your opponent is going to offer. Do this not by stating the opposing contention and then arguing it down (that is defensive and in some jurisdictions improper), but by aggressively describing the evidence you have that will prove your case and automatically disprove your opponent's. If you know that the opposition will contend that the construction zone was inadequately marked, don't make a defensive statement such as, "You'll hear that the construction zone was not well marked, but we'll show you that it was." Don't even mention the opposition claim. Just offer a positive statement ("The area was marked.") and show photos of the two hundred orange barricade barrels, the hundred red pylons, the ten signs, and the two flagmen.

Any opposition contentions that you do not undermine in opening will be dangerously potent afterwards.

Preparing this section of your opening provides you with an excellent way to gauge—in advance—the strength of your case. If, in preparation, you cannot figure out how to successfully undermine every opposition contention in opening, you will not be able to do it later in trial either. The earlier you find that out, the better you can serve your client.

10. HOW DO YOU KNOW?

It may hurt your feelings to be told that you are the least credible person in the courtroom, but you are. Jurors will not take your word for anything, especially not in opening. That means you have to tell the jurors how you know—and by extension how they will know—the truth of everything you have been telling them. This is when to talk about your experts, your evidence, your authoritative foundations (such as textbooks), and any other ways you have of supporting your assertions.

Don't ask jurors to take your word for anything. Show how they can know you are right. Ironically, the more you do that, the more they will accept your unsupported assertions as the trial progresses. This principle dictates that you

---

2. The sections "Who You Are Suing and Why" and "Undermining the Opposition" were initially named and developed by Diane Wiley of the National Jury Project.

delay mention of your less supportable assertions until after you have shown jurors how fully you can support your earlier assertions.

As a general rule, it is a persuasion-technique blunder to make unsupported assertions in opening and delay the "how you know" until testimony. For example, it is not persuasive merely to profess that the standard of care did not require an X-ray. Explain how you know that your understanding of the standard of care is accurate ("The head of neurology at Duke will show you three textbooks . . . . ")

Unsupported assertions raise questions. Your opening should resolve, not raise, questions.[3]

11. JUROR EMPOWERMENT and LARGER SIGNIFICANCE.

Tell jurors that they are the reason this event is taking place. Let them know how their role is central: that it is solely up to them to judge the facts and weigh the evidence. Tell them what they will be asked to decide. Come as close as you can to using what the jury instructions will say.

Then show the jurors the larger significance of this case: why it is important beyond itself. Remaining within proper boundaries (see below), explain how people just like these jurors—not only your client—are affected by the issues in this case. (See Chapter 7, p. 130, "Larger Significance.")

It is useful but insufficient to say merely that jury service is important. Given current attitudes in vogue about the court system, you must make jurors see why service is important *on this particular case*.

Present larger significance properly. Offer it as upcoming evidence—something, for example, that an expert is going to say. (Caveat: If you are a criminal prosecutor, it can be a mistrial to do it at all.)

THREE MORE POINTERS:

1. Get into the habit of noting every effective opening tactic you ever see, including those used against you. Employ them yourself next time.

2. After trial, ask jurors what they remember from the openings and how they felt after each counsel's opening. Incorporate what you learn into the next opening you do.

3. Practice your opening. The best structure and preparation in the world fall apart when unrehearsed.

---

3. Writing communications expert Katharine M. Wilson points out that the failure of expository writers to include "how do I know" validations is their most harmful persuasive omission, and that such an omission can *single-handedly* undermine such introductory oral communications as opening statements.

I: TRUTH

Being believed by jurors is not easy. Credibility does not reside simply in your honest smile, believable voice, and trustworthy demeanor. Even with all three working in your favor, jurors don't automatically believe you.

Though jurors may not believe that you are always telling them the truth, they do believe that both you and your opponent *know* the truth. Yet because you are each claiming the truth for your own side, common sense tells jurors that one (or both) of you is mistaken or lying. To help decide whom to believe, jurors scrutinize every clue as to which counsel can be trusted and which counsel is lying or in error. Because neither counsel overtly lies or makes gross errors, jurors rely on subtler clues.

The following techniques help you control those clues. They will also start you thinking in terms of creating, protecting, and enhancing your credibility at every instant you are in court.

LEAD JURORS TO THEIR OWN CONCLUSIONS

Don't tell jurors what to think. "Stanley Brown is a generous person" tells jurors what you want them to think but gives them no reason to think it. The statement asks them to take your assertion on faith. Sometimes they will, sometimes they won't. Not good enough.

Instead of providing pre-digested conclusions that jurors may or may not swallow, you should provide facts, authoritative support, and logic that lead jurors to arrive at your conclusions on their own. For example, the statement "Every year Stanley Brown gives half his income to the poor" provides a fact that helps lead jurors to the conclusion you want.

Concrete facts not only support your contentions. They are also a compelling, memorable means of communication. This is because visual and tactile facts such as "wind gusts" and "sideways sleet" or behavioral examples such as "gives his income to the poor" communicate vigorously and are remembered. Abstracts such as "bad weather" and "generous guy" communicate weakly and are easily forgotten.

Many adverbs and some adjectives are conclusions because they can be debatable value judgments. "He drove *recklessly*" is one such adverbial conclusion. "He was a *nice* guy" is adjectival. Instead of "He drove recklessly," say, "He was doing 90, cutting through traffic, and trying to dislodge a cassette from the tape player." "Driving carelessly" is a debatable value judgment. Doing 90, cutting through traffic, and fiddling with the tape are facts.

Note how the facts not only provide credibility but convey that the driving was worse than merely "reckless."

Jurors don't like being told what to think. They are not persuaded by it. They prefer building blocks that help them structure their own conclusions.

SUPPORTING YOUR ASSERTIONS

Don't support an assertion or conclusion with another assertion or conclusion. "We know our client was driving safely because she looked at her
speedometer and it said 35." That is like saying, "We know our client was
driving safely because she says she was." It carries no weight. Worse, it implies
that you have no evidence, thus arousing greater question than if you had
never said anything at all.

Insofar as possible, validate every assertion either with demonstrable *fact*
("We know Sally was driving safely because the state trooper clocked her at
30"), or with reasonable *argument* ("We know Sally was driving safely because
if she had not been, the state trooper behind her for ten miles would have
noticed"), or by citing a believable *authority* ("We know Sally was driving safely
because this graph of her speed was recorded automatically by the trooper's
radar system.")

Often, trial attorneys don't validate an assertion right away because they
know it will be fully and easily validated later. But this is poor persuasive
technique. By the time the assertion is validated, temporary doubt about it can
have affected the jurors' responses to many other assertions. Thus, an assertion
should be immediately followed by its validation, or at least an indication of
how you will validate it ("We know it was daytime because that's what three
witnesses will tell us.")

This article is full of unsupported assertions. But we are not in court and
I am not trying to persuade you. I am merely offering suggestions from which
you can pick and choose. In court, however, you don't want jurors to regard
your assertions as mere suggestions, and you don't want jurors to pick and
choose.

You gain control in court by using facts, logical arguments, or authorities
(experts and textbooks) that jurors can believe. Support every assertion, fact,
argument, observation, and opinion by making clear *how you know it to be true.*
Jurors expect you to show them why they should believe your contentions.
When you fail that expectation, they lose faith in you—even when you are
accurate and truthful.

USE THE BS PRINCIPLE

Before you decide to make any statement, consider the potential reactions
of jurors who might disagree with you. O.J. Simpson Prosecutor Marcia Clark
undermined her own credibility when she said in closing that L.A. cops could
not have gotten into Simpson's Bronco had it been locked. Any jurors still
capable of listening critically must have been astonished to hear her say such
a thing. After all, when you are locked out of your car, who do you call? A cop!

A Bad Statement (BS) is one that is not only obviously false but also calls
into question your general good sense and veracity. Such damage to your

credibility can ripple through everything else you say. This is especially dangerous in closing, because undecided jurors who are looking for ways to decide the case will be affected by any undermining of your credibility.

Before you make a questionable assertion that you cannot prove, apply the BS Test to discover any possible worst-case reactions of jurors who disagree most. The BS Test consists of examining your proposed statement from the point of view of a rabid disbeliever: "The statement is BS because _____" (for example, " . . . because cops can easily open any locked vehicle"). Then weigh whether such a potentially damaging conclusion will do more harm to your general credibility than the statement is worth in the first place.

USE TIME LINES

You gain credibility by showing jurors how your version of the facts fits logically and plausibly into a time line. Unfortunately, few attorneys provide time lines. As a result, even informal studies show that many jurors begin deliberations confused or uncertain about time sequence, and consequently can make enormous errors in judgment. Not only does your overall case need a time line, but subsections of your case (such as specific events during a physician's office visit) also need a time line.

You will find that assembling a time line is difficult. But if it is difficult for you, think how much harder it will be for jurors. When you offer no time line, jurors use your opponent's. When neither of you offers a time line, jurors make their own. Their inaccuracies can undermine your case.

As early as opening, but no later than the early part of your case-in-chief, provide a clear time line. And use it in closing to organize your review of the evidence.

BE YOURSELF

The problem: Mannerisms, behavior that is unnatural or artificial, or the technical vocabulary of any profession can make jurors think that you are pretending—i.e., not completely trustworthy. To be credible in court, you have to act like the real you. To act like the real you, you first have to know who the real you actually is. Here are two ways to find out:

1. Next time you go to court, bring someone who knows you well: a spouse, an older child, a sibling, a close friend—someone comfortable telling you the truth even when you might not want to hear it. Have that person note everything you do that seems different from the way you do it in real life.

2. Have someone videotape you at home and in the office. He should follow you around with the video camera for a few days until you get used to it and ignore it. The result will be a video of how you talk and act in real life.

Then have yourself videotaped in court (if possible) or working in front of a group of mock jurors hired for a couple of hours.

Carefully compare the two videos for differences in how you talk, how you move, and how you behave. Ask yourself which version of you seems easier for a real human being (such as a juror) to attach credence to.

Caveat: "Being yourself" does not mean being *all* of yourself. We all have characteristics that don't belong in court. Perhaps you have a quick temper and easily become caustic. Or perhaps in confrontational situations you tend to bully people. You may even have personal habits that are less than mannerly. On court days, leave *those* parts of the real you at home under the bed. Bring only the parts of you that help you be persuasive, personable, and credible.

In brief: Change your courtroom behaviors that are not part of the real you, and eliminate "real you" behaviors that don't belong in court.

AVOID FORMALITY

Speaking in formal tones undermines your rapport, your persuasive powers, and your credibility. Acting stiffly formal keeps jurors from taking you seriously.

Unlike in earlier eras, formal courtroom speech and behavior today arouse juror suspicion. Jurors expect you to talk like a real person, not like an orator. Certainly there are times when heightened oratory is appropriate. But heightened oratory that is successfully persuasive (such as Martin Luther King's) remains person-to-person and even seems conversational.

The courtroom is formal enough. Don't add to its formality by speechifying when you speak, or by behaving stiffly, artificially, or stuffily. Be serious but be human.

Avoiding formality does not mean being disrespectful, sloppy, clownish, or otherwise inappropriate. It merely means being relaxed, open, and confident enough not to fall back on artificial behaviors and mannerisms.

To break through the courtroom's formality and sound real, you need learn nothing new. You already sound real when you speak in real life. So in court talk nonformally and conversationally: person-to-person and *human*.

It is easier to do this if you *look* at your jurors. They are real people, not Greek statues. Make eye contact. Talk to them face-to-face and seriously about the case—as if you were having lunch with a friend or your dad and telling him about your case. Your dad would look at you most strangely if you suddenly stiffened up and elevated your conversational tones into speechifying. He would think three things: that something has gone wrong with you, that you have turned unbearably stuffy and insecure, *and that you are making something up*. In other words, he would stop believing you.

When you force jurors to listen to your formal speechifying, they just want you to siddown and shaddup. In the narrow confines of a courtroom, speechifying is stiff, unnatural, confrontational, hard to follow, and less persuasive than any other form of discourse except screaming. Worst of all, it masks counsel's humanity.

When I am in court, I have a simple test to determine whether counsel is formally speechifying or being real: I shut my eyes. Counsel's sound clearly reveals stuffy oratory—or just good old plain talking, the way people talk to each other in real life.

Jurors interviewed after a recent trial noted that aside from deciding 10-2 on a verdict, the jury also decided 12-0 that plaintiff's counsel, a formal puffer and huffer, talked like a pompous ass and marched around the courtroom (in the words of one juror) "like a chicken." That juror said, "We'd never buy a used car from him. Eggs, maybe." Yet that attorney does not come across that way outside of court. He is normal, real, and relaxed. Moral: Be your normal, informal self. Talk real. Act real.

If your opponent takes the formal route, tell her she's doing great.

DON'T TURN YOUR BACK

Few attorneys readily accept this wisdom, but centuries of theater experience and decades of communications research show it to be true: *Never turn your back on jurors—not even momentarily.*

The reasons not to turn your back are multiple and complex. Simply put, your backside is less credible than your face. (With some people the opposite may be the case, but that presents a dilemma beyond my powers to assist you with.) Turning away implies that you have something to hide. So even at a bench conference, stand at an angle that lets jurors see you from the side. Let your opponent aim rump at the jury.

Every time you show the jury your back you chip away at your credibility. Over the course of trial those tiny, subliminal chips add up.

There are many ways to make your honesty apparent to jurors. The first step is to begin to pay attention to the process at every moment that you and the jury are in the same room.

It is necessary but hard to be sufficiently credible at all times. It is harder still to do so without seeming as if you are *trying*. But you must succeed. A trial is a credibility battle between opposing counsels. Truth is useless to you unless jurors trust you.

J: READING THE JURORS

Many attorneys reading this will think they are no good at determining how jurors are reacting at any given time. But you can develop your ability to perceive at least some juror reactions. It is not a fuzzy-feely process. It is a learnable skill composed of learnable techniques.

These techniques will help you read juror reactions well enough to provide some clues as to how things are going: when you are doing well, when you are not, when you need to try something different (or differently), when to do something again, and even how to do it.

Before explaining the techniques, here is an example of what you can do based on a jury's reactions:

CHOOSING EMOTIONAL TONE ON CROSS

1. *Mirroring.* "Lawyerese formal" is rarely an effective tone for you to use for every cross-examination topic and witness (or for anything else, for that matter). Of all possible tones (such as anger, sympathy, interest, disinterest, concern, disgust, aggressiveness, neutrality, or friendliness), the dreary tone of "lawyerese formal" most makes jurors tune you out—or want to kick you out. A more effective choice of cross-examination tone is best made according to how jurors are feeling at that specific moment about that specific topic and that witness. For example, if jurors are sympathetic to the plight of a witness, you might choose to mirror their sympathy.

Don't let your attitude toward a witness contradict the jury's feelings about that witness. Don't be hostile or overbearing to a witness the jurors feel sorry for (unless you are certain that the results of your cross will get them angry at the witness). Conversely, don't be friendly to a witness the jury hates. And unless you have a reason for wanting to seem aggressive, don't be formal with a witness who is obviously scared of the courtroom environment. In other words, try to align your emotional tone with what the jury seems to be feeling.

In films and stage plays, a character whose tone conflicts with the audience's feelings alienates the audience. This is the basis of creating effective villains. The good guy is the one whose tone mirrors the audience's.

It is the same in court. Alignment between your tone and the jurors' feelings creates rapport and trust and makes the jury feel as if you are working *with* them. But disjuncture between your tone and the jurors' feelings can cause jurors to regard you—not the witness—with detachment, hostility, or suspicion.

This makes a neutral tone safe because it does not conflict with any juror feeling. It is the tone of choice when you are getting a variety of different feelings from the jurors. But in *needless* safety lies mediocrity; overuse of a neutral tone bores jurors into listening less carefully. Eventually, many of them stop listening altogether.

Overuse of a neutral tone also masks your passion for the case and your interest in your work. That makes you less credible and, in jurors' eyes, ultimately less worthy of prevailing. (If jurors think you don't care, they often assume it is because you don't think your client should win.)

So don't settle for neutral just because it is safe. If you can develop a sensitivity for how jurors are feeling, you will be able to mirror their feelings. That makes you more interesting to them than a neutral tone can, and will align you with them.

2. Underplaying. In terms of tone, it is important not to seem *more* suspicious (or whatever) than are the jurors. Be slightly *less* so, or jurors will feel you are trying to shove your feeling down their throats.

In other words, decide how the jury is feeling, and slightly underplay that feeling. If jurors are angry at a witness, your tone should reveal an anger slightly less than what you think the jury feels.

This is important because you cannot change how a jury feels about a witness by exhibiting a feeling (or intensity of feeling) about that witness that the jury does not already have. Jurors often resent it when you try. Unless you are a speaker of great charisma, it rarely works—and can sometimes backfire.

Igniting juror feelings is like igniting a fire: Start with a small spark. Fan the spark by mirroring and underplaying. If you fan the spark too hard, it goes out. Proceed gently; don't get ahead of what the spark can support.

You light a fire with a tiny match, not by screaming, "Conflagration!"

When you mirror and underplay what jurors are already feeling, you verify and reinforce juror feelings, create rapport instead of suspicion, and you will not come across as "too much." And when you have a sense of what jurors are feeling and how intensely they are feeling it, you will be more comfortable and confident letting your own similar feelings come to the fore.

This technique is so useful that even by itself it makes it worth your effort to develop your juror-reading skills. There are many such useful techniques. In fact, the usefulness of almost every persuasive skill you ever learn increases proportionally with your jury-reading skills.

So how do you sharpen those skills?

To start with, *reposition the jurors in your priorities.* So much competes for your attention in court that it is easy to ignore the jury. But jurors know when they are the last thing on your mind. Make them the first.

There are five ways to do that. Three are to be done in court, the fourth is for real life, and the fifth is something to do after your next (and every) trial.

I. LOOK AT JURORS

The more you look at your jury, the more you will perceive their feelings. And certainly when you don't look you will perceive nothing.

Some attorneys worry that looking at jurors makes jurors uncomfortable. It is true that if you look only rarely, your occasional glance may seem odd and even suspicious. If you conduct hours of testimony without looking their way, when you finally look it is jarring. But if you establish early on that the jurors are the audience for whom you are working, and if you look their way regularly instead of once in a while, then looking at them will seem open and appropriate, and they will be comfortable with it.

Every attorney looks at the jury during voir dire and opening. But many stop when testimony begins, and until closing barely glance that way again. This rudely breaks off the two-way communication and feeling of juror participation created in voir dire and opening. It is like a colleague inexplicably wandering away right in the middle of an important conversation.

To solve this, make an extra effort to make visual contact with the jurors when you begin examining or cross examining your first witnesses. Look over at the jury as you listen to the witness's answer. Study the jury as if they are the ones who can tell you what the next question should be. As you look at the jurors, ask from their point of view, "What question do *we* want next? What do *we* want to know?"

Of course, you can go too far. You will discomfit jurors—if not freak them out—if you just stare at them or look only at certain ones. But if you watch them comfortably, naturally, and easily, moving your glance from juror to juror the way you do when talking with any group of people, you will make no one uncomfortable. (If you are not sure how to do this, pay attention to how you do it in real life when you are talking with any small group of people.)

In a recent North Carolina trial, the eyes of one of the nation's most famous criminal defense attorneys were on the jury 58 percent of the time (measured by stopwatch) during a three-hour cross-examination. One of New York's most successful plaintiff attorneys—Tom Moore—watches the jury even more than that—on direct as well as on cross. If such outstanding lawyers need to watch jurors that much, so do you. Not looking at your jurors is like hiding your head in the sand.

Frequent visual contact with jurors creates rapport, trust, and empathic identification. It makes jurors pay closer attention to you, and they tend to perceive what you say in a more favorable light. Most important, it is the first step toward developing your jury-reading abilities.

Not watching the jury is like shutting your eyes while driving fast. In your car that is called negligence. Is court a safer place?

II. GO TO A JURY CALL

For a variety of reasons, including the development of your jury-reading abilities, it is worth your time to participate in a jury call.

Cajole the jury clerk into letting you sit in on orientation for a newly arriving venire panel. (Do this at a time far removed from any trial of your own.) Juror orientation consists of remarks by the clerk and sometimes the showing of a videotape. There may also be materials either mailed to jurors to read in advance or distributed at the jury call.

Make your participation as real and complete as possible. Start the day by parking in or near the same lot as the jurors, making the same walk to the courthouse, and continuing with the day exactly as they do.

Wait around with them for the hours or morning or whole day(s) it takes before they are finally called into court.

Don't bring any work with you. Most jurors don't, and you want to experience for yourself the awful feeling of wasted time they carry with them into voir dire.

Go with them into the courtroom (though you will have to sit in back). *And sit there no matter how long voir dire takes.*

You will gain a whole new understanding of juror attitudes.

You will learn how jurors feel at the start of voir dire and as it drags on, and what makes them feel that way. That is a big first step in understanding juror mind-set and feelings during trial. And it is of inestimable help next time you do voir dire.

Participate in the experience and you will understand the feelings.

For example, here is a true story: Last year on a bad-weather morning (forty degrees, gusty winds, wet sidewalks, and grey sky), I was walking to court. An unexpected rain had started, and four people, including an elderly, frail woman, took refuge beneath an awning. I joined them. It quickly became apparent that they were unhappy about something other than the rain.

What they were unhappy about was the decision of some bureaucrat. Despite the spacious and mostly empty parking deck directly across from the courthouse, the bureaucrat had decreed that jurors would park several long blocks away.

Every juror who makes that hike, especially in bad weather, arrives at the courthouse and spots that roomy parking deck across the street. Some of them worry about the prospect of making that long walk back, perhaps alone, late in the day when downtown streets may not seem safe. Result: Jurors entering the courthouse may not only be nervous and wet, but justifiably annoyed at the system. Jurors don't know who runs the system, so their annoyance attaches not just to the bureaucrats but to everyone—including counsel. In fact, you are almost the only one they get to talk to.

The parking situation is merely the first of a series of indignities, inconveniences, and outright rudenesses to which jurors are subjected in many courthouses before they walk into voir dire. Thus, when conducting voir dire, extra warmth and hospitality on your part are essential. More human gratitude and less lawyerly formality will show jurors that you are not one of the uncaring bureaucrats who are oblivious to the comfort, dignity, and safety of citizens doing their duty.[1]

The treatment of jurors affects how they feel in voir dire and throughout trial. If you have taken the trouble to experience a juror's voir dire day for yourself—whether it is good or bad—you will better understand what jurors are feeling when they first get to your voir dire. That will help you to begin reading juror feelings and continue reading them all through trial.

Do you need further convincing that jurors are not always the merry group of volunteers you might take them for? When you go to a jury call, *don't take your cellular phone*. During the day, try making a phone call. In most courthouses, you are forced to wait in line for the same few phones during the same recess as all the other jurors, observers, participants, and witnesses—because the courthouse will not come up with a few hundred bucks a year for a local-calls phone in the jury waiting room.

There is not even a sign informing citizens where they can find other phones. Thus, because no one has time to go exploring during a brief recess, there is usually a line at the fifth-floor phone and no one at the third. And recesses often end before everyone has managed to make the call they needed to.

It gets worse. There are no pay phones in many federal courthouses. There is no way a juror can make a phone call. If a juror needs to check on a babysitter or arrange a ride home, it cannot be done. Prisoners get one phone call; jurors get none. Jurors get the message loud and clear: "The court system does not think much of jurors." And jurors consider you part of the court system.

For these reasons or others that are similar, when jurors come in for your voir dire, they usually have reason to be angry or at least out of sorts. Some will associate you with the jerks who removed the phones, provided too few chairs in the waiting room (if there is a waiting room), forced them to park blocks away, and brought them in at the crack of dawn to do nothing for an hour or a morning or an entire day. Jurors know it is easy to treat people better,

---

1. Fortunately, the courthouse I was walking to on that rainy morning—like many others across the country—is blessed with a wonderful jury clerk. She is hospitable to every venireperson. She even started providing coffee for jurors when the grinches who arranged for remote parking also removed the courthouse snack bar. This jury clerk and some of her courthouse colleagues help make jurors feel less shoved around. Not much else about the system even tries to do that.

so many of them resent the court system—of which you are a part—for placing them at the bottom of the priority list.

Critics analyzing what is wrong with the jury system, as well as attorneys gauging the mood of jurors at the start of voir dire, might start with this: Consider how jurors feel when they are called at 8:30 a.m. and voir dire does not start till 4:00 p.m. Cramming seventy people into a comfortless room, holding them incommunicado, barring them from reading newspapers (even when the case is so trivial it would not make the papers in a town of 250), and forcing them to do nothing all day is no way to precondition an important decision-making body. Some judges believe it is possible to get honest and open voir dire answers under such conditions. But folks who feel abused don't answer their abusers as openly and honestly as folks who have been well treated.

Moreover, angry jurors are more likely to want to get off the jury. This conditions, limits, and warps their voir dire responses. Result: many prospective jurors try to maneuver their way off, some succeed, and the jury is that much less of a cross-section.

Only when you have shared the jurors' treatment will you know what you are dealing with at the start of trial.

Perhaps that will lead you to decide that on a late afternoon when the jurors you are about to voir dire have been held captive for six desolate hours, it might be better to ask the judge to let them go home and to start the next morning with a new, less abused batch. (Unless, of course, that same group would just have to come back again.)

In brief: Jurors who have had to fight off drug dealers to get at the outdoor pay phone in the rain across the street are going to be mad at the courts, the phone company, the world in general—and at you and your client.

Maybe things are different in your jurisdiction. Jurors might be treated so well that they are happy campers by trial time. You don't know until you have gone through the day with them.

Either way, you need to know so you can adjust your behavior accordingly. The way to find out is to participate with real jurors in a voir dire day. Do it a few times. It will vastly improve your juror-reading skills throughout trial.

III. WATCH JURORS AT SOMEONE ELSE'S TRIAL

You did not learn to read books by glancing at book covers now and then. Your first-grade teacher forced you to scrutinize words and sentences until they made sense.

Invest a few hours a month going to other lawyers' trials and paying attention to the jurors. A few hours a month may seem a burden, but it is the best investment of time you can make.

Go and watch. Study the jury. With nothing on your mind but observing, you will be able to see, for one of many examples, that when counsel inappropriately bullies a witness on cross, jurors don't go along with it. They subtly withdraw to being guarded, cooly neutral observers who are unhappy with counsel and the situation, not with the witness. (See above, p. 237, "Underplaying.")

Another example: When counsel draws close to the jury at the start of opening, do jurors lean forward subconsciously mirroring the attempted intimacy, or do they sit stiffly, waiting for counsel to back off? Watch and you will find out.

Observing the trials of other lawyers requires an investment of time that may not be easy to come by. Much of the experience will be boring. You will not be enlightened in dramatic leaps and bounds. But over the course of a number of observations, you will learn new trial skills and become far more astute at perceiving juror feelings.

When mediocre actors go the theater to see other actors in a play, they watch the play. *Brilliant actors watch the audience.* When you go to court and watch the jury instead of all the things you normally must dwell on when you are at work, you will understand why the brilliant actors are right. By watching the audience instead of the play, they are mastering the most important part of their work: the audience.

Your equivalent of the audience is the jury.

IV. OBSERVE REAL LIFE

Get into the habit of paying conscious and constant attention to people in real life. Watch everyone wherever you go. Always ask yourself, "What is that person (or those people) feeling right now?" Look at people in the supermarket picking out which can of beans to buy. Watch drivers in cars going past you. Look at people walking down the street. Constantly compare them to each other, and try to guess what they are feeling.

It makes no difference if you are right or wrong. The important thing is the process.

This may sound like New Age snake oil. Maybe you are too logic-based to believe it works. But it works because human beings are programmed for it to work. Evolution (or whatever you believe shaped us) has given us the capacity to perceive how others are feeling. It is an instinctive, powerful, and essential defense mechanism. Our predecessors who lacked it, being the least likely to survive, did not. Those who possessed it survived and passed it on to all of us, just like intelligence.

Like intelligence and other inherent capacities, it can be ignored and wasted—or maximized and put to good use.

If you are so logic-based that observing people to gauge their feelings sounds fuzzy-feely to you, then you are the very sort of person who can eventually do it best. This is because it requires the application of logic and experience to those very faint readings you get by watching people.

V. FOLLOW UP

This final suggestion is the easiest. It is also good manners and helps build future business.

A couple of weeks after every trial, your paralegal should interview by phone every juror and alternate. In this way, you will find out how jurors reacted to you, your case, and your opponent at each stage of trial: what did they like, dislike, believe, disbelieve, etc.—and most important, *what did they feel about each witness, each line of argument, and you?* (See also Chapter 4, p. 82, "Ask Questions Afterwards.")

A leading jury expert, Oregon's Joyce Tsongas, suggests that you also ask jurors if they felt that there was anything important about them or other jurors that was not brought out by voir dire questions. New Mexico jury expert Lin S. Lilley suggests that you ask if any such biases or attitudes affected deliberations. The answers to these questions will improve your next voir dire.

(Caveat: In some jurisdictions, post-trial juror interviews require court permission. In others, questions about voir dire responses and juror biases might be frowned upon as unsanctioned digging for juror misconduct. In such jurisdictions, clear your plans with the judge beforehand.)

Follow up your post-trial juror interviews with thank-you letters to the jurors for their service during trial. Remember that jurors gave up a lot to serve—not just their time, but often expenses (such as baby-sitting fees) and lost income. Jurors deserve—and will appreciate—your thanks. Your letter should also thank them for talking with your paralegal. Explain how this kind of follow-up helps with future cases. This thoroughness makes you a strong candidate in their eyes when they or someone they know may need a lawyer.

Ask them to call you if other thoughts eventually occur to them regarding their reactions to you or to the trial. If they call, be sure to talk to them or call back *promptly*. Call them yourself; don't have a colleague or assistant call. You are dealing with potential future clients who already think well enough of you to want to talk to you.

But most important: Asking the right questions in post-trial juror interviews reveals how jurors felt during key moments of the case. This helps you make giant steps in your future ability to read—and consequently to win over—juries.

K: PARALEGALS IN COURT

We use a third of our brains, a fifth of our computer's capabilities, and about a tenth of our paralegals' potential.

Paralegals and legal assistants (the terms are used here interchangeably) can become skilled courtroom professionals who know your work, your case—and maybe the jury—better than anyone else.

Using your paralegal in court only for clerical tasks is like using your computer only to type letters.

What can paralegals do in court? Foremost, they can *watch* and *listen* to help monitor and study jurors and others—beginning before voir dire and continuing through post-trial interviews long after the verdict.

HELPING ON VOIR DIRE:

While you are concentrating on questioning a juror in voir dire, your paralegal can watch other jurors for tell-tale reactions to questions and answers. Paralegals don't have to interpret behavior; they just have to spot any visible reactions and let you know what they see.

For example, your paralegal might cue you, "Ask #7 what he thinks about the answer #2 just gave." While you questioned #2, your paralegal saw #7 roll his eyes at #2's response. No interpretation is required; *any* reaction should be followed up. So you can ask, "Mr. Smith, what do you think about that? What do you most agree—or disagree—with about what Miss Jones said?" (See Chapter 3, "Voir Dire.")

If your paralegal knows that rolling eyes might mean disagreement, so much the better. That cues you to probe for differences of opinion among jurors. Jurors who exhibit disagreement with each other in voir dire may never agree about anything—especially not a verdict.

Any visible response your paralegal notices can be a sign that one of the jurors has feelings about something you asked of a different juror. That is sufficient to alert you to follow up.

You will often spot such clues yourself, but your paralegal, unencumbered by having to concentrate on asking questions, can better scan the jury.

For voir dire purposes, it is useful if your courtroom paralegal is the opposite sex from you, because men and women judge people differently. In voir dire you want both perspectives. (The same is true with regard to race: You will know more about jurors at every stage of trial if you have a racially-mixed trial team.)

Incidentally, when you use a female paralegal in court, remember to be careful how you treat her (even if you are a woman yourself). Rude or condescending behavior on your part—such as gesturing her over to you with a crook of your finger, or a condescending manner of touching or talking to her—will offend some jurors. Because of their own workplace experiences, some jurors take offense when they see anyone treated with anything less than respect and dignity. (See also Chapter 1, p. 13, "Gender.")

HELPING AFTER VOIR DIRE:

In addition to monitoring jurors during voir dire, paralegals can help monitor juror reactions throughout trial. For example, during your opening or when you need to have your attention focused on a testifying witness, your paralegal can spot clues that can alert you to when jurors are losing attention, when they are staying with you, when they don't understand, and when they disagree with a point.

To make it easier for your paralegal to observe the jury, arrange seating so your paralegal has to look past you to see the jury (i.e., you are between the paralegal and the jury). That way, jurors will not feel stared at, because the paralegal will seem to be looking at you.

Your paralegal's ability to monitor jurors during and after voir dire can be improved by books and courses about interpreting such visual clues as body language,[1] clothing, conversation groupings and behavior in the hall during recesses, where jurors look during trial, how jurors respond to you vs. to your opponent or the judge, what specific points jurors react to, and other signs.

MONITORING FAMILY:

Your paralegal can monitor family members in the gallery. Though family members may be out of your sight behind you, jurors scrutinize them. If you don't know that your client's sister is shaking her head in disbelief during your client's testimony (such things happen more often than you think), you are unaware that she has one hundred percent impeached your client.

Even if it is not as obvious as a sister's head shaking in disbelief, jurors note facial expressions and can interpret them in damaging ways. Your paralegal can let you know when this is occurring.

MONITORING THE TRIAL TEAM:

Paralegals can also monitor other members of your trial team to make sure they are not distracting jurors by rummaging through files looking for things, reading documents, appearing bored, or exhibiting other such behavior while you are trying to make jurors pay attention.

Caveat: It is important for your paralegal to report trial team problems *to you* for correction and not try to handle them on his or her own. This

---

1. But be careful. Though reading body language was once trendy, it does not work. There is no such "language." You can learn something by comparing a juror's physical behavior in one circumstance to her physical behavior in another circumstance—i.e., her posture when she is listening to your opponent versus her posture when listening to you. You paralegal can learn to spot these differences, but trying to read body positions as if they are some kind of consistent language can have disastrously inaccurate results.

precaution prevents office politics and egos from oozing into court, and ensures that you run the show.

MONITORING THE OPPOSITION:

Your paralegal can spot when your opponent makes a note of something you or a witness says. This can alert you to your opponent's concerns and possible strategies.

MONITORING COURTROOM PERSONNEL:

Your paralegal can even monitor courtroom personnel. Does the sheriff still have the handcuffs in view as he brings in your prisoner-client? Is the bailiff making clear his dislike or disbelief of your witness? Is the judge doing something you need to address? Is the clerk or court reporter doing anything distracting? (Again, your paralegal should alert *you* to such concerns so that you are the one who deals with them.)

In addition to being an extra set of ears and eyes in the courtroom, your paralegal is useful in other ways, including those that follow below.

ORGANIZING:

Charge your paralegal with knowing the location of every piece of paper and shred of evidence at all times—so you never get yourself into that unfortunate mode of grinding the proceedings to a halt while you seek that doggone chart you had yesterday. Paralegals can develop foolproof systems for tracking everything. (See Chapter 5, p. 92, "Props List.") If a nurse can do it for a surgeon, your paralegal can do it for you. With or without computer assistance, your paralegal can make sure that you never temporarily "lose" something in court.

There are excellent organizational aids that can help your paralegal organize. Pre-fab trial notebooks (such as Tom Vesper's, published by the Association of Trial Lawyers of America) and numerous software programs not only help but encourage you and your paralegal to master this essential task.

CREATING RAPPORT:

Paralegals can help create rapport between your client and the jury.

When jurors see a friendly, comfortable relationship between your paralegal and your client, they assume it is because your client is the sort of person with whom someone would be friendly and comfortable.

But if your paralegal has had little opportunity to be around your client in the days, weeks, and months before trial—so that they hardly know each other—their relationship will naturally seem cool. Jurors may draw negative conclusions as to why.

GUIDING AND CRITIQUING:

Because your paralegal sees you every day, he or she is well qualified to tell you how you are doing. You may be the boss, but you cannot see yourself. Your paralegal can.

If you want your paralegal to offer constructive criticism, remember that it is hard for employees to be open with you unless you emphasize that you need and relish criticism (as well as an occasional compliment).

Friends, colleagues, family members, and even some judges (if you ask them) will provide you with useful critiques of your work. But few people are likely to know you and your work as well as your paralegal does, so encourage as much paralegal feedback as possible.

Some criticisms are mundane: "Talk louder."

Some are embarrassing: "Stop picking your ear in court."

Some are subtler: "When you say 'God knows' or 'by God,' Juror McPew seems offended."

Some are substantive: "No one understood your complicated explanation of what the doctor did." You may or may not believe such a critique, but you must consider whether it might be true. Ask your co-counsel, reread it in the record, and after the trial ask the jurors. That way you can evaluate the quality of the advice you are getting from your paralegal.

Everyone who "performs" in any way—athletes, performing artists, trial attorneys, teachers—benefits from constructive input. That is why there are coaches, directors, and conductors.

Caveat: You need to be a relatively emotionally secure person to accept, weigh, and use such input. If you don't have that kind of emotional security, explore ways to develop it. As much as any other factor, it makes the difference between adequate trial attorneys (or athletes, performing artists, teachers) and superb ones. If you have that level of emotional security, encourage your paralegal to offer honest criticism—not flattery—of your courtroom performance.

Caveat: *Never* make your paralegal feel bad for telling you what he or she thinks, or for offering a criticism that might be wrong. Don't explain, don't complain, don't make excuses. Above all, *do not argue*! Just say, "thank you," make a note of the criticism, and then use it or ignore it as you see fit.

When you find a paralegal's criticism helpful, be sure to acknowledge it. Everyone takes pride in having advice acknowledged. This also helps your paralegal learn what kinds of advice can be helpful, and encourages more of it.

Even when a criticism may be wrong, it often signals something else that needs correction. Ask yourself, "What am I *really* doing wrong that led my paralegal to give the criticism she did?" For example, your paralegal may say,

"You talked so fast that the jury was confused when you explained standard of care." Was it really that you talked too fast? Or might the problem have been your use of complicated words?

In other words, your paralegal may not always pinpoint the cause of a problem. That is your job. But your paralegal can do something you cannot always do: notice that there is a problem in the first place.

KEEPING BUSY:

Having your paralegal monitor jurors, keep you organized, and evaluate your work precludes a common problem: With too little to do in court, paralegals get bored. I have seen them space out and even snooze during the boss's passionate closing! When *any* member of your trial team is less than eagerly alert, jurors take what you are doing less seriously, and they pick up the same uninterested attitude.

So keep your paralegal busy in court.

TRAINING:

Some attorneys are skilled at helping paralegals improve courtroom skills. Others rely on classes, associations, and books. Either way, once you have decided to tap your paralegal's full potential, you will begin to think of more and better ways to use him or her.

If you are near a school that offers night courses for paralegals, offer to foot the bill. Encourage—no, *require*—your paralegal to join whatever organizations your state has for legal assistants, as well as the National Association of Legal Assistants. Such organizations provide training, publications, and informative conventions.

If your paralegal is not thoroughly familiar with a text such as R.D. Blanchard's *Litigation and Trial Practice for the Legal Assistant* (West Publishing Co., St. Paul), buy a copy for the office and expect it to be read. It would not hurt to read it yourself, too.

Every paralegal has different potential strengths—but few paralegals are encouraged or even allowed to use them. Not only does this frustrate some of the most capable people in our profession, but it also minimizes what should be a major resource.

One secret of great lawyering is the ability to maximize the unapparent abilities of the people you work with. You can have a superb paralegal—not by searching and hiring but by helping, encouraging, training, and consequently trusting the one you have.

L: THE CARE AND FEEDING OF EXPERTS

Fed. R. Evid. 702: The purpose of an expert is "to assist the trier of fact to understand the evidence or to determine a fact." Unfortunately, the purpose of your opponent's expert is to assist the trier of fact to understand the evidence *differently* or to determine a *different* fact.

When experts collide, jurors rarely have enough information or expertise of their own to decide whom to believe, so they tend to resolve the dilemma by ignoring both. Like two opposing Senators who agree not to show up for a vote, you and your opponent have expended considerable resources merely to neutralize each other (or, at most, to avoid a directed verdict).

It is dangerously tempting to rely on superior credentials to help your expert dominate your opponent's expert. Surprisingly, in gauging an expert's credibility, jurors give credentials little weight. That is something you probably don't want to hear, especially if you have just coughed up $500 an hour for that Mayo Clinic neurologist. But jurors are not very swayed by experts' credentials.

Neither are you. Even after you hired the best-credentialled expert available, you had to see her on the stand before you were certain she was credible. If credentials alone cannot convince you, then they cannot persuade jurors either.

Why not? Because jurors know what you know. First, plenty of numskulls have impressive credentials. Second, there are experts who will make themselves believe (or at least say) anything for the right price.

Moreover, the courtroom experience itself (dueling experts) teaches jurors that fifty percent of the credentialled experts who come to court are wrong.

Other than extremes (for example, a leading physician at Harvard vs. a local retired midwife), research shows that "seldom do jurors consider a difference in credentials in determining the weight of the evidence."[1] When counsel begins an expert's testimony by dragging her through a litany of credentials, jurors' minds wander. Right when counsel should be arousing juror attention, she deflects it. The litany of credentials grows more and more monotonous and less and less relevant, *diminishing* juror interest in the expert's upcoming testimony. And the poor expert brags and drags on about this degree, that publication, this honor, that position . . . .

This scenario is common partly because jurors see only a vague relationship between an expert's credentials and the issues of the case.

Solution: Make the litany of credentials persuasive. One way to do that is suggested by Raleigh attorney and professor Donald H. Beskind: A qualification

---

1.   V. Hale Starr & Mark McCormick: *Jury Selection*, 2nd Ed., 1994 Supplement, p. 62.

should tell jurors how your expert's training and experience relate *directly and specifically* to what she is here to testify about.

For example:

Q: "Are you going to be able to tell us why the mine roof collapsed?"

A: "Yes."

Q: "How do you know how to do that?"

A: "When studying for my degree in mining engineering, I . . . ."

In another kind of case, you might ask: "Doctor, our concern in this case is drug interaction. When and where did you first study drug interaction?"

A: "In 1978 in an undergraduate honors organic chemistry seminar at Brandeis University."

Q: "Was that your only course on drug interactions?"

A: "As an undergraduate, yes. But as a student at the Harvard Medical School I took X and Y drug-interaction courses. I then interned under Dr. Robert Mixum at Duke University, the country's leading specialist at the time in drug interactions. Since then, I've conducted three government-funded research projects on drug interaction and written up the results in a dozen articles and a book. And for five years I've run the drug interaction intervention group at the Center for Medical Error in Pittsburgh."

Q: "Has this training and experience helped you to identify the drug interactions in this case?"

A: "Yes, it has."

Rather than lulling jurors to sleep with credentials, this method offers your expert's credentials as the specific lenses through which she will view and present the issues of the case. The jurors are primed to hear more.

CREDIBILITY FACTORS

Starr and McCormick[2] report that the following factors weigh more heavily than credentials:

—Demonstrated expertise

—Reliability

—Trustworthiness

—Objectivity

—Dynamism

---

2. Op. Cit., p. 61.

To help your expert's opinions outweigh those of your opponent's expert, build your expert's credibility on some combination of those five. Some ways to do that are suggested below, along with other strategies to help your experts establish and sustain credibility.

SUPPORT EXPERTS VIA LAY TESTIMONY

When jurors are not emotionally bonded to your expert's opinion, they are vulnerable to competing opinions. Thus, your task is to emotionally bond jurors to your expert's opinion. But it is difficult to emotionally bond jurors to anything as cerebral as an expert's opinion.

Solution: Because expertise is clinical and often detached, place it in a humanized context. For example, before your expert testifies, use a lay witness to establish the human situation. Then your expert can explain each point (each symptom, each observation, each problem) that your lay witness has described.

To illustrate: In a recent case, Kentucky attorney Gary C. Johnson had a teenage girl testify what it was like to live with her brain-damaged mother. The girl talked about her mother's short temper, bad memory, inability to tolerate even such small noises as the crinkling of candy wrappers, and the deep depression that kept her mother in bed nearly twenty hours a day. The daughter's moving testimony created a humanized context for a neuropsychiatrist's expert testimony of how the mother's depression, temper, memory loss, noise intolerance, and endless sleeping related medically to specific brain injuries suffered in a car wreck.

Because the daughter's testimony established the human situation, the jury emotionally bonded with her—and then bonded as well with the expert's testimony. Additionally, the daughter's testimony lent extraordinary credibility to the expert's testimony, and vice versa.

The sequence: First, present a lay witness describing the situation from a human point of view. Then immediately present your expert's explanation of that situation. This potent combination can win cases by giving emotional impact to your expert's testimony—yet requires that you merely re-sequence witnesses you were going to use anyway.

DEMONSTRATIVE EVIDENCE

Use at least one exhibit for each key point your expert makes. Visuals support experts with two central components of persuasion: clarity and reinforcement. And in your closing, the same visuals instantly remind jurors of the expert's testimony on each point.

AUTHORITATIVE TEXTS

In addition to charts, graphs, X-rays, diagrams, and relevant records and documents, make liberal use of authoritative texts to accompany and support expert testimony. Jurors believe excerpts from books and articles because the texts were written by people uninvolved in the case and before the case ever came up. Texts provide experts with two components of persuasion: neutrality and authority. (Indeed, the root of the word "authority" is "author"—a person who creates texts.)

When looking for publications to use in court, be thorough and creative. Consider using the books you see on the shelves of opponent experts during depositions. Master the research software at your local medical library. And don't look only for books. You are more likely to find what you need in journal articles because there are more of them. There are on-line indices to every professional journal; it is a rare topic for which authoritative, peer-reviewed, learned research or analytic articles cannot be found. Articles have another advantage over books: Being shorter, there is less chance that articles will contain anything your opponent can use back against you. (For guidance in displaying texts and other visuals, see Chapter 5, p. 83, "Demonstrative and Real Evidence.")

PUBLICATIONS BY YOUR EXPERT

Peer Review: Explain the significance of your expert's publications. In many professions, publications are peer-reviewed. That means that the submitted text is accepted or rejected not by text editors *but by the author's learned colleagues.* Jurors rely heavily upon demonstrated expertise to gauge credibility, and your expert's expertise is effectively demonstrated by peer acceptance. But you must explain the peer-review system if your jurors are to understand the validation that peer-acceptance carries.

Who Uses the Publication? Reciting a list of publications is as ineffective as reciting a list of credentials. But publications help persuade jurors that the expert is credible *if you show where and how the publications are used.* Let the jury know that your expert's book is the primary text in use at thirty engineering schools, and name the most prestigious of those schools.

PREPARING EXPERT WITNESSES

Don't be so intimidated or impressed by your expert's credentials or demeanor that you fail to prepare her to testify. Don't assume that her wisdom and professional experience will make her an expressive and effective—or even communicative—witness. Being a brilliant cardiologist has nothing to do with being an adequate communicator. It is a gamble to put your expert on the stand without a dry run to see what help she needs.

Among things to pay attention to:

Taking Sides #1: Coach your expert not to take sides. When jurors think an expert is your partisan, they give her testimony less weight and may even reject it altogether.

On direct, ask your expert a few questions on non-critical points which she can answer in ways that favor the other side. Jurors rarely believe that the other side's experts can be wrong about every single thing, so if your expert shows where the other side is right as well as wrong, she gains trust based on her objectivity.

If you know that your opponent will ask questions your expert must answer in ways that hurt you, *ask those questions yourself on direct*. The answers will be heard either way, but on direct they make your expert seem neutral and forthcoming (instead of partisan)—and you will seem willing to reveal rather than hide the truth. Moreover, harmful answers on direct can be controlled, whereas on cross they are emphasized and presented in their worst light.

Taking Sides #2: There is an effective way your expert can take sides: to wage battle on behalf of decent professional standards in her field. A plaintiff's expert can be professionally offended at what the defendant has done; a defendant's expert can be professionally offended at what the plaintiff's experts have claimed.

This approach is effective but requires care. The fragile distinction between battling for your side and battling for high professional standards must be kept clear.

Forthrightness on cross: Coach your expert to forthrightly and fully answer on cross—*especially questions she fears might work against you*. Shying away or trying to evade such questions does not diminish the harm her answers might do. If she shies away she will seem partisan, less authoritative, and even less honest.

Passion: Your expert's testimony should be driven by passion—not the passion of a partisan but the passion of a professional who is energized by her strong interest in the nature of her work as it relates to this case. Jurors tend to believe experts who are reasonably passionate about their work. Jurors tend to distrust, ignore, or forget experts who seem disinterested or uninvolved. Such experts can appear to be concealing uncertainty or even dishonesty.

Passion does not mean high emotion or dramatics. It means enthusiasm and strength of expression that come from devotion to the task at hand.

Language: Coach your expert to speak plain English. A very modest use of jargon and technical terms might serve to impress, but such terms turn against you when they make your expert hard to understand.

Moreover, in this era of suspicious jurors, *testimony delivered in the technical language of any profession can annoy jurors and arouse their distrust*.

Assertions: Don't let the credibility of your expert rest on her assertions. ("Yes, Miss Smith's temperature should have been a warning *because it was too high*." Or, "In my opinion, it's below the standard of care *because it's not good enough*." Or, "The girder was not strong enough for a structure like that *because you're supposed to use a different kind*.") Such supporting of an assertion with another assertion is a Composition 101 error in logic, but experts do it all the time. It severely undermines them because jurors, regardless of educational level, expect expert conclusions to be based upon explainable and demonstrable foundations—not upon assertions.

So have your expert explain *how she knows* her opinions are valid. When possible, introduce text references, research studies, or other authority. And have your expert provide clear explanations of each of the steps that led her to her conclusions. Omitting such support and step-by-step explanations is an invitation for your opposition to mount an effective challenge and for jurors ultimately to doubt your expert's testimony.

You may be tempted to forgo step-by-step explanations because you believe that jurors will not understand them. But this is a losing strategy. Jurors understand virtually anything if you pay sufficient attention to how it is conveyed. Moreover, if jurors understand the step-by-step basis on which your expert's opinion is founded, then you gamble less on whether they will take her at her word.

Analogies: Help your expert find analogies to explain complex concepts. Analogies are not merely clever little comparisons, but rather comparisons of a particular kind: They express something difficult to explain by comparing it to something familiar the listener already understands.

"Centrifugal force propelled the car toward the edge of the curve *like spinning a ball on a string propels the ball away from the spinner.*"

Analogies are best when they relate to the life experiences of your jurors. ("Sending Mr. Jones to Miracures, Inc., was *like your physician sending you to a witch doctor instead of a hospital,*" or "When the atomic particle generator went out of control, it speeded up the electrons so fast that they smashed through the wall of the containment chamber *like a rock crashing through your picture window.*")

Skillful use of analogies and other such methods allows your expert to explain virtually anything to a jury.

LIMITING TESTIMONY

Limit what your expert says. Don't let her stray beyond the specific issues in contention. The more she says, the greater the chance she will say something impeachable. Moreover, by saying too much she can drown her important points in a sea of unimportant details. Focus. Don't stray. Here is the drill:

"*What did you look at* to arrive at your conclusions?"

"*What methods of analysis* did you use?"

"*What conclusions* did you draw?"

"*How do you know* you're right?"

"How do you *explain the conflicting view* offered by the opposition?"

"How do you *know the opposition is wrong?*"

Stop.

Too much never impresses a jury. Less is more.

LEADING QUESTIONS

Don't lead your expert. If you do all the talking, jurors cannot judge her credibility, so they are never quite convinced.

For the same reason, if your opponent leads his experts, let him!

SELECTING EXPERTS

Some expert witnesses—including some of the most highly paid—think their fee is merely for the hire of their authoritative expertise. Such experts can be poor communicators and even resist your guidance in improving their ability to communicate.

Experts are useless unless they communicate credibly and clearly—or can be coached into doing so.

If you want a credible, authoritative, forceful, and memorable expert, it is almost always worth your while to spend an hour coaching her presentation skills before putting the fate of your case into her hands. But that will not help if she is not open to being coached. To determine whether she is willing and able to benefit from your suggestions and guidance, *before signing her on* ask her how she would explain a particular complexity to lay jurors. Then see if she responds positively to your guidance for improvement.

You can do this by phone. But if the scope of the case warrants it, meet in person. How a person comes across is largely visual. Moreover, many experts do well in their own offices. You want to see how they do in an environment removed from their familiar haunts—like court.

You can also check with other attorneys who have used your prospective expert.

HANDLING YOUR OPPONENT'S EXPERTS

Attack Facts: It is usually impossible to effectively attack an opponent expert's opinion simply by disagreeing or by offering a conflicting opinion.

But you can attack the accuracy of underlying facts. The first step: Get your opponent's expert to specify the facts on which he has based his conclusions. Then get him to agree with the principle that if underlying facts change, conclusions can change. (He cannot deny that principle without looking foolish.) After he has agreed with that proposition, *and after he has left the stand*, show the difference between the facts he used and the actual facts of the case. By showing the disparity later with a different witness, the expert who used the wrong facts has no chance to waffle out of it.

Demarcate Areas of Expertise: Carefully delimit your opponent expert's specific area(s) of expertise. Ask questions that reveal which areas of concern in this case lie outside her specialty. A particularly dramatic way to do this:

"Doctor, would you go to the anatomy chart and erase each anatomical structure that your specialty does not cover?" It is fun to watch the jury watching body parts integral to the case disappear under the expert's eraser.

Use Prior Statements: In researching an opposition expert's testimony in prior cases, don't look only for statements that contradict her current assertions in this case. Go an extra step and seek prior statements that might speak to omissions the expert has made in this case, or that support your own expert—or both.

Sometimes you will find direct links: "Doctor, you haven't mentioned sightlines today, but in 1987 you said under oath in a different courtroom that four-track crossings require 300 yards of sightline clearance, didn't you?" Other times, the link may be less direct but still useful: "Doctor, under oath in 1993 you stated that the mechanical engineering department at Carnegie Mellon University is absolutely reliable, didn't you?" and "Did you know that in 1987 Professor MyWitness was chair of that department?"

This technique supports your case, validates your own expert, and impeaches the integrity (or at least the memory or consistency) of your opponent's expert.

Validate Your Expert's Credentials: You can often get opposition experts to agree that your experts are recognized authorities respected by their colleagues. Opposition experts can also be questioned about the quality of your expert's credentials. For example, "What is your opinion of the neurology department at the University of Minnesota?" The opposition expert may have difficulty criticizing the institution your expert is from.

Experts are heavy artillery. Military science teaches that heavy artillery must be prudently deployed. When you enlist an expert solely on the basis of credentials and rely on her expertise alone to make her credible, you imprudently risk turning your heavy artillery attack into a game of Russian roulette.[3]

---

3. For more on expert witnesses, see Chapter 9, p. 141.

M: COURTROOM TECHNOLOGY: TIPS & CAVEATS

Some fool gave one of my favorite trial attorneys a high-tech gift: a laser pointer. Counsel was as pleased as a kid on Christmas. The pen-sized marvel could project its tiny red dot as clear and sharp as Satan's eye all the way across a courtroom.

"Technology's great!" counsel crowed.

Without rising from his chair, he could pick out items on a chart ten feet away. Without leaning forward, he could designate the faulty rivets on a structure model over on opposing counsel's table.

Great?

No! The laser pointer turned counsel into a courtroom couch potato. Charts and models provide reason to get up and move around—and thus to gain focus and provide variety. The laser pointer lets you sit dully in your chair. Laser pointers are to jury persuasion as TV remote controls are to aerobic exercise.

The laser pointer did manage to amuse jurors when counsel inadvertently zig-zagged it across Her Honor's face. After trial, one juror gravely remarked that the little red dot looked like the electronic gun-sight projector of a high-speed rifle.

The laser pointer also kept two jurors on the alert because they had read someplace that laser beams cause eye damage. They tensed whenever it was turned on, ready to leap out of the way should it come in their direction.

But the laser pointer did nothing to help counsel persuade jurors. Amuse and alarm, yes. Persuade, no.

So leave your toys at home. Don't bring anything to court unless it helps you persuade.

THE ULTIMATE QUESTION for technology in the courtroom: *Does it make you a better persuader?* The fact that it is fast or amazing or new or easy or labor-saving is meaningless unless it is also—and mainly—persuasive.

Even if it is persuasive, there are seven more points to consider:

1. OPERATION. *Will it work?* Will your case be doomed if your VCR, Elmo, or cassette player suddenly goes on the fritz? Is your spare ready to go? Something as simple as the special bulb on an X-ray viewer can burn out. By the time a replacement is found, counsel's only expert is on her flight back to Yucca. If a simple bulb can cause such damage, what can a failed hard-drive or broken animation cassette do?

2. OPERATOR. *Do you know how to work it?* Rehearse with your recorders, projectors, and even easels and charts, so you can make them do what they are intended to do. You must be able to work them while simultaneously

saying—without being distracted—whatever must be said or asked at the time. While your attention is on figuring out the CD-drive or the easel legs, you are not persuading. You are looking inept and confused.

3. APPEARANCE. *Does it make you seem to have infinite dollar resources?* Will you come across as a rich lawyer with tens of thousands of dollars' worth of equipment lined up against your poor opponent party who has nothing to carry his case forward but a guy in a suit?

Just as you should not wear a Rolex or drive a Mercedes to court on trial days, neither should you fill your table with thousands of dollars' worth of computers, portable printers, video equipment, etc. Wear a Bulova. Drive a two-year-old Buick. Bring last year's laptop. If you have a 30" video monitor, let your opponent use it, too—so jurors don't know who owns it.

3a. APPEARANCE OF NECESSITY. Will it be clear to the jury that your use of technology is necessary? Or will it seem distracting, show-boating, or even intentionally diverting from main issues?

4. ADMISSIBILITY AND EFFECTIVENESS. Videos, models, and computer animations and simulations can clarify complex expert testimony. But your best (and most expensive) demonstrative aids—especially those generated by technological means—may not get in if you don't take pains to anticipate potential objections and to prepare counters and briefs. Several grounds for such objections are discussed below in the section entitled "Animations."

Because technology progresses rapidly, you must help judges who are unfamiliar with decisions regarding high-tech aids to be comfortable ruling in your favor. Prepared arguments are always more effective than impromptu arguments, and good briefs are better than oral arguments alone.

For purposes of admissibility (as well as persuasive power and clarity), animations and day-in-the-life videos are best presented either in brief segments alternating with an expert's testimony, or simultaneous with expert or other testimony being delivered "voice over" (live or recorded). This provides credibiity and helps convince the judge that the animation or video is a legitimate adjunct to the expert's testimony.

With respect to persuasive power and clarity, the "voice over" method combining visual and verbal testimony is generally the most effective way to present evidence. Visual communication alone is 100 percent more effective than verbal communication. But visual communication *plus* verbal communication—"show and tell" or "voice over"—is 700 percent more effective.[1]

---

1.   Ellenbogen, Marc A. "Lights, Camera, Action: Computer-Animated Evidence Gets Its Day in Court." *Boston College Law Review.* 9/93, p. 1101.

5. BEWARE BOOMERANGS. However effective your document blow-up, video, piece of real evidence, photo, or animation may be in your favor, it is that much more effective in favor of your opponent if she uses it to make her own case back against you. (For example, your animation of the wreck inadvertently shows that your client could not have had the sightlines he claimed to have.) Boomerangs are powerful persuaders. (See Chapter Five, p. 90, "Tit-for-Tat: The Boomerang.") So examine your visual offerings from the point of view of opposing counsel looking to make use of them.

In a recent case, a video that showed how a landlord neglected to fix a stairway had a background that inadvertently showed how meticulously the landlord maintained the grounds and parking area. In another case, a set of financial records blown up by laser-disk projection to show a particular mistake made by the defendant also showed how meticulously he maintained his books—thus making jurors feel that the one mistake was a forgivable aberration.

So be sure that your day-in-the-life video of your suffering, disabled client does not reveal his track shoes on the floor and his new Cadillac outside the window.

6. APPROPRIATENESS. Animations and other visuals can implicitly convey impressions that trivialize or otherwise undermine your case. A recent Kentucky jury smiled at a $28,000 computer-generated animation of a car wreck. They smiled not because the wreck killed two small girls and their mother, but because those little cartoon cars and the cartoon dump truck were just so *cute*!

7. PIN-POINT CLARITY. Do the main points you intend to make with your visual aid come across quickly, easily, and clearly? Or must jurors squint or interpret or puzzle them out? Visual evidence is useless if its main points cannot be taken in at first glance.

PERSUASION. If your planned use of technology passes those seven tests, then re-ask the ultimate question: *Does it persuade?*

A high-tech visual display can clarify your version of how the wreck occurred. It can make the wreck frightening to the jurors and etch it into their memories. But that is not enough. Technology may be clarifying, emphatic, and memorable—but so was *Star Wars*, and no one over the age of twelve ever believed that the Wookie or those space ships ever existed. And therein lies the problem with courtroom visual-aid technology: In itself it carries little credibility, and therefore by itself it does not persuade.

Jurors are TV viewers who have come to court. They have seen hundreds of movies and TV shows use state-of-the-art technology *not to convey truth but to fabricate*. Jurors are thus conditioned to subconsciously associate high-tech visuals with creative fabrication—such as realistic beer-thirsty frogs, dancing gasoline pumps, and talking lumps of cookie dough. Such high-tech wonders are clear, emphatic, and memorable. They represent some of the most brilliant visual work anyone is doing. They may even make you buy a particular brand of beer, gasoline, or cookie mix. But they *never* persuade you that Budweiser-loving frogs, dancing gas pumps, and talking cookie dough actually exist.

High-tech visuals can effectively convey your contention of *how* something happened but they cannot convey *whether it actually happened that way*. High-tech visuals can clearly, memorably, and emphatically show how a crew of three-headed Martians negligently landed their flying saucer on your client's convertible. If you could only make those visuals in and of themselves *persuasive*, you would get a handsome judgment against Mars (respondeat planetus superior). But persuasion requires you to do something more to attain credibility.

CREDIBILITY. Because high-tech visuals are rarely credible in themselves, a credible expert is an essential companion to animation. Believable testimony bolsters a day-in-the-life video. Documentation of such factors as size, weight, and mass, along with textbook blow-ups of engineering principles, strengthens the credibility of structural models and animated simulations.

In the absence of such credibility-providing means, high-tech visuals are highly vulnerable to opposition experts and textbooks.

To support or undermine high-tech visuals, blow-ups of relevant statements from recognized authoritative books are particularly powerful. Such excerpts can be extraordinarily credible because the textbook was written before your case came about. If you point this out to jurors, they will conclude that the book is unbiased with respect to this case. Often textbooks can be found that were written by a dozen or more experts (the more authors, the more authoritative the book will seem to jurors), or published by the field's professional organization, and possibly used at some of the leading schools in the field.

Example: An animation can show the process by which the rash has eaten away at your client's skin. But it is just a cartoon, no matter how sophisticated the artwork. Add *credibility*, such as a leading pharmacist on the stand pointing (with wooden pointer, not laser) at a blow-up of a paragraph from the *Physicians Desk Reference* on side effects: "Corrosive rash, discontinue use."

Remember: A $25,000 computer animation is not credible by itself, but can be given credibility by even one page of an authoritative textbook. At the same time, watch out for the boomerang: The animation's credibility can be just as easily destroyed by your opponent's textbook. (See also Application L, p. 240, on authoritative texts.)

TECHNOLOGY THAT WORKS:

If you bear firmly in mind that credibility is not intrinsic to most high-tech displays, you can safely look for useful possibilities among the following suggestions of high-tech as well as low-tech options.

TIME LINES. You must visually show your time sequence of events. Jurors can hear your chronology a dozen times and still not know it. A clear, simple, and LARGE time line of events lets them see your chronology and prevents your opponent from muddying your waters. You can create an effective time line on your laptop and enlarge it to a few feet wide at your local copy shop.

A time line should be skeletal: no explanations, no details; just critical events. Exclude items your opponent can discredit; otherwise, the entire time line can be discredited by extension.

Black-and-white time lines are sufficiently effective, but an inexpensive color printer (a few hundred dollars) will allow your paralegal to make even better time lines at virtually no expense. If you have color, you can color code similar events—for example, doctor visits in blue, symptom manifestations in red, medications in green, etc. But remember that because many people are color-blind and cannot distinguish between, say, red and green, you still need textual and shape differences to distinguish various categories of events.

An office CD-ROM gives you access to thousands of pieces of clip art from which to select time line icons. For example, doctor visits can be indicated by a clip-art caduceus (the medical profession's familiar staff-and-serpent symbol). Travel dates can be indicated by airplanes. Dates on which notice was received of an existing danger might be indicated by a skull and crossbones. Such icons reinforce clarity, add interest and memorability, and inject persuasive points of view.

If permitted, give an 8 x 11" version of your large time line to each juror so they have it to refer to when your large one is removed.[2]

STORYBOARDS. Storyboards are used to plan movies. A courtroom storyboard is a series of pictures—like a cartoon strip, but with art that is more representational than fanciful—that illustrates key moments of your version of the case. A storyboard is an illustrated time line. For example:

FRAME 1: CAR leaves the left toll booth as BUS leaves the right toll booth.

FRAME 2: CAR and BUS progress side by side, as MOTORCYCLE pulls out of the right booth a few car lengths behind BUS.

FRAME 3: CAR in the left lane adjacent to BUS; MOTORCYCLE very close behind BUS in the right lane.

---

2. For more on time lines, see Chapter 5, p. 83, "Demonstrative and Real Evidence,"; and Application I, p. 233, "Use Time lines."

FRAME 4: MOTORCYCLE pulling onto the right shoulder to pass BUS.

FRAME 5: MOTORCYCLE alongside and passing BUS by using the right shoulder.

FRAME 6: MOTORCYCLE passing BUS approaches barricade blocking right shoulder.

FRAME 7: MOTORCYCLE pulls onto highway, cutting off BUS. An icon indicates that BUS blows its horn.

FRAME 8: MOTORCYCLE in right lane forces BUS left across the white line toward CAR. CAR cannot swerve left due to guard rail.

FRAME 9: BUS hits front fender of CAR. MOTORCYCLE continues away.

FRAME 10: CAR hits guard rail. BUS hits back fender of CAR. MOTORCYCLE is no longer in picture.

FRAME 11: The position of CAR and BUS after they have come to rest following the wreck.

It is a simple wreck, but jurors listening to it have even more trouble following it than you just had reading about it. A simple storyboard makes it visual and clear. Until jurors have a clear picture of it, they will not understand it the way counsel does.

When using a storyboard, reveal its frames one at a time. This keeps jurors from getting ahead of you or being distracted by upcoming frames as you talk about the one you are on. It also bolsters clarity and provides an effective sense of forward movement.

Credibility: If you have a photograph of the vehicles as they came to rest after the wreck, use it for the storyboard's last frame (#11). If your artist makes her drawings match the photo with respect to color, shape, scale, distance, and background, the realism of the final photo adds credibility to the whole storyboard.

Technology-assisted storyboard: With inexpensive software, your artist can scan the photo into a computer to use as the basis for all her drawings.

Computers can also help you be your own artist. For example, you can obtain software that allows you to show human figures in any position. These images can be superimposed over scanned-in photos of any interior or exterior location. You can show the step-by-step process of, say, how your client was hurt in the wreck.

You can combine a photo of a motorcycle with a human figure to show the direction the driver was looking at each moment before the wreck.

Learning to use such software is not easy, but once mastered, it will be useful on many cases—first for a negotiation tool, later in trial. You will quickly create clear illustrations of each important moment of your case story. Print the pictures, enlarge them, mount them in sequence—and you have the kind of storyboard that would have cost you thousands of dollars just a few years ago.

You can do last-minute changes even in court. You need only your laptop and access to a printer (or a laptop that includes a printer).

If you lack the considerable time or patience it takes to master this kind of software, your paralegal can pick up a valuable skill by learning. (The only risk: your paralegal will be in demand by other firms.) Whether used for individual illustrations to clarify particular moments, or for creating multi-frame storyboards to guide your jurors through the case, the computer-assisted storyboard can become one of your best trial tools.

ANIMATIONS. Until recently, good animations cost tens of thousands of dollars. Software now gets it done for a tenth of that figure. Though it cannot provide the judgment and knowledge you get from a professional animator, new software means that animations are becoming more and more common in court.

You can make good use of animations to clarify difficult, complex, or dense testimony.

Admissibility: Familiarize yourself with both sides of admissibility arguments. Animations are more easily ruled out than you might expect. They can be barred for such reasons as speculative interpolations, inescapable error and distortion, omissions, false impressions, cumulativeness, and prejudice.

Speculative interpolations. Animations by definition present continuous motion—but invariably there is evidence only about specific *unconnected* moments. Insofar as the animation shows what happens *between* those moments, it is showing information that is not in evidence.

For example, there is testimony that the dump truck turned left onto Main Street and 125 feet from the corner drifted across the solid line into oncoming traffic. But though the animation purports to show the dump truck's path, no one can testify to any such path. There can be no such testimony unless the dump truck was leaking paint onto the road and thereby tracing its path. Did the dump truck move down the street in a straight line, a simple arc, or a gentle S-curve? More crucially (and virtually impossible to find testimony to support): did it move at constant speed, or varying? There is no way to know these connecting factors—yet animation represents them. At best, they are the animator's interpolations, not a witness's.

Some such interpolations involve case-determinative matters, such as which way the driver was looking. An animator's assumption, wild guess, or careless error can make its way into the animation—and thereby, if unquestioned, become hard evidence in the jurors' minds.

Inescapable error and distortion. Even in the unlikely event that an animator knows everything about the shape, location, and movement of the objects and people involved, it is impossible to represent virtually any event with complete visual accuracy. In other words, the limitations of visual representation mean that an animator cannot avoid outright errors.

The geometry and physics of motion and momentum, location, impact, and other components of animated representation are highly technical. Animators are rarely engineers or physicists, and even when they are (or when they consult with them), errors are inevitable.

Moreover, images can *never* be fully accurate, not even in documentary film or live TV. The laws of physics make it invariable that camera lenses (and the human eye) distort reality. Distances, perspectives, shapes, and movement are seen differently by different lenses—and no lense is the same as the human visual system, because the human visual system processes information in three dimensions whereas camera lenses process information in two dimensions. Distortion is thus inevitable.

When examining an animation, scrutinize the ways—both minute and gross—that this distortion misrepresents reality. Repeated examination of an animation will reveal elements that seem accurate at first glance but are, in fact, distortions. For example, the animation's *apparent* distance from point A to point B may appear different from the distance in real life. And the movement of, say, a car pulling away from you in real life will not look the same as the movement of a car in an animation pulling away from the viewer of the animation.

When it is your animation, be prepared to show that the distortions carry no relevant weight. When it is your opponent's, point out every distortion you can find.

Sometimes such errors and distortions are not apparent for a dozen or more viewings, but sooner or later emerge to careful scrutiny. They are there because they are inseparable from the process of creating animations.

Omissions: Every representation of reality requires the producer to exercise selectivity: what to include and what to exclude. No representation can include everything—not even a photo (the photographer must decide depth of field and where to locate the edge of the picture). Whatever is excluded (such as, say, a dark sky) or only partly included (such as weather conditions or road texture) can skew reality. Scrutinize every animation for what has been left out and note how the omissions change the impression the animation creates.

False impressions: Animations create false impressions for many other reasons. For example, an animation might make a dump truck look like a highly maneuverable vehicle. It is small, it zips around with no trouble, and it is cute. The actual dump truck's momentum and cumbersome handling qualities would have prevented the driver from swerving and would have caused the truck to tip over even if he had managed to make it swerve. But the animation conveys the opposite impression. This false impression can sway jurors even when there has been credible testimony from several experts that the driver could not have swerved without tipping over. When there has been no testimony on that point, the false impression becomes the only impression, and as such it is usually accepted—particularly by jurors who have never driven heavy trucks.

When defending an animation from your opponent's charges of interpolations, distortions, or false impressions, argue that such things are unavoidable *and irrelevant* by-products of the animation process.

When you are the one offering the animation, you (not your opponent) should be the one to tell jurors the difference between what represents admitted evidence and what had to be estimated for the sake of this visual display.

To attack an animation, use your opponent's own expert to point out every guess and error in the animation. And ultimately argue that all those problems make it unlikely that the animation accurately and fairly conveys the points in contention. Impeach the animation the way you impeach a witness: Show where it is in error, and then argue that since it is in error about one thing, it can be in error about all things.

Emotional impact. An animation can ignite emotions. For example, an animation might show a fire engine ramming a car sideways into a ditch, smashing the car's occupants out through closed windows, and strewing them in bits and pieces across the highway. The proponent must be prepared to show how each segment of the animation is illustrative and the only (or best) way to depict what happened. The opponent should resist that argument, and point out that moving images have extraordinary power to unfairly ignite juror emotions.

Perhaps a contradiction seems apparent: I am saying that your opponent's animations can harm your case, yet earlier I argued that animations are not very persuasive. Remember that they are unpersuasive *by themselves*. In combination with other offerings (such as an expert or a textbook) they are credible and compelling. If you are the proponent, add the credibility fortifier (such as a textbook blow-up). If you are the opponent, fight to bar the animation so it cannot be used in combination with a credibility fortifier.

Bonus: When your opponent comes to court armed with an expensive animation, she relies heavily on it. After spending all that time and money on animation, she may have no other effective means of unraveling the complexities of her experts' testimony. But if the animation contains so much distortion or omission that you can successfully argue against its admission, she may have nothing else prepared to clarify her complex evidence. (Warning: When trying to have an animation ruled inadmissible, remember that jurors love animations. So object in limine.)

To protect yourself, when you plan to use an animation or some other high-tech visual, have an unannounced effective back-up ready to go—such as a storyboard or some other set of effective charts.

Fighting animation with languge: When discussing your opponent's animation, always refer to it as that "expensive cartoon."

PHOTO RETOUCHING SOFTWARE.[3] A technological virus is infecting the once reliable use of photographs.

Readily available, low-cost, easily-learned software allows photos to be undetectably retouched. You can turn a blue car green, smooth a rough highway, add or eliminate a puddle, turn a green light red, eliminate or add bruises, or wreak any other kind of change on a photo. You can alter the distance between vehicles, enlarge or diminish visibility-masking shrubbery, make a thin person fat or vice-versa, put sunglasses or a beard or feathers on someone, or do anything else you want.

Obviously, you would never engage in such unethical practices. But even though prosecutors never alter evidence, they still must prove chain of custody. In the future, it may be wise to insist that your opponent do the same regarding photographs. Perhaps you should insist already. Don't rely on your opponent's ethics because even if she is trustworthy, she may have obtained the photo from a desperate client whose ethics—unbeknownst to counsel—were less reliable.

The implications are enormous. For example, you may be able to keep *any* legitimate opponent photo out of evidence by retouching a copy and showing both to the proffering witness. If he cannot tell which is real, then he is *ipso facto* incapable of credibly stating that either is fair and accurate.

Not even an examination of the film negatives can reveal the deception, because negatives, too, can be retouched. And soon it will be possible for your opponent not merely to retouch photos, but inexpensively to create *from scratch* realistic, full-color photos of anything imaginable—even one of you and your client flying around the courthouse on a pumpkin with the Easter Bunny. This is no exaggeration. It (creating images, not pumpkin flying) can be done now, if you can afford it. The capability will soon be inexpensive enough to show up on everyone's laptop.

---

3. See also Chapter 5, p. 86, "Deceptive Videotapes, Films, and Photos."

VIDEO TABLES. This is similar to the old-fashioned overhead projector, except it uses a video camera to show your display on a TV monitor. These inexpensive tables are portable and allow you to create effective visuals even on the spur of the moment: You can zoom in on important areas of a photo or document, you can turn the display off and on at exactly the appropriate instants, you can compare images side by side on the same screen, and you can get a clear image without turning out the courtroom lights the way most overhead projectors require.

Caveat: Video tables can also be used to project onto a flat screen, but as of this writing (1997), the image quality is terrible. Do not project video images. Jurors are rarely affected by images they can barely see.

MULTI-MEDIA. Think of the marvels your teenager can do at home by combining video, stereo, computers, software, disks, and CD-ROMs. You can do the same in court: Animations, stills, graphs, charts, diagrams, voice-overs, video depositions, documents, and sound can be produced and displayed in any order or combination with a few keystrokes.

You can play the words of a deposition while showing a rotating computer diagram of the structure in question. You can stop, start, go back, enlarge, change angles, and fast forward. All the materials of your case are available in a single display system.

Such systems can be so expensive and complex, and use such rapidly-developing technology, that they are often rented, not purchased. Some cannot function without a trained operator. And if there are any such systems that do not malfunction with some frequency, they have not been brought to my attention.

But there is a greater drawback: It is difficult to present something credibly when jurors know you can manipulate your material in any manner you choose.

Moreover, if both sides do not have equipment at this high level of sophistication, your use of it may incur juror suspicion: If your case is any good, why do you need all that expensive stuff? You can answer this question in a variety of ways (for example, you can say that communicating the complexities of the case requires this level of high-tech assistance), but make sure that your use of the equipment is consistent with your explanation. (Don't claim that you need the equipment because the case is complex, and then use it merely to display material that you could have shown on a hand-drawn diagram.)

There are those who believe that courtroom multi-media presentation technology is the wave of the future. Others call it the Edsel of trial practice: Sounds good in advance, but do you want one in your driveway? This does not mean that you should ignore the possibilities of multi-media presentation. But balance the values against the drawbacks.

THE NOTEBOOK COMPUTER. In addition to all of technology's current and rapidly arriving marvels, consider the simple possibility of a small notebook computer at your table. Notebook computers are so inconspicuous that they don't tend to arouse juror suspicion, yet they are as powerful as desktop computers.

A laptop allows you to find in seconds anything you want in any deposition, record, or document. If your opponent's witness says from the stand that she never saw the weather report that night, and you seem to remember her saying the opposite, you needn't fumble through her 200-page deposition to find it. Your notebook computer will give you page, line number, and the full quote—or more than one, if they exist.

You don't even have to type all those documents into your computer. An inexpensive scanner and some optical recognition software turn documents into computer text files.

You can scan into your computer copies of visual evidence, too: graphs, charts, blow-ups, and photos. This allows you instantly to find anything you need.

Select a laptop with a quiet keyboard and a control to squelch its beeps. And consider the usefulness of a laptop that incorporates a printer. Aside from providing documents, you can create instant visuals.

SOFTWARE. A program called ADAM lets you show visuals that can peel away a human being layer by layer to reveal any internal anatomical structure. You can highlight the structure and even operate on it—properly or negligently, as your case may require.

For every area of litigation, such software is available to help explain, maneuver, and display spatial relationships, strengths of structures and materials, chemical and other processes, financial flow systems, maps of every highway and city street in America, charts and graphs . . . whatever you need, there is probably software to produce it in a useful form for trial. (Remember that any displays produced by such software require authoritative support to be credible, persuasive, and resistant to opposition attack. See pp. 251-252 above, "Persuasion" and "Credibility.")

The only drawback is the difficulty of learning these programs. But that very drawback represents a great courtroom advantage: The harder a program is to learn, the less likely your opponent will have learned it.

YE OLDE OVERHEAD PROJECTOR. Jurors regard the simple overhead projector as the most credible means of visual presentation. This fact is less astonishing when you consider that we trust a real person we see working the overhead projector more than we trust unseen electronic circuits, absent technicians, and sophisticated results. When jurors see your hand sliding the projection into place, they feel in contact with the material. And your fingers seen on the screen help to humanize you.

Ultimately, if technology by itself helped anyone to determine the truth, we would be living on a more honest planet than a hundred years ago. But technology has yet to change the fact that the testing of truth in court is a *human* pursuit. Juries are human beings who gauge truth via such human attributes as tone of voice, facial expression, body language, forthrightness, simple logic, gut feelings, and *vibes*—all as evaluated through the filter of complex human attitudes and human experiences that each juror brings to court.

Without great care, every technological device used on the trier of fact has the potential of *reducing* that human quotient of the case. This is why display technology can be clear, memorable, and emphatic—but not in itself persuasive.

For at least the next half century, new and more flexible presentation technologies will come along faster than anyone can keep up with them. Deciding which to use will become more and more difficult, unless you simply ask the only questions that matter: if and how the new technology will help you persuade.

SELECTED BIBLIOGRAPHY and SUGGESTED READINGS

THEATER and FILM TEXTS

Ball, David. *Backwards and Forwards*. Carbondale: Southern Illinois University Press, 1983.

Bartow, Arthur. *The Director's Voice*. New York: Theatre Communications Group, 1988.

Benedetti, Robert L. *The Actor at Work*. 3d ed. Englewood Cliffs: Prentice-Hall, 1981.

Brockett, Oscar G. *The Theater: An Introduction*. Historical Edition. New York: Holt, Rinehart and Winston, 1979.

Brook, Peter. *The Empty Space*. New York: Atheneum, 1978.

Carra, Lawrence. *Controls in Play Directing*. New York: Vantage Press, 1985.

Chekhov, Michael. *Lessons for the Professional Actor*. New York: Performing Arts Publications, 1985.

Cole, Toby and Helen Krich Chinoy. *Actors on Acting*. New York: Crown, 1949.

_____. *Directing the Play*. New York: Bobbs-Merrill, 1953.

_____. *Directors on Directing*. Revised ed. New York: Bobbs-Merrill, 1963.

Dean, Alexander and Lawrence Carra. *Fundamentals of Play Directing*. 4th ed. New York: Holt, Rinehart and Winston, 1974.

Esslin, Martin. *The Field of Drama*. New York: Methuen, 1987.

Funke, Lewis and John E. Booth. *Actors Talk about Acting*. New York: Random House, 1961.

Grebanier, Bernard. *Playwriting: How to Write for the Theater*. New York: Crowell, 1961.

Guthrie, Tyrone. *Tyrone Guthrie on Acting*. New York: Viking, 1971.

Hagen, Uta. *A Challenge for the Actor*. New York: Scribners, 1991.

_____. *Respect for Acting*. New York: Macmillan, 1973.

Kindem, Gorham. *The Moving Image: Production Principles and Practices*. Glenview: Scott, Foresman and Company, 1987.

Lessac, Arthur. *The Use and Training of the Human Voice*. New York: Drama Book Specialists, 1967.

Linklater, Kristin. *Freeing the Natural Voice*. New York: Drama Book Specialists, 1976.

McGaw, Charles. *Acting Is Believing*. New York: Holt, Rinehart and Winston, 1966.

Mekler, Eva. *The New Generation of Acting Teachers*. New York: Penguin Books, 1987.

Phillips, Henry Albert. *The Universal Plot Catalog*. Springfield: Home Correspondence School, 1920.

Phillips, Walliam H. *Writing Short Scripts*. Syracuse: Syracuse Univ. Press, 1991.

Savran, David. *In Their Own Words: Contemporary American Playwrights*. New York: Theatre Communications Group, 1988.

Sayles, John. *Thinking in Pictures*. New York: Houghton Mifflin, 1987.

Scanlan, David. *Reading Drama*. Mountain View: Mayfield, 1988.

Stanislavski, Constantin. *An Actor Prepares*. New York: Theatre Arts Books, 1973.

_____. *Building a Character*. New York: Theatre Arts Books, 1949.

_____. *Stanislavsky on the Art of the Stage*. New York: Hill and Wang, 1962.

Styan, J.L. *Shakespeare's Stagecraft*. London: Cambridge Univ. Press, 1967.

Whiting, Frank M. *The Theatre: An Introduction*. 4th ed. New York: Holt, Rinehart and Winston, 1979.

GENERAL TEXTS

Bailey, F. Lee. *Secrets*. New York: Stein and Day, 1978.

Dement, William C. *Some Must Watch While Some Must Sleep: Exploring the World of Sleep*. New York: Norton, 1972.

Elgin, Suzette Haden. *The Gentle Art of Verbal Self-Defense*. New York: Prentice-Hall, 1980.

Hogshire, Jim. *You Are Going to Prison*. Port Townsend, Washington: Loompanics Unlimited, 1994.

Knapp, M.L. *Nonverbal Communication in Human Interaction*. 2d ed. New York: Holt, Rinehart and Winston, 1978.

Monroe, Alan H. and Douglas Ehninger. *Principles of Speech Communication*. Glenview: Scott, Foresman and Company, 1969.

Pabst, William R. *Jury Manual*. Houston: Metro Publishing, 1985.

Ryan, Mary and David Svadli. "Women in the Courtroom: Increasing Credibility through Nonverbal Behavior Change." *Trial Diplomacy*, 11/93.

Tannen, Deborah. *You Just Don't Understand*. New York: Ballentine Books, 1991.

TRIAL PRACTICE

ATLA. *Excellence in Advocacy*. Washington: ATLA Press, 1992.

Bailey, William S. "Storyboards: Inexpensive and Effective." *Trial*. 9/94:64.

Bailey, F. Lee and Henry B. Rothblatt. *Investigation and Preparation of Criminal Cases, Federal and State*. Rochester: Lawyers Co-operative Publishing Co., 1970.

Bennett, Cathy E. and Robert B. Hirschhorn. *Bennett's Guide to Jury Selection and Trial Dynamics*. St. Paul: West, 1993.

Blanchard, R.D. *Litigation and Trial Practice for the Legal Assistant*. St. Paul: West, 1990.

Brain, Robert D. and Daniel J. Broderick. "Demonstrative Evidence: Clarifying Its Role at Trial." *Trial*. 9/94:73.

Chaney, Elaine M. "Computer Simulations: How They Can Be Used at Trial and the Arguments for Admissibility." *Indiana Law Review*. 19:735.

Christy, Gary. "A Storybook Approach." *Trial*. 9/94:68.

Ciresi, Michael V. and Jan M. Conlin. "A High-Tech Case: Lessons from *Honeywell v. Minolta*." *Trial*. 9/92:23.

Condon, Paul T. "The Process of Forensic Animation." *Trial Diplomacy Journal*. 17:171.

Ehrlich, J.W. *The Lost Art of Cross-Examination*. New York: G.P. Putnam's Sons, 1970.

Ellenbogen, Marc A. "Lights, Camera, Action: Computer-Animated Evidence Gets Its Day in Court." *Boston College Law Review*. 9/93:1087.

Field, George P. "Using a Computer at Counsel Table." *Trial*. 9/92:30.

Genevie, Louis. "Juror-Friendly Animation in the Courtroom." *For the Defense*. 7/94:28.

Heninger, Stephen D. "Cost-Effective Demonstrative Evidence." *Trial*. 9/94:65.

Imwinkelried, Edward J. *Evidentiary Foundations*. Charlottesville: Michie, 1989.

Krauss, Elissa and Beth Bonora, eds. *Jurywork*. Deerfield: Clark Boardman Callaghan, 1992.

Labe, Jacob, III. "The Blackboard is Obsolete." *Trial Lawyer*. 7/93:37.

Lisko, Karen Ohnemus. "Hollywood in the Courtroom: Use of 'Day-in-the-Life' Videos." Paper Delivered at Annual Meeting of American Society of Trial Consultants, Chicago, 1990.

Lubet, Steven. *Modern Trial Advocacy: Analysis and Practice*. Notre Dame: National Institute for Trial Advocacy, 1993.

Martin, E.X. III. "Using Computer-Generated Demonstrative Evidence." *Trial*. 9/94:84.

Mauet, Thomas A. *Fundamentals of Trial Analysis*. 3d ed. Boston: Little, Brown and Co., 1992.

Rosen, William W. "Altered Photographs: New Evidentiary Considerations?" *Trial.* 9/94:66.

Rothstein, Paul F. *Evidence.* 2d ed. St. Paul: West Publishing, 1981.

Saraceno, David A. "Creating Demonstrative Evidence." *California Lawyer.* 12/94:59.

Seltzer, Robert. "The Keys to Admissibility." *California Lawyer.* 12/94:59.

Simmons, Robert and J. Daniel Lounsbery. "Admissibility of Computer-Animated Reenactments in Federal Courts." *Trial.* 9/94:78.

Starr, V. Hale. *Jury Selection: Sample Voir Dire Questions.* 1995 Edition. Boston: Little, Brown and Co.

Starr, V. Hale and Mark McCormick. *Jury Selection.* 2d Edition. Boston: Little, Brown and Co., 1993.

Tanford, J. Alexander. *The Trial Process: Law, Tactics and Ethics.* Charlottesville: Michie, 1993.

Turbak, Nancy J. "Accentuate the Positive." *Trial.* 9/94:63.

Vinson, Donald E. and Philip K. Anthony. *Social Science Research Methods for Litigation.* Charlottesville: Michie, 1985.

Wellman, Francis L. *The Art of Cross Examination.* New York: Macmillan, 1903.

Younger, Irving. *The Advocate's Deskbook.* Clifton: Prentice-Hall, 1988.

PLAYS (for examples of techniques explained in this book)

Aeschylus. *The Oresteia.*

Albee, Edward. *Who's Afraid of Virginia Woolf?*

Anonymous. *Everyman.*

Beckett, Samuel. *Waiting for Godot.*

Buechner, George. *Woyzeck.*

Duerrenmatt, Friedrich. *The Visit.*

El Guindi, Yussef. *Hostages.*

Euripides. *Medea.*

Gogol, Nikolai. *Inspector General.*

Ibsen, Henrik. *Peer Gynt, Ghosts, A Doll's House.*

Kushner, Tony. *Angels in America.*

Mamet, David. *Sexual Perversity in Chicago, Glengarry Glen Ross.*

Marlowe, Christopher. *Dr. Faustus.*

Miller, Arthur. *Death of a Salesman, The Crucible.*

Moliere. *Tartuffe, The Miser.*

Mowatt, Anna Cora. *Fashion.*

Noonan, John Ford. *A Coupla White Chicks Sittin' Around Talking.*

O'Neill, Eugene. *Long Day's Journey into Night; Ah, Wilderness!*

Orton, Joe. *Loot, What the Butler Saw.*

Rabe, David. *Sticks and Bones.*

Rostand, Edmond. *Cyrano de Bergerac.*

Shakespeare, William. *The Taming of the Shrew, Romeo and Juliet, A Midsummer Night's Dream, The Merchant of Venice, Henry IV Part 1, Henry V, Julius Caesar, As You Like It, Hamlet, Othello, King Lear, Macbeth, Antony and Cleopatra.*

Shaw, George Bernard. *Arms and the Man, Major Barbara.*

Sheaffer, Peter. *Amadeus, Equus.*

Sheridan, Richard Brinsley. *The School for Scandal.*

Simon, Neil. *The Odd Couple, Brighton Beach Memoirs, Broadway Bound.*

Sophocles. *Oedipus the King.*

Stoppard, Tom. *Rosencrantz and Guildenstern Are Dead.*

Terry, Magen. *Viet Rock.*

Wilder, Thornton. *The Matchmaker, Our Town.*

Williams, Tennessee. *The Glass Menagerie, Cat on a Hot Tin Roof.*

INDEX